J l Nuron

Manchester 1997.

Financial Liberalization in Developing Countries

For Geraldine, Mom and Dad

I would like to thank all the people at the University of Strathclyde for their support and input. In particular Roger Perman, Mozzamel Huq, Harminder Battu, and Mark Mcfarland for insight, patience, and friendship. I would also like to thank the anonymous referees and Max Fry for comments on earlier drafts. Any remaining errors remain the responsibility of the author.

Financial Liberalization in Developing Countries

Trevor M. Sikorski

Previously with The University of Strathclyde

Edward Elgar
Cheltenham, UK • Brookfield, US

Published by
Edward Elgar Publishing Limited
8 Lansdown Place
Cheltenham
Glos GL50 2HU
UK

Edward Elgar Publishing Company
Old Post Road
Brookfield
Vermont 05036
US

British Library Cataloguing in Publication Data

Sikorski, Trevor M.
  Financial Liberalization in Developing Countries
  I. Title
  330.91724

Library of Congress Cataloguing in Publication Data

Sikorski, Trevor M. 1967-
  Financial Liberalization in Developing Countries /
  Trevor M. Sikorski.
    p. cm.
    1. Monetary policy. 2. Free enterprise. 3. Monetary policy -
  Pacific Area - Case studies.   I. Title.
  G230.3.S55 1996
  332.4 91724 - dc20   95-36673
                                                                           CIP

  ISBN 1 85898 244 8

Printed and bound in Great Britain by Hartnolls Limited, Bodmin, Cornwall

Contents

Tables

Figures

1. Introduction

MAIN OBJECTIVES

An extensive descriptive literature exists outlining the experiences of developing countries with financial and monetary policy. A large portion of the literature concentrates on the failings of existing monetary regimes and on episodes of policy change, the so-called 'financial liberalizations'. Less work has been done on the theory of monetary and financial policy in a context particular to development.

This text is meant in the way of a theoretical exploration of the way monetary policy has been thought of in development economics. It seeks to hold up to the fine light of scrutiny the conventional theoretical foundations which serve as a base from which policy prescriptions have been drawn. It further seeks to move towards a paradigm which can provide a coherent and unified theoretical framework capable of explaining the way monetary policy works in repressed and liberalized financial regimes. The benefit of such a theoretical body is that it can then suggest a general strategy for the reform of the financial system which will minimize the adjustment costs of policy change. The aim of the book is, then, to work towards a theoretical framework successful in description and prescription, with regards to monetary and financial policy in developing countries.

SOME INTRODUCTORY ISSUES

The story begins with a period of optimism, the 1960s, characterized by a view that developing countries were economically young, full of potential for growth, and that the government was going to be the benevolent parent assisting that growth at all levels. An intellectual attitude then existed which had a spirit of faith in government intervention, based on economic advice, to put right any existing structural weaknesses in the markets. Markets in developing countries were seen to be shallow, weak, prone to failure; and such flaws were seen as being best mitigated by astute government

1

intervention. In financial markets, a primary weakness was seen to be the less than socially-optimal levels of capital provision which existing financial intermediaries were providing. The shortage of capital, at this time, was seen as a paramount reason for underdevelopment, and capital provision was prioritized by most developing country governments. To provide more socially-optimal levels of capital, to make sure this was done in synchronization with government development plans, and to provide finance for government budget deficits, the government intervened in domestic financial markets. Intervention led to more intervention and soon the financial markets were dominated by government interference in terms of both the direction and the price of credit. A prevalent feature of this period resulting from the controls on the financial system was very low, and often negative, interest rates both on deposits and loans.

Like most intervention, a mixture of non-benevolence, corruption and weak administrative ability introduced distortions, rent seeking and inefficiency into all aspects of financial markets. Firms which were given access to cheap finance appropriated rents from depositors, who were induced to withdraw their resources from the intermediaries. Commercial banks became reliant on governments for everything from whom to lend to, to the funds which they were going to lend. Direct attempts at money control, and the resulting dis-intermediation led to excessively fragmented and dualistic financial sectors. Capital left the country and savers refused to hold domestic financial assets, a glaring case of government failure.

The pathology of the patient, or the excesses of the intervention, were first catalogued by McKinnon (1973) and Shaw (1973) in their now seminal books which set out the case for financial liberalization. The diagnosis was that the mass of controls on the financial system were 'repressing' it and causing it to malfunction. The solution to this 'financial repression' was then going to be 'financial liberalization' - the removal of government controls. Financial liberalization theory was predicated on an unashamed faith in markets and a not unreasonable belief that 'government failure' was best combated by removing the government. As a result, policy prescription called for the freeing of financial markets from their administrative shackles in order to let the forces of market-clearing work. The centre-piece of the policies was the removal of the ubiquitous interest rate ceilings which were identified as the primary, but not sole, culprit of repression. Allowing this central price to reach its market-clearing level would increase both the quantity and quality of investment, curing much of what was wrong in these markets. The story told by financial liberalizers was that a liberalization resulting in significantly higher interest rates would increase investment and growth by providing a greater amount of savings to be used in such pursuits. Moreover, by allocating credit at a higher price reflecting its 'market' worth, only those investment projects which were productive enough to meet payment obligations would be undertaken, thereby lowering the number of unproductive investments absorbing credit. Savings was very much the dominant nexus, the dog that would wag the investment tail. Increasing savings, by causing domestic agents to forego consumption, was to be the engine of growth.

With the passage of time, the McKinnon-Shaw prescriptions became a new orthodoxy and received a large amount of academic interest. Elaborate theoretical justifications and empirical examinations marked the growing body of literature. A major element in the theory of liberalization was the belief in the necessity of reform being of the rapid "big-bang" nature (eg. Mathieson, 1980). Policy calls focused on programs in which distortions were all eliminated in one fell swoop of government disintervention. The justifications of the big-bang policy flowed directly from neo-classical concepts in which market adjustment is rapid and thus the gains to liberalization would be quickly reached. Rapid reforms would provide strong signals to economic agents who would respond quickly to the incentives. Additionally, a large dose of the medicine would not give vested interests the time to mobilize and block future progress. The faster it was over, the quicker the economy could benefit from the ensuing efficiency gains. Such ideas had come to be thought of as self-evident truths.

Coinciding with the ideological triumph of liberalization theory was the beginning of a dreadful period in which the developing world became so indebted that it could no longer borrow of its own accord. The developing world had opted for dollar-denominated debt to pay for its development. Such heavy borrowing at world interest rates left most of these countries highly vulnerable to large increases in the price of credit. When this occurred, the heavily indebted countries could no longer meet existing payment obligations. Developing countries were now very ill patients, dependent on the IMF and World Bank lending to meet their financial requirements. Those institutions were optimistic that their policy conditions could set right these imbalanced economies. The IMF became responsible for stabilization, and based its stabilization policy largely on the imperative of getting prices right. Financial liberalization, with its emphasis on market-clearing interest rates and the congruent importance of interest rates in combating inflation, was in the limelight. The theoretical orthodoxy now had teeth and was ready to bite.

The results from the periods of liberalization in the first half of the 1980s, were at best mixed and at worst disastrous. Most frequently financial liberalization led to periods of financial crash and chaos (Cho and

Khatkhate, 1989; Corbo, de Melo and Trybout, 1986; Diaz-Alejandro, 1985). Governments were forced to either re-enter the financial market or tough it out and try to salvage what was left in the end. With hindsight, it would seem that any existing market failure was obscured by the thick veneer of excessive government tampering. As most patients became worse, the resulting dissatisfaction with liberalization was relatively quick and two major areas of response emerged.

The first response was to question the logic of liberalization, and this was enshrined in the new-structuralist critique. The new-structuralist critique catalogued the negative effects of liberalization which highlighted the working-capital cost-push nexus (e.g. Buffie, 1984). This element of liberalization, and the effect it has on the productive sector, was the most important aspect of the critique. Unfortunately, the formal theoretical critique eschewed the cost-push effects and concentrated on a critique which focused on the curb or informal financial markets (e.g. van Wijnbergen, 1982). According to this story, the failure of financial liberalization is due to the fact that the resultant increase in interest rates in the official market decreases the quantity of finance available to firms because it draws resources out of the unorganized market. The recipient of these funds, through household asset substitution, is the formal market, which is less efficient in intermediation than the curb market because of the prevalence of high reserve requirements.

The critique is not entirely plausible because of the picture of fragmented, and inefficient, unorganized markets that has emerged from the largely descriptive literature of these intermediaries (Burkett, 1989; Owen and Solis-Fallas, 1989). Also, it is likely that the curb market is not important in the macroeconomic adjustment of the economy to policy changes, as the firms it serves contribute very little to measured aggregate investment. Thus, the curb market explanation is not convincing in describing either the financial instability following a financial liberalization program, or for explaining the large drops in investment noticed after liberalization programs (Greenaway and Morrissey, 1992). The unconvincing nature of the formal theoretical models of the new-structuralists has led to the marginalization of this critique.

The alternative response was by the proponents of financial liberalization themselves who sought an explanation as to why the reforms were not successful. The logic of reform was not held up to scrutiny, but the implementation of reform was examined. The lesson that emerged was that for financial liberalization to work:

1.   Reform must be attempted only after an initial series of

preconditions had been met. Of these, the most important was macroeconomic stability. Macroeconomic instability, characterized by raging inflation, made the domestic financial system too weak and susceptible to collapse in the face of any large-scale reform measures (McKinnon, 1989). Such a condition presented a dilemma, because financial liberalization was originally envisaged as a key element of stabilization. Requiring macroeconomic stability as a pre-condition to liberalization seriously dampened policy options. The result was that the bulk of the stabilization process was to be borne in the area of fiscal policy, true austerity. The ability to rein in the fiscal deficit before liberalization would allow the government to forgo the use of the inflation tax, and therefore not undermine the basis of the reform with rapid inflation. Such drastic spending cuts were normally concentrated in those fields which could mobilize the least political resistance. Health and education were notable targets and thus the welfare costs to stabilization were borne inequitably by those most dependent on such spending - the poor, rural and female. Hence, adjustment felt more like an earthquake with the massive spending cuts turning masses of workers out of employment. With no social security nets to ensure and augment welfare, demand and wages tumbled, dragging down inflation. The World Bank had then to institute programs to save the poorest from starvation. Stabilization was to be very costly.

2. Reform must be sequenced. Generally, liberalization of domestic financial markets was best seen as preceding the liberalization of capital controls. Otherwise, the resulting large flows of capital (either inwards or outwards depending on what happened to the real interest rate) would destabilize the markets and undermine the reform progress. Improper sequencing would thus have pernicious effects on the economy and could lead to policy failure and policy reversal (Dooley and Mathieson, 1987). Trade liberalization was also seen as best coming before financial market liberalization, a nod to the importance and difficulty of restructuring the productive sector.

3. Reform must be credible. Policy reversal has come to be viewed with as great a disdain as persisting with the old bad habits. A failed policy reform is seen as imposing very high adjustment costs, leaving the economy worse-off and damaging the credibility of the government in its reformist intentions. Credibility, broadly defined to encompass commitment, political stability and design of

reform, is thus a crucial element that, if lacking, could hinder the potential success of any program (Greenaway and Morrissey, 1992).

The response sheds some light on the problems of implementing reforms in an atmosphere of macroeconomic instability. The question must be, though, is this 'mitigating conditions' approach to policy analysis an acceptable way of advancing?   Would financial liberalization be successful, by its own criteria, if it was undertaken by a credible government, in relative autarky and an atmosphere of macroeconomic stability?   If the answer to this question is 'no', the value of financial liberalization as the theoretical basis for policy prescription must be open to doubt.

Why must the answer be 'no' to this question? The idea of necessary preconditions is not necessarily wrong, it is just that the preconditions suggested do not tell a convincing story of why financial crisis follows from liberalization.   The response misses the basic failings of financial liberalization, and these basic failings have large implications for policy prescriptions. In fact, the basic failings are severe enough to imply that it is not just a case of preconditions, but that liberalization is inappropriate for developing countries given their *current institutional realities*. This is not to say that change is not needed, but that a protracted period of financial repression has introduced additional distortions into the financial markets which act as significant barriers, or limits, to the amount of freedom financial markets should be given. It is not a question of freeing up markets once some fortuitous circumstances are upon us, but rather that developing country financial markets need large amounts of freedom like a fish needs a bicycle.   Given the institutional realities, widespread liberalization is simply not a beneficial option.

The dominant limit to institutional change flows from the interaction of banks and industry under repression, which creates a highly-leveraged industrial structure.   Under repression, firms with access to credit in the official markets are those favoured under development policy goals, often linked to programs of industrialization.   Such firms which dominate the aggregate economies of these countries, have and continue to rely on bank credit, and the associated subsidy, for the majority of their financial requirements (Villanueva and Mirakhor, 1990). The banks, for their part, connive with these large industrial firms as lending to such bodies often comes with implicit guarantees of repayment from the government.   Over time, the firms establish customer relationships, providing the banks with financial information about these customers which reinforces the direction of credit.   The commercial banks are usually characterized by severe asymmetric information, adverse selection and moral hazard, which hinder them from serving the small- and middle- sized firms in the market. Such firms would be credit-rationed regardless of whether or not credit is explicitly directed away from them. Repression just serves to make the rationing more severe for the larger of these borrowers. The asymmetric information of banks coupled with the credit demands of large firms which shy away from equity, thus conspire to produce dangerously high debt - equity levels.

The problem of high debt-equity ratios follows from the fact that the *sine qua non* of financial liberalization is a significant increase in interest rates. High and rapidly rising interest rates put such leveraged firms into a Ponzi-game of doubly increasing costs.[1]

In this game, firms experience an increase in interest cost on outstanding debt. The rise in costs comes as an exogenous shock to the firms in that it was not a part of past expectations on which borrowing was based. In order to meet the new costs firms must borrow more, and this process of entering into new debt contracts just to meet repayment obligations becomes a second source of cost increase. Firms are borrowing just to survive. Commercial banks are drawn into this game through a vicious moral hazard in which their loan portfolios are highly exposed to these firms and their viability would be threatened if these firms failed. Thus, it is a matter of solvency for them to continue lending to these firms even though these assets are rapidly becoming non-performing.[2]

The ability of the commercial banks to satisfy this Ponzi-boom is dependent on the monetary policy stance of the authorities. If the authorities, in the direct aftermath of the liberalization program, fully accommodate the needs of the Ponzi-boom, the solvency of the system will be maintained in the short-run. However, the double-bind of increasing costs will consistently worsen the financial positions of firms and the portfolios of their banks. The continuation of such accommodation is unsustainable as it leads to a large build-up of non-performing debt in the

---

[1] A Ponzi-game is a situation in which a firm must borrow to meet an increase in payments on outstanding debt. The additional borrowing, however, serves to increase the debt load, worsening the financial position of the firm. The firm borrows to survive, but in doing so makes its own position more hazardous (Minsky, 1986).

[2] If the bank stopped lending immediately, the failure of the firms would then cause the failure of the bank. Thus, the bank continues to lend to stave off its own immediate failure, in the slim hope that firms will eventually begin to perform on the loans. This is a severe moral hazard.

system. Realizing this to be the 'road to hell', the monetary authority will be required to adopt a new policy stance, in order to place the economy back on a stable path. Its policy options are two-fold.

First, the authorities could pursue a non-accommodating stance whereby it refuses to satisfy the needs of the Ponzi-boom. A general debt deflation occurs which brings down inflation by eliminating a large amount of income generating capacity through firm bankruptcy and the consequential insolvency of financial institutions. The layering of financial claims means some contagion effects will occur and the liberalizing country may be left with a full-scale financial crisis. The welfare losses will be felt primarily in the industrial sector with the constituent loss of productive capacity and an upsurge in the unemployment of labour. The negative income effects of this aggregate supply shock will have further multiple negative effects on aggregate demand and the entire economy. Price stability will have been achieved, but only at a very high cost to the productive capacity of the economy.

The alternative option is to retreat from the program of liberalization by reinstating interest-rate controls and trying to salvage the units in the economy through industrial and financial restructuring. The most financially troubled firms will need to undergo painful restructuring often at a very sizeable cost. Because of the large restructuring costs, it is usually most feasible for the government to use the banks as the main channel of adjustment. That is, the government will require the banks, rather than industry, to absorb the losses by writing off *de facto* sizeable chunks of non-performing assets. Such a step requires the government to become more pervasive in financial markets, as it must give banks an additional degree of financial and administrative support to compensate them for absorbing the large costs of adjustment. The net effect is to increase the level of financial repression in the economy and to damage the reformist credibility of the government. However, although it loses in credibility, it reduces the short-run welfare loss associated with a simple non-accommodating stance.

Thus, the whole tiering of financial claims under repression, which produces firms with very high debt-equity ratios and banks over-exposed to those firms, undermines the applicability of liberalizing policy prescription. Even with macroeconomic (price) stability and proper sequencing, a program of financial liberalization which leads to a rapid change in the price at which credit is created is not feasible for a developing country with the stated institutional structure. The only precondition that would damper this conclusion would be to require a full previous industrial restructuring and a full overhaul of banks' portfolios. Such a precondition implies that these countries must stop displaying the problematic characteristics that constitute the barriers to development. The countries must stop being, in other words, developing countries. The value of such a policy prescription is limited.

In practice, there has been a steady realization that although existing government intervention creates inefficiencies, the unfettered market is an unsuitable and unsustainable option. This realization has led policy makers to adopt a more pragmatic approach, recognizing limits to change and that a more balanced approach to the mixed economy is needed. Such a pragmatic approach is often implicitly cloaked in the language of gradualism. A gradual process to change is usually championed by a combination of arguments (Greenaway and Morrissey, 1992). The first argument rests on the ability of a gradual change to mitigate the adjustment costs borne through the increasing unemployment of labour and capital. The factor specificity of both labour and capital will allow a gradual reform to achieve more socially optimal write-off and retraining rates. The welfare losers will be easier to compensate as the incidence of loss is spread over a longer time horizon.

The second justification for gradualism is on the grounds of income distribution. Income redistribution is favoured because gradual change slows down the rate at which rents to factors are reduced, providing a longer adjustment time for the old favoured sectors to diversify their income sources and reduce their reliance on rents.

The final argument commonly invoked for a gradual approach is the credibility issue, whereby the government introduces a series of gradual reforms on which it can demonstrate commitment and thereby build up a reformist reputation.

So, the order of the day has become an economic pragmatic approach in which small incremental changes are tried, and the big-bang liberalizations to which the IMF still pays lip-service are viewed with scepticism. The question then remains: what role is left for theory in a pragmatic atmosphere? Is theory redundant, only able to provide a glimpse of distant goals to which the policy maker can merely hope the economy will one day converge? The answer to the last question should be a resounding 'No'. Theory based on an understanding of the institutional realities can play an important role in identifying both the limits to change and avenues for advancement. The failure of financial liberalization theory, both of the neo-classical and new-structuralist varieties, to outline adequately the various roles of government and the market is that it has been based around a faulty understanding of institutional structures. Once those institutional structures are built into an alternative paradigm, the value of theory and the policy emanating from that theory is enhanced. The goal of this book is to work towards such a theory.

STRUCTURE OF THE BOOK

In order to discuss fully the issues outlined above, this work will assess the fundamental assumptions behind the way financial and monetary policy is thought about, and carried out, in a developing country.

Chapter 2 is an overview of monetary theory, focusing on the exogenous versus endogenous money debate. The exogenous money position contends that money is exogenous to real income, prices and interest rates.[3]

In conjunction with money's exogeneity, approaches consistent with the assumption, including the quantity theory, new classical theory and Keynesian-synthesis models, usually ascribe some causal impact from money on to one or all of those variables. In order to describe an exogenous money theory, the approaches must specify a mechanism for how monetary changes occur (a supply mechanism) and for how those changes are transmitted to changes in other macroeconomic variables. In order to do so, these approaches generally rely on a money-multiplier approach in which monetary changes engineered by the monetary authority are related in a stable fashion to macroeconomic variables by virtue of a set of knowable and predictable coefficients. The main weaknesses of these multiplier approaches is that relying on fixed coefficients to predict the results of policy changes involving vast institutional change, such as a liberalization, is open to the greatest of doubts. The ability of static, fixed coefficient approaches to fully capture changes in a dynamic and changing environment is unlikely. However, most approaches tend to continue to use a money-multiplier approach in analysing the transmission mechanism of monetary policy.

The endogenous money story told by the post-Keynesians, on the other hand, postulates that money is endogenous to real income, prices and interest rates. The argument is essentially that economic activity, broadly defined, requires money which the banking system creates in response to the demand. The transmission mechanism of the post-Keynesians is then specified by looking at the role of the banks and the financial system as a whole in the process of money creation. The post-Keynesians realize the ability of the banking system in creating money is constrained, and the exact nature of the endogeneity of money is still a source of some debate.

---

[3]The term exogenous here is used in a very loose sense, implying that the mechanism by which money is created is outside the determination of real income. For a more rigorous definition, see chapter 2.

However, the touchstone of the story is that money is demand determined, responding to the needs to finance increments in investment, production and consumption. Thus, the post-Keynesian view of the policy transmission mechanism between money and income (and, by extension, growth) is firmly rooted in the premise that money is credit-driven and credit is demand-driven. The theoretical foundation from which post-Keynesians then view the results of policy changes is fundamentally different from the analytical basis of the new classical and associated schools.

Chapter 3 assesses the financial repression paradigm and the first decade of liberalization theory. The key issues which emerge from the McKinnon-Shaw literature are the importance of increasing the quantity of credit, increasing the quality of credit allocation, and the importance of intermediation to development. The formal theoretical models encasing these ideas are assessed and it is demonstrated that all of the formal starting points begin with money as exogenous. The exogenous money assumption in these models causes them to rely on the premise that savings and investment are always equilibrated through the workings of a market rate of interest. Essential to this concept is the idea that a repressed financial system fails to both adequately mobilize savings and efficiently allocate resources because the relevant price (the market rate of interest) is controlled administratively. With repressed interest rates, credit is over subscribed and a shortage of savings is encountered. If savings in the official financial market were increased, by increasing the rewards to saving, these savings will be intermediated to investors encouraging capital growth. As a result, *savings* are going to be the prime engine of growth. Policies which foster the mobilization of resources, by improving the functioning of financial markets, will therefore be growth enhancing. The supply of financial resources (savings) to the financial system is the key. An increase in savings, then, leads to an increase in growth.

However, believing that savings will always equal investment, and will be so maintained by a market rate of interest is an unimaginative and static view of the economy. It is a misinterpretation of the way a modern credit economy works, completely negating the special role which credit plays. The salient feature of credit is that it allows a separation of the decision to save and the decision to invest. The investment decision is then going to be governed by perceptions and rationales completely distinct from those governing the decision to save. The issue is then which factor is going to be the dominant force.

If one was to proceed from the premise that expenditure governs output, and output (national income) governs saving, it would appear that the only way to increase savings in the current period is to reduce consumption, or alternatively, expenditure. As expenditures drop, entrepreneurs make losses and this reduces national income. As income falls, savings must fall. Thus, an attempt geared at manipulating the quantity of savings directly through inter-portfolio substitution, stimulated by increasing the rate of interest, is ultimately folly. A policy geared at increasing investment, however, has the opposite consequences. As investment increases, income is enhanced, and as income grows, savings grow. Thus, investment provides the saving which will finance it: the future income which will meet the future financial obligations contracted by current-period investment expenditure. Investment is then the causal force and savings (money) is the endogenous respondent. In reversing the causality, a clearer picture of the workings of the monetary transmission mechanism will begin to emerge.

The chapter proceeds to argue that the new classical liberalization models will then be subject to the same weaknesses as the traditional monetary models relying on the exogenous money assumption. In particular, these models only take a partial look at the monetary transmission mechanism and ignore the role of banks in the money creating process.

Chapter 4 looks at the response of theory to the failings of financial liberalization as a sustainable policy for developing countries. The first theoretical critique is that of the new-structuralists. The new-structuralists' critique is a two-tiered attack, with the first tier being the cost of credit nexus. The second tier is an asset-demand framework which highlights the importance of the unorganized or curb money markets in these countries. The formal theoretical models are discussed and it is argued that the failure of the new-structuralists to endogenize the money supply led to logical inadequacies in the critique. As a result of these weaknesses in the critique being exposed, the critique has been primarily discounted in the subsequent debate over liberalization. The chapter then goes on to discuss the informational theories of banking and how they have been employed to explain the failures of liberalization. In particular, theories of asymmetric information and moral hazard have been introduced to explain the often negative results of liberalization programmes. The chapter then argues that despite the insights which these approaches provide, they do not constitute an alternative theory and thus the neo-classical exogenous money assumption still governs the thinking about monetary and financial policy.

Chapter 5 suggests an alternative by applying post-Keynesian monetary ideas to the ideas of development economics. A description of financial systems under repression is used to argue that the money supply in developing countries is endogenous under a repressed regime responding to the credit needs engendered by development policy. The crux of the matter is that under repression, the directed credit policies of the government's development policy are generally combined with accommodative arrangements through the discount window. This required accommodation by the Central Banks to credit demands engendered through development policy creates a large source of monetary endogeneity in the economy. The endogeneity requires, or gives rise to, further repression to maintain some semblance of monetary stability. The repression influences the direction of credit and creates particular institutional features which influence how the monetary transmission mechanism works in these countries. The chapter then goes on to analyse changes in monetary policy under repression, the ensuing credit rationing, and where adjustment to policy changes will be concentrated.

Chapter 6 goes on to expand the ideas developed in chapter 5 by analysing the response of a repressed economy to a change in monetary regime (a liberalization). The chapter has a heuristic discussion, followed by a formal dynamic control model which seeks to encapsulate the main ideas. It is argued that given the institutional realities of countries under repression, financial liberalization is not going to be a sustainable policy. The reason is that under repression, firms benefiting from the government policy umbrella and with access to credit tended to rely on credit to fund expansion and growth. As a result, these firms which dominate the macroeconomies of these countries, become very highly leveraged and will view any large increase in interest rates as a massive price shock. The price shock could then stimulate distress borrowing and/or a complete debt deflation in the economy. The large reductions in liquidity and demand following these debt deflations, and the simultaneous fiscal 'responsibility' are then successful in stabilizing the price level. However, this price stability is only bought at the price of a large reduction in productive capability and aggregate demand. The following contraction in the economy then holds long-term implications for the future growth path of the economy.

The chapter also argues that an extended period of liberalization may not be in the best interests of a developing country. As a liberalized monetary regime takes hold, the ability of the banks to create credit independently of the monetary authority grows (this is surely a primary rationale for liberalization). As such, the conditions of credit expansion (price and availability) will become more open to the banks' influence. The banks, for their part, will be both responding to and altering business expectations and attitudes. This interaction, between the expectations of entrepreneurial agents and financial establishments, will then determine the direction and quantity of credit created. If both businesses and banks share optimism (or perhaps a speculative fever) with regard to particular enterprises, credit will then be created and allocated to finance those activities. Thus, as the scope for independent credit creation grows, credit will respond more directly to the particular business climate. Congruently, the ability of the government to influence these conditions in line with a concerted effort at development is reduced.

A problem arises, however, if financial intermediaries in developing countries lack the skill and sophistication to adequately assess and monitor credit risks. Greater freedom for such institutions in creating and allocating credit may then mean greater freedom to finance speculative and unproductive activities. In particular, if such activities become attractive as part of an upswing, banks and businesses may then divert too many credit resources into these activities. Thus, a liberalized climate of finance has the potential for encouraging the emergence of large systematic risks and debt overhangs. As banks, responding to the herd instinct, over-finance any one given activity - for example, the property market - the financial system can become grossly unbalanced. Once liquidity conditions become too loose, possibly because of government attempts at indirect monetary control being stymied by market imperfections, large speculative and aggregate demand bubbles may appear. With the large debt overhang, a debt deflation becomes inevitable to cool off an economy that has begun to be overwrought and over-hot. As the monetary authority strives to rein in liquidity, by pushing up interest rates, the price and availability of credit must change rapidly. The resulting debt deflation will be successful in stopping the overheating, but will not plant the seeds for growth. As business pessimism is generated by a downward swing, the ability of the economy to grow and develop is subsequently reduced. Hence, liberalized finance becomes a source from which large swings in the development cycle may emerge.

The centrality of credit in the process of development means monetary concerns will be a main cause of domestic shocks. Entrepreneurs must have reasonably well-formed expectations of the level of future payments obligations (rates of interest), and of the level of future access to credit. When these expectations prove to be grossly wrong, financial instability is encountered both for firms and for financial intermediaries. Therefore, a goal of policy makers should be to limit broad swings in the availability and cost of credit. The freeing-up of credit conditions by a financial liberalization makes greater swings in the allocation and price of credit both possible and likely. In increasing the volatility of credit, this is actually increasing the endemic uncertainty in developing countries, thereby serving to discourage investment and make the task of development that much more difficult. Liberalization, by removing government guidance, removes the potential stabilizing and guiding roles of intelligent government action. By increasing the uncertainty in the economy, it damages investor confidence and the growth prospects of an economy in transition.

Chapter 7 presents a selection of case studies from the south-east Asian developing countries. Case studies are presented for Korea, Malaysia, Indonesia and the Philippines. The case studies reinterpret the experience of these countries in a post-Keynesian light. The cases argue that the post-Keynesian paradigm is successful in accounting for and explaining the past history of monetary developments in these countries and their brushes with liberalization. This chapter is used to present illustrative evidence of the theoretical ideas developed throughout the text.

Chapter 8 includes a summary of the work and looks at conclusions in terms of policy prescription. It is argued that an active role by policy makers is desirable in the financing of development.

2. Endogeneity v Exogeneity - A Monetary Debate

INTRODUCTION

The issue of the endogeneity or exogeneity of the money supply is a recurring, unsolved dilemma running through the history of monetary theory. The origin of the debate can be traced back nearly three centuries to the 'real bills doctrine versus Bullionist' controversy. In a nutshell, the real bills doctrine proposed that bank notes which are lent in exchange for 'real bills' (titles to real value in the process of creation) could not be issued in excess, and given a finite non-bank public demand for currency any superfluous notes would return automatically to the issuer. Hence, notes which were advanced upon real bills of exchange were demand determined by the needs of trade and in this manner over-issue was constrained. Money supply, in terms of the real bills doctrine, was endogenous. Bullionists such as Ricardo disagreed, finding a refusal to discount any bills except for those of bona fide transactions as impractical, and of little value in limiting circulation. The money supply was proposed to be exogenously determined, corresponding solely to the will of the issuers (see Green, 1989; and Laidler, 1989). The seeds of the modern debate, to which attention in this chapter is turned, were sown.

The debate about the characteristic of money is significant as it underlies the way economists view the relationship between the quantity of money and national income, and ultimately, the way they view monetary policy in its function. Sitting at the core of traditional monetary analysis is an assumption that money is a quantity uniquely defined, measured and effectively controlled by the monetary authority. The pertinent policy question to answer is, then, through what transmission mechanism did the stock of money influence both nominal national income and its dual components real income and prices. The discovery of this transmission mechanism pointed to the relevant policy prescriptions to be used in effectively managing the economy. A key element in such an approach is

16

the assumption of the exogeneity of money to the real productive sector. Such an approach characterizes much of the work done in (development) monetary economics which sought to describe the monetary transmission mechanism, through the use of paradigm and formal model, and to quantify the significance of those relationships with empirical work.

The traditional approach, broadly aligned to monetarist (and classical) economics has been questioned by a growing body of literature aligned to the post-Keynesians and members of the banking school who find traditional monetary analysis guilty of telling only half the story. In particular, the role of financial intermediaries and the behavioural and institutional characteristics of the economy in the money creation process are ignored. In an economy with a financial system characterized by a variety of financial intermediaries and a large spectrum of financial assets, relevant theoretical and policy questions concern the mechanism of money creation and the ability of the Central Bank to control the monetary supply. It is this focus on the mechanism of money creation in a credit money economy which illuminates the claim that the money stock is endogenous, responding to changes in national income and prices. The importance of the interaction between the public and banking sectors in the money creation process, then, becomes a determining factor in the consequences of monetary policy on the economy.

The purpose of this chapter is to present an overview of the debate which has characterized monetary economics. This debate is a pertinent starting point as development monetary economics is largely influenced by the issues arising from the debate. The chapter begins with a conceptual clarification of the definitional aspects of exogeneity and endogeneity. This is followed by a look at theories associated with exogenous money supply assumptions - the monetarist and Keynesian theories. The alternative tradition of assuming money supply endogeneity will be discussed by looking at post-Keynesian theory.

CONCEPTUAL CLARIFICATION: EXOGENEITY

The general debate, while adopting the terms exogenous and endogenous, has tended to use them in a varied and imprecise manner, often conflating them with related issues. In the simplest of worlds an endogenous variable is one whose value is determined inside a given model, while an exogenous variable is one which is determined externally. The issue then becomes a function of model size and whether a given model is sufficiently extensive to encompass the process by which a given variable is determined. The debate over money supply exogeneity, however, concerns a much broader concept relating to the very nature of the money supply creation and how money should appear in economic models. Briefly put, an exogenous view of the money supply would consider one or all of a cluster of variables - price level, interest rate, real output - and postulate them as being determined by movements in the money stock. Conversely, the endogeneity view postulates that the stock of money in circulation is determined by one or all of the variables mentioned above. Central to this issue is, then, the direction of causality - money to other variables or other variables to money.[1]   The direction the causal arrow takes will determine how proponents view the monetary transmission mechanism as working, as well as which monetary policies should be prescribed. The above debate as it appears in this form is static, with causality flowing in a one-way, one-time format. Once posed in a dynamic context, the distinctions derived in the rigorous reworking of the concept of exogeneity by Engle, Hendry and Richard (1983) become relevant. A simplified version of the Engle et al. framework is found in Desai (1989), who specifies a small model within whose context exogeneity may be defined.

Consider a macroeconomic model consisting of the variables: P, Y, R and M whose exogenous/endogenous status is being questioned. For simplicity, the three non-monetary variables P, Y and R are labelled X, the monetary variable is labelled M, whereas other truly exogenous variables - such as international variables - are grouped under the vector of variables Z. Observing the variables X and M to be correlated and jointly conditional upon Z, the question of the exogeneity of money is whether the correlation between X and M can be written in terms of X being a function of M and Z (exogenous money) or M being a function of X and Z. An important partition to make is to derive a conditional distribution of X on M and Z and a marginal distribution of M on Z (exogenous M) or to derive a conditional distribution of M on X and Z and a marginal distribution of X on Z. Hence, an exogenous money supply is exogenous with respect to X variables, but it could still be determined by Z variables. The symmetric case holds for the X variables being exogenous.

From here it is possible to distinguish between three types of exogeneity.

---

[1]Strictly speaking, a third causal alternative exists which is dual, or simultaneous, causality. If two variables are linked by simultaneous causality, a feedback process exists where changes in one variable are caused by, and cause changes in, the second variable. In this case, neither variable is strictly exogenous.

If M is influenced by the past values of X as well as by Z, though not by current values of X (that is a system in which feedback exists), M is *weakly* exogenous. Thus, M may be controlled by monetary authorities but they may be reacting to past behaviour of X variables. M is determined then by a reaction function and is only weakly exogenous. M would be *strongly* exogenous if it was wholly independent of any past or present values of X. In other words, feedback from X back to M would be absent. Furthermore, if the systematic variations in M are such that economic agents can fully anticipate them, so that M exerts a scale effect on X, and has no effect whatsoever on the real variables in the system at all times, then M displays *super* exogeneity. A super exogenous money supply would be consistent with the neutrality hypothesis as proposed by some quantity theorists (see Patinkin, 1989).[2]

Rarely has the theoretical debate concerning money exogeneity risen to the level of rigorous definition as suggested, or demanded, by the preceding discussion. More typical of the participants in the debate is the tendency to conflate or treat as synonymous the related concept of a variables controllability by policy. Money is treated as exogenous by some writers if it is strictly under control of the monetary authority. In the strictest definitional sense, exogeneity is a separate concept, not requiring policy control. The obvious example is that whilst rainfall is universally agreed to be exogenous to agricultural output, it is not (yet) controllable by policy. The question must then be asked, why has the debate concerning the exogeneity of money supply been largely couched around a discussion of policy control? The answer lies in the very close relationship of the two concepts in terms of the money supply debate. For if M is exogenous with respect to X (any internal processes), then the obvious external process by virtue of which the money supply could be caused - and perhaps the only one left given the marginal distribution of Z - is the monetary authority's policy function. However, the participants lose a certain amount of rigour by treating exogeneity as controllability, as an endogenous money supply theoretically may be effectively controlled by the Central Bank given certain restrictive assumptions.

---

[2]The implications for empirical work which the Engle et al. distinctions hold will be discussed fully in chapter 7.

THE QUANTITY THEORY TRADITION

The present section seeks to present the theories, models, and paradigms that have become associated with monetarist and neo-classical monetary economics. The importance of these theories in terms of policy influence has been vast in both the developed and developing world. The theories will be discussed with particular emphasis placed on the nature of money, and the transmission mechanism which connects money to nominal income and its component parts of real output and prices.

The salient features of the monetarist models discussed below include:

1. An implicit assumption that the quantity of money is well defined and that the monetary authority is capable of effectively controlling it up to a random component. Implicitly this is the justification for assuming the money supply is exogenously determined.
2. None of these models, either implicitly or explicitly, gives a role to the banking system in determining the stock of money. Although the banking system may create 'inside' money, the behaviour of banks is constrained by simple mechanistic operating rules which imply that the Central Bank has complete control on the total quantity of money created, except for the effect of unanticipated shocks on the base or monetary base multiplier.
3. The models tend to abstract from the effects of wealth and capital accumulation on the demand for, and supply of, productive goods and financial assets.

The Fisherian and Cambridge Approaches to the Quantity Theory of Money

Table 2.1: The Fisherian approach

$$m + v = p + y \tag{2.1}$$

$$y = \bar{y} + \epsilon_y \qquad v = \bar{v} + \epsilon_v \tag{2.2}$$

$$p = m + \bar{v} - \bar{y} + \epsilon_p \qquad \epsilon_p = \epsilon_v - \epsilon_y \tag{2.3}$$

The simplest, most succinct and fundamental concept to monetarist economics is the quantity theory of money. The earliest formulation of the quantity theory is associated with Irving Fisher (1911) and starts with the accounting identity, the equation of exchange: $MV=PT$ which is expressed in a log-linear form in (2.1). The equation of exchange relates the quantity of money in circulation (M) to the volume of transactions (T) in a given period and the price of articles traded, (P).[3] M is proportionally related to PT by V which is the 'transactions velocity of circulation', a measure of the average number of times a unit of money is employed in performing transactions during that year.[4]

The basic quantity theory of money supplements this identity with two key propositions. The first is that money is 'neutral', and thus it does not affect aggregate real income ($dy/dm=0$). The reason for money neutrality is based on the market clearing assumptions of the classical economic paradigm. The specific assumption made is that the markets for all goods and services (particularly labour) systematically clear through the continuous adjustment of relative prices. Resources are thereby fully utilized so that employment and output tend to equilibrium at "full employment" levels determined by tastes and preferences of the labour force. The economy is only moved from full employment output levels due to the effects of transitory or random shocks. Here money serves only as a numeraire and a medium of exchange and has no consequences for real economic magnitudes - it is neutral. The second proposition states that velocity is a real variable determined by institutional, behavioural, or technological characteristics and is independent of the quantity of money ($dv/dm=0$) as well.

The two propositions are expressed in equation (2.2) with both income and velocity being determined by non-monetary factors, deterministic as well as random. A bar above the y variable denotes "full employment" levels of real income, whereas v bar denotes the component of velocity which is determined by institutional factors - assumed to be independent of M and to

---

[3] A variant of the quantity theory relates money to national income ($MV=PY$) where Y is real national income. Here, V becomes the 'income velocity of circulation'. I will treat $Y=T$ for reasons of simplicity in exposition.

[4] Some debate remains in monetary economics over how to define what constitutes M, the stock of money (how to give empirical content to the concept of money). In general, the set of assets referred to as money, and which are postulated here as determining the price level, has broadened over time. Fisher (1911) dealt with the issue by broadening his statement of the quantity theory to incorporate bank deposits (which are indicated by a prime): $MV + M'V' = PT$.

change slowly over time.   Combining the identity in (2.1) with the propositions in (2.2) yields (2.3), the simplest form of the quantity theory which states that, other things being equal, the price level varies in proportion to the quantity of money.[5]

The alternative approach to the quantity theory, but displaying continuity with Fisher, is the Cambridge formulation associated with the work of Marshall (1923) and Pigou (1917). The Cambridge formulation emphasizes the importance of money demand in determining the effect of the supply of money on prices.   The demand for money balances is assumed to be proportional to aggregate nominal income as captured by the equation of exchange $M^d=kPY$ (2.4).

Table 2.2: The Cambridge approach

$$m^d = k + p + y \qquad (2.4)$$

$$m^s = m, \quad m^s = m^d \qquad (2.5)$$

$$y = \bar{y} + \epsilon_y \qquad k = \bar{k} + \epsilon_k \qquad (2.6)$$

$$p = m - \bar{k} - \bar{y} + \epsilon_p \qquad \epsilon_p = -\epsilon_k - \epsilon_y \qquad (2.7)$$

The Cambridge formulation shares Fisher's classical orientation with income being at its equilibrium (full employment) level except when moved off through random disturbances (ϵ_y). Velocity, or its Cambridge equivalent the k (such that $v=1/k$), is also a constant, institutionally determined variable, with deviations from equilibrium due only to random disturbances (ϵ_k). With these "constants" and the classical assumption of an exogenous supply of money (2.5), the equilibrium condition $m_s=m_d$ requires that aggregate money demand adjusts, through the price level, to match the

---

[5]Empirically, this is taken to require (imply) a unit coefficient on the price variable in a money demand equation.

existing supply of money according to (2.7).[6]   The significant contribution
of the Cambridge formulation is the story that was told focusing on the
public's demand for money, especially the demand for real balances, as the
key factor determining the equilibrium price level consistent with a given
quantity of money.   Under this formulation, people have a definite real
quantity of money they wish to hold, determined by institutional features in
the economy - prices, expectations, incomes.   An unexpected exogenous
increase in nominal money balances will set off a chain of portfolio
adjustments as individuals attempt to spend their surplus balances, and
return to their desired holdings of real balances.   However, as a group they
are constrained and cannot succeed, given that each purchase creates income
for someone else engaged in production.   The resulting excess nominal
balances continue to flow through the system until they are eroded away by
increases in the price level.   Money retains its neutrality in the sense it
cannot affect real output, and therefore must be reflected in changes in
absolute prices.   In terms of our discussion, it would be possible to draw a
causal arrow as such: $M \Rightarrow P$.

The Phillips Curve and Monetary Neutrality

The Cambridge tradition's reliance on real balances as the transmission
mechanism linking money to nominal income began to wane. The simplicity
of the assumptions concerning the nature of money demand - that it was
insensitive to the interest rate and displayed unit elasticity with regard to
prices - as well as the classical view of fully   flexible (labour) market
clearing began showing limitations beyond a first approximation.
Additionally, the neutrality of money came into question with the
generalization of the output-inflation trade-off in the Phillips (1958) curve.
The primary implication of the Phillips curve undermined classical notions
of money neutrality.   The Phillips curve established the existence of a
continuum of equilibrium output levels associated with different inflation
rates, both in the short run and in the long run.   The policy implication was
that employment could only be reduced at the cost of a permanently higher

---

[6]Parkin (1987) employs three alternative money supply policy rules to $(m^s = m^d)$:
1. $m = \mu + \varepsilon$ with any deviations from a deterministic path of the money supply being random.
2. $m = m_{t-1} + \mu + \varepsilon_t$ where money supply follows a random walk with drift.
3. $\Delta m_t = \Delta m_{t-1} + \varepsilon_t$ where changes in the money supply follow a random walk.
Parkin shows that all of the growth rules have different implications for the exact nature of the
relationship between money and prices, although all of the broad conclusions are consistently
monetarist (they retain neutrality).

rate of inflation. A higher rate of inflation requires a higher rate of money growth. As a result money was not neutral, it could influence real output.

Friedman (1968) and Phelps (1968) challenged the long-run non-neutrality implied by the Phillips relationship, arguing that the Phillips statistical relations could not be permanently stable. Phillips relationships were only short run characterizations because they were the result of the actions of economic agents induced by unanticipated price fluctuations, under conditions of imperfect information. Errors in expectations could persist, resulting in transitory output fluctuations. In the long run, however, actual and expected price changes would not differ systematically (i.e. $P=P^*+\varepsilon p$ where * denotes an expectations term). As a result, a 'natural' rate of employment output exists at an equilibrium which is invariant to permanent inflation. More specifically, the natural rate of employment is that rate of employment consistent with a labour market in which all inflationary expectations are fulfilled. The existence of the 'natural' rate suggests that in the long run the Phillips relationship should be vertical. While it was possible for short run changes in the money supply to cause unanticipated but persisting price changes, resulting in output fluctuations, in the long run money was neutral. The extent of money neutrality in these models does depend critically on assumptions held concerning the nature of expectations formation. Rationally held expectations imply that changes in the money supply cannot affect output systematically over any time horizon. Monetary policy actions are neutral in the long and short runs, unless they are unanticipated, in which case they could lead to fluctuations in output due to the short-term error effect on expectations.

Employing Keynesian assumptions regarding market clearing also changes the analysis. If price and output adjustments are constrained by overlapping wage and price contracts, even with rationally held expectations, a fully anticipated monetary policy may affect output in the short run. The reason for this is that overlapping contracts pose a barrier to market adjustment in response to changes in the supply of money. As a result inflation may show some inertia and the change in the supply of money may be reflected in output. In general, however, the key theme in all these formulations remains the same: that inflation and transitory changes in real income are always and everywhere primarily monetary phenomena.

To sum up, the Friedman-Phelps formulation of the vertical 'expectations-augmented' Phillips curve quickly became a core analytical tool in monetarism, supplementing the quantity theories transmission mechanism of the connection between output and national income.[7]   What is particularly interesting for this discussion is the direction in which the causal effect is seen to work.   By causal it is implied that the occurrence of the cause is both necessary and sufficient for the effect to take place.   Such a notion of causality does not require temporal precedence of the cause before the effect.   Rational expectations obviates the need for that condition as perfectly rational agents (those with perfect foresight) will forecast changes in the causing variable and act in anticipation of a change (Laidler, 1991).

Nevertheless, the causal relationship in the monetarist theory, as so far discussed, is such that changes in an exogenously determined money stock bring forth changes in real income (although only in a transitory fashion) and changes in the price level.   Replacing the equality in the equation of exchange with a causal arrow, monetarists would view the transmission mechanism as: $MV \Rightarrow PT$, or alternatively, $M \Rightarrow kPY$.   Friedman (1989) encapsulates this viewpoint by stating: 'substantial changes in the supply of nominal money balances can and do occur independently of any changes in demand.   The conclusion is that substantial changes in prices or nominal income are almost always the result of changes in the nominal supply of money.' (p.3).

A fundamental assumption of the monetarists' view of the monetary transmission mechanism is the exogenous nature of the money supply.   As changes in exogenous nominal balances drive the system, the monetarists had a theoretical 'black box' to fill.   The story they told had to be supplemented by a theoretical specification of a process through which such exogenous changes might occur.   That is, by which process does monetary creation come about?   The story so far told is underpinned by a theory of money demand which ignores or assumes away the method by which money is created.   For the monetarist propositions to be theoretically tight, a supply story is needed justifying the exogeneity assumption - in particular, a story showing money to be directly and effectively controlled by the Central Bank.[8]

---

[7]Friedman's (1989) restatement of the quantity theory is broad enough to encapsulate the expectations-augmented Phillips relation explicitly.

[8]This last requirement is needed for the theoretical case and not for an empirical case of exogeneity.

THE MONEY-MULTIPLIER APPROACH

The theory of the money supply process which is most consistent with the label 'monetarist' is the money-multiplier approach associated with, amongst others, Brunner and Meltzer (1989).[9] The salient feature of this approach is the key role of certain fixed behavioural ratios. The behavioural ratios aim to capture the portfolio behaviour of the banks and non-bank public, and relate these to the supply of money and the authority controlled money aggregates (the monetary base).   As a first approximation, the discussion will begin with a model assuming that the only financial assets are currency (C) and demand deposits (D).

The analytical essence of the model stems from a group of related accounting identities. The first identity defines the high-powered monetary base (H) as the Central Bank's holdings of the liabilities of the banking sector. It is from this base that the remainder of the money supply is eventually created.   The liabilities of the banking sector held by the Central Bank consist of currency (C) and reserves (R)(2.8). It is proposed that banks will maintain cash reserves (R) equal to a fixed proportion (z) of deposits, reflecting either regulatory requirements or firm specific liquidity needs. Additionally, the deposit-holding public will hold a constant fraction (h) of their deposits in currency (2.9). The next identity simply defines (narrow) money (M) as the sum of currency and deposits (2.10). Substituting the "behavioral" ratios of (2.9) into (2.8), solving for D, then substituting into (2.10) yields a relationship between the supply of money and the monetary base (2.11).[10]

From these simple identities it is demonstrated that the money supply is a multiple, μ, of the base. From this, the theory postulates that the Central Bank can directly control the money supply (M) because the base (H) is directly under their control, and because h and z are knowable and constant (or at least predictable).[11] Succinctly put, the money supply is 'exogenous' because the monetary authorities control M, since they control H and know

---

[9]Typical expositions of the approach can be found in Friedman (1989), Cuthbertson (1985), and in a development framework, Coats and Khatkhate (1980). The following discussion owes a great debt to the exposition in Papademos and Modigliani (1990).

[10]See Appendix 2 for full mathematical derivation of all solutions.

[11]Although the asset ratios are usually assumed to be constant for simplicity, most authors (e.g. Brunner, 1989) require only predictability of the ratios for the logic to work.

h and *z*.

Table 2.3: Money-multiplier approach

$$H = C + R \qquad (2.8)$$

$$R = zD; \quad C = hD \qquad (2.9)$$

$$M = C + D \qquad (2.10)$$

$$M = \mu H \qquad \mu = \left[\frac{1 + h}{h + z} \right] \geq 1 \qquad (2.11)$$

The intuitive rationale for the existence of the multiplied relationship between base and money supply provides the behavioural theory of the money supply process. The intuition can be most clearly envisaged by considering an increment of H caused by a Central Bank policy action. This Central Bank expansionary action is accomplished by causing bank reserves to rise by the full change in H. With the assumption of a fixed z $(=R/D)$, banks now have excess desired reserves (deposits left unchanged) and use these to acquire earning assets in the form of loans or securities. In creating loans, the banks create new deposits equal to the magnitude of the new assets, less the cash balances that the public wants to hold - which will be determined by h. The increment in deposits will lead to a further increase in reserves, which will set off another round of expanding loans, deposits and cash. The withdrawal from this circle into cash and reserves means that in each subsequent round the increment in deposits becomes smaller. The money supply will continue to expand until this increment in deposits becomes zero. The eventual total increase in the money supply will then be determined by μ and the magnitude of the initial change in H.[12]

The multiplier approach can be generalized to incorporate a broader spectrum of bank assets, as well as to deal with the complications of borrowed and excess reserve holdings (for discussions, see Papademos and Modigliani (1990)).   The key restriction is that additional financial assets must be assumed to be held in some defined, and known, fixed proportion to demand deposits. However, despite the broadening of the model's scope, the essential features of the money supply process are not altered. Briefly restated they are that the supply of money is a well-defined multiple of the monetary base and the size of the multiplier is determined by the fact that the growth of reserves maintained by banks is a constant fraction of their deposits. The constant level of desired reserves leads banks to respond to an increase in reserves created by the Central Bank in a predictable fashion, expanding the money supply by some known multiple. In the nature of the models presented, the conclusions rely on the assertion that asset preferences of the banks and the public, which affect the process of deposit expansion, are invariant to changes in the values of financial or real variables (Y or r), at least to a good approximation.

Following from these assumptions, the money supply process is not influenced by economic variables, but only by institutional, technological, and stochastic factors influencing asset-holding behaviour. The supply of money can be taken as a quantity determined exogenously by the monetary authority up to a random component.[13]   The multiplier money supply formulation retains its compatibility with the quantity theory, and with the long-run neutrality of money as hypothesized by the expectations augmented Phillips curve.

---

[12]In symbols, $\Delta D = \Delta H - \Delta C = \Delta H - h\Delta D$ which gives $\Delta D = \Delta H (1+h)^{-1}$. The change in the money supply will then be $\Delta M = \Delta C + \Delta D + h\Delta D + \Delta H (1+h)^{-1} = h(\Delta H (1+h)^{-1}) + \Delta H (1+h)^{-1}$. The total increase in the money supply is then $\Delta M + (1+h)(h+z)^{-1}$.

[13]Brunner adds a degree of rigour to the assumption of Central Bank control of the money supply by redefining controllability as 'the variance of the probability distribution of the forecast error of the money stock conditional on some policy variables' (p.266). The degree of monetary control (DCA) is then equal to: $DCA = 1 / (V [m-m^*] / IR)$ where V is the variance of the forecast error ($m-m^*$) conditional on the choice of policy variables (σ) and on the institutional regime (IR). Citing a study by Johannes and Rasche (1987), Brunner goes on to assert the money base and hence supply is perfectly controllable to the last dollar (potentially) by a Central Bank able and willing to use suitable strategies and tactical procedures.

THE KEYNESIAN NEO-CLASSICAL-KEYNESIAN SYNTHESIS

An alternative viewpoint of the transmission mechanism of monetary policy and the role of money in the economy in relation to national income is based around Keynes's work in the *General Theory* (1936). The body of work has been known variously as simply 'Keynesian' theory and as the 'Keynesian-Neo-classical synthesis' reflecting the fact that it is an interpretation of Keynes' work consistent with classical general equilibrium concepts.[14] The formulation of the theory begins with a money demand formulation similar to the Cambridge quantity theory approach.

The first theoretical innovation introduced by Keynes follows from his work on liquidity preference, which found the existence of a systematic effect of nominal interest rates on people's demand to hold money. In Keynes discussion money balances are held for, amongst others, 'precautionary' and 'speculative' motives. Speculative balances are held with the desire to secure profit from 'knowing better than the market what the future will bring forth'. Differences in individual expectations are the key, and these cause portfolio shifts of the public based on expected interest-rate differentials. Precautionary balances are held due to uncertainty about the future, and thus individuals desire to hold money balances as there is no risk involved. Holding money balances provides certainty as to the future cash equivalent of their resources (see Harris, 1985). Both of these motives, and their relative importance, will thus respond to changes in the interest rate. In focusing on precautionary and speculative motives, Keynes highlights the role of *uncertainty* and *expectations* in economic processes and in determining individuals' demand for money balances. It is the presence of uncertainty and future expectations which begins to give money its special characteristics in an economic system.

Liquidity Preference with Flexible Prices

Before proceeding to a fully Keynesian case, it will be illuminating to analyse a case which incorporates just this first insight of liquidity

---

[14]More radical devotees of Keynes such as Joan Robinson vehemently deny such theory is truly Keynesian and have labelled the synthesis 'bastard Keynesian'. The key bone of contention has been the assumption concerning money supply exogeneity and how true the assumption is to the spirit of Keynes. Such concerns are usually labelled post-Keynesian and will be discussed in greater detail.

preference. As a result, the immediate discussion will concentrate on a model retaining classical assumptions regarding full employment equilibrium and the independence of real income and the interest rate (2.13).

Table 2.4: Keynesian liquidity preference with flexible prices

---

$$m^d = p + \alpha y + \beta i + u_{md},$$
$$\beta \leq 0 , \alpha \geq 0 \tag{2.12}$$

$$y = \bar{y} + \epsilon_y \qquad r = \bar{r} + \epsilon_r \tag{2.13}$$

$$m^s = m + u_{ms} \qquad m^s = m^d \tag{2.14}$$

$$i = r + \pi^* \qquad \pi^* = p^*_{t+1} - p \tag{2.15}$$

$$p + \beta(p^*_{t+1} - p) = m + \bar{v}(\bar{r}, \bar{y}) - \bar{y} + \epsilon_p \tag{2.16}$$

where:

$$\bar{v}(\bar{r}, \bar{y}) = -\beta\bar{r} + (1 - \alpha)\bar{y}$$

$$\epsilon_p = -u_m - \beta\epsilon_r - \alpha\epsilon_y \qquad u_m = u_{md} - u_{ms}$$

Incorporating the Keynesian ideas on liquidity preference into a stylized log-linear money demand equation yields equation (2.12). Money is then influenced by prices, income and interest rates. β here is the semi-elasticity of money demand with respect to the nominal interest rate, i, and α is the elasticity of money demand with respect to real income. The coefficient on the price level p is set to unity. In keeping with the money demand basis, money is assumed to be exogenous but with a stochastic component reflecting imperfections in monetary controls (equation 2.14). Incorporating Keynes's concern with uncertainty and expectations, the nominal interest rate is then the sum of the real interest rate and the expected rate of inflation (2.15), where * denotes an expectation.

Combining (2.12)-(2.15) and solving for the equilibrium price level gives a relationship (2.16), which implies that the equilibrium price level in the next period will depend on the existing quantity of money and the expected price level in that next period.   To solve the equilibrium conditions, however, it becomes necessary to specify the determinants of anticipated inflation. As discussed, the anticipated inflation rate affects the equilibrium price level by influencing the demand for real money balances through the speculative and precautionary motives - i.e. by influencing the opportunity cost of holding money. The magnitude of this 'liquidity preference' effect will theoretically be determined by the assumed process through which an individual's expectations are formulated.

The key implications of this approach can be highlighted by drawing the assumption that people expect zero inflation - an assumption consistent with an environment where variations in the money stock are a random walk around a constant non-inflationary rate of monetary expansion. In this case the equilibrium condition reduces to:

$$p = m + \bar{v}\,(\,\bar{r}\,,\bar{y}\,) - \bar{y} + \epsilon_p \qquad (2.16a)$$

Here, the price level moves in proportion to the quantity of money, with the proviso that the velocity term, v bar, fluctuates in response to variations in equilibrium levels of real income, y, and real interest rates, r.   That is, changes in the equilibrium rate of interest will have an effect on trend velocity by influencing the demand for real balances, whereas changes in the real income equilibrium level will have a positive effect on real balances if the income elasticity of money demand is less than one.   The new implication for monetary policy that this analysis holds is that price stability is best achieved by adjusting the quantity of money so as to offset predictable shifts in velocity due to changes in y bar and r bar.   Such reasoning underlay attempts in the late 1960s to fine-tune the economy by the appropriate use of monetary policy.

Liquidity Preference with Wage Rigidity

The second fundamental contribution of Keynes was 'wage-rigidity' in the face of persistent unemployment. The key insight is that the average wage rate will fail to adjust quickly when aggregate demand falls short of its full employment level, due to the inherent stickiness of wage contracts and prices. Aggregate output and employment can then deviate from their full employment levels for a potentially long period, depending on the ultimate flexibility of wages. The implication of this proposition is that monetary policy can in fact be non-neutral by influencing output when the economy is at an unemployment equilibrium.

A stylized formulation of the Keynesian model with liquidity preference, price inflexibility and aggregate demand begins with the equilibrium condition in the money market (2.17). This condition is the same condition as in the previous model and represents a version of the Hicksian LM relation. Building wage stickiness insight into the Keynesian money demand framework is then done by employing Keynesian aggregate demand concepts. The aggregate demand equation will describe the mechanism through which an insufficient quantity of money can lead to an equilibrium with unemployed resources. In this case, aggregate demand is specified (2.18) as a function of deviations around equilibrium levels of real output and real interest rates. If either the real interest rate or real income is not at its long-run equilibrium, aggregate demand will deviate from its full-employment equilibrium. The real disturbance term, u_d, is seen to incorporate the net effects of fiscal variables affecting aggregate demand. Additionally, equations (2.19) and (2.20) embody standard assumptions about the nominal interest rate, i, real income, and expected inflation. For simplicity, it is also assumed that the analytical period is short enough for average price and wage levels to be unchanged - hence anticipated inflation is zero.

Substituting these definitions into (2.17) and solving for the relationship between the equilibrium level of real output and the quantity of money yields a solution which is expressed in two alternative, though equivalent, expressions (2.21a) and (2.21b). The first relationship (2.21a) expresses the deviation of real output from its long-run equilibrium level as being: (1) proportionate to the real quantity of money, with the proportionality factor μ being the elasticity of equilibrium real output with respect to m, given p, and (2) influenced by a multiplied effect running from the difference between trend velocity and the equilibrium rate of real output, with a random component.

Table 2.5. Keynesian liquidity preference with fixed wages

$$m^d = p + \alpha y + \beta i + u_m$$
$$\beta \leq 0 \, , \, \alpha \geq 0$$

(2.17)

$$y^d = \bar{y} + c\,(\,y - \bar{y}\,) + d\,(\,r - \bar{r}\,) + u_d$$
$$0 < c < 1 \, , \, d < 0$$

(2.18)

$$i = r + \pi^*; \quad \pi^* = p^*_{t+1} - p;$$
$$M^s = M^d; \quad M^s = M + u_{ms}$$

(2.19)

$$p = \bar{p}, \quad \pi^* = 0, \quad y = y^d + u_y$$

(2.20)

$$y = \bar{y} + \mu\,(\,m - \bar{p}\,) + \mu\,(\,\bar{v} - \bar{y}\,) + \epsilon_d$$

(2.21a)

$$y = \bar{y} + \mu(m - \bar{m}) + \epsilon_d$$

(2.21b)

where:

$$\mu = (\,\alpha c\,)^{-1}$$

$$\bar{v} = -\,(\alpha d + \beta)\,r + (\,1 - \alpha\,)\,\bar{y} \qquad , \quad \bar{m} = \bar{p} + \bar{y} - \bar{v}$$

$$\epsilon_d = (-d\bar{r} - u_d + u_y)c^{-1} \quad , \quad u_m = u_{md} - u_{ms}$$

Employing the familiar equation of exchange $(M=P+Y\text{-}V)$ allows a re-parameterization of the relationship which clarifies the model's implications. The new parameterization, (2.21b) shows very clearly, then, that deviations of real income from its long-run equilibrium value will be due to deviations in the money supply from its long-run equilibrium value. In this case swings in economic activity (or the business cycle) are seen to be a largely monetary phenomena. Monetary disequilibria has the power, then, to push real income away from its long-run equilibrium value.

An interesting point here is that causation still runs from changes in an exogenously determined money stock to the vector of national income. A money supply story was still required theoretically to complete the tale.

Although both of the models discussed employ fairly simple assumptions about the nature of wage-price flexibility and the market-clearing mechanism, these models can be extended to incorporate a range of dynamic responses of nominal income to changes in the money stock. However, the basic logic remains the same, relying on assumptions about the exogeneity of the money supply imparting a uni-directional impact on national income variables. As no mechanism allows for feedback from national income to the supply of money, the quantity of money would be assumed to display strong-form exogeneity. The fundamental difference, however, from the case of the monetarists is that wage rigidity and sticky prices allow money to have a non-neutral impact on the economy.

THE PORTFOLIO BALANCE APPROACH

The implications of Keynes's liquidity preference insights meant that the money-creation story told by the classical economists, which relied on portfolio preferences being invariant to changes in rates of return, now had to be altered. Rather, the money multipliers of the classical case, μ, had to be amended ('endogenized') by making them sensitive to interest rate effects and economic factors such as wealth. Once the multipliers are re-specified, they would still be 'knowable' and 'predictable', allowing the Central Bank to control the money supply to a fairly exact level. The approach to endogenizing the money multipliers is known as the 'portfolio balance approach'. The key proposition here is that the portfolio choices of the bank and the non-bank public will be influenced by existing rates of return: e.g. the interest rates on demand and time deposits, r_d and r_t, the market rate of interest on government securities, r, interest rates on bank loans, r_l, the average return on banks reserves, r_r, and the discount rate on bank borrowing from the Central Bank, r_{cb}. The precise behavioural relationships of each of these rates of return will be determined by institutional and regulatory factors.

The impact of liquidity preference on the currency ratio ($h = C/D$), and the time deposit ratio ($t = T/D$), is felt through the non-bank public's real demand for currency and bank liabilities. The real demand for an individual asset depends upon the asset's own rate of return, the return on competing assets, real income and real wealth (W/P). Gross substitutability amongst assets is assumed and demand for all assets is homogeneous of the first degree in income and wealth. The ratios, h and t, are respecified in a behavioural parameterization in (2.22) and (2.23) respectively. The intuition for the expected signs of the partial derivatives is derived from the assumption of gross substitutability amongst assets. In terms of the currency ratio, the effects of increases in the term deposit rate, r_t, and the market rate, r, will both be positive, based on the assumption that while both would tend to reduce the demands for currency and demand deposits, demand deposits are a closer substitute to the other financial assets than is currency. Thus, the currency-deposit ratio would be expected to increase since reductions in holdings of demand deposits are greater than reductions in currency holdings. An increase in real income has an expected negative effect on the currency ratio, which is consistent with the income elasticity of the demand for currency, $\acute{\eta}_{hy}$, being smaller then the interest elasticity of the demand for demand deposits, $\acute{\eta}_{dy}$. The ambiguous effect of income on the time deposit ratio stems from uncertainty regarding whether income has a stronger speculative effect (positive relationship) or transactions effect (negative effect).

Supplementing the equations expressing the non-bank public's portfolio behaviour is (2.24) which expresses the commercial bank's portfolio behaviour. The most important behavioural factor for the banks is their ratio of free (excess) reserves to demand deposits, $(f=R_e/D)$. Applying simple profit maximization to the behaviour of the banking firm suggests that the desired level of excess reserves held by the bank is negatively affected by their marginal revenue, the rate of return on the bank's earning assets, r, and positively influenced by their marginal cost, or the effective cost of borrowing from the Central Bank, r_{cb}, and the rate of return on such reserves, r_r. An increase in r_{cb} should induce banks to maximize their holdings of reserves, in order to be able to meet any large unexpected withdrawals.[15]

Employing a standard relationship between $M0$ (narrow or non-borrowed monetary base controllable directly by the Central Bank) and broader monetary aggregates MJ $(J=1,2)$ of the form: $MJ = n_j M0$; $n_j = (1+h+t+f)\mu_j$ $(J=1,2)$; where μ_j is the money multiplier on the Jth aggregate, and substituting in the portfolio behavioural relations (2.22)-

---

[15] The effect of borrowing from the Central Bank (r_{cb}) may actually be ambiguous as the demand for such borrowing may increase with the market rate, reflecting an increased demand for credit by the public.

(2.24), provides an expression (2.25) for the money supply as a function of incomes and interest rates.[16] The exogenous policy variables are $M0$, z_d and z_t, the required reserve ratios on demand and time deposits, and r_r and r_{cb}.

Table 2.6: Keynesian money multipliers: the portfolio balance approach

$$h = h \; (\; r_d \; , \; r_t \; , \; r \; , \; py/w \;) \qquad\qquad (2.22)$$

$$t = (\; r_d \; , \; r_t \; , \; r \; , \; py/w \;) \qquad\qquad (2.23)$$

where:

$$\partial h/\partial r_d < 0, \quad \partial h/\partial r_t \geq 0, \quad \partial h/\partial r \geq 0$$

$$\partial h/\partial y = - \; \partial h/\partial(w/p) = \eta_{hy} - \eta_{dy} < 0$$

$$\partial t/\partial r_d < 0, \quad \partial t/\partial r_t > 0, \quad \partial t/\partial r < 0$$

$$\partial t/\partial y = - \; \partial t/\partial(w/p) = \eta_{ty} - \eta_{dy} \; \substack{< \\ >} \; 0$$

and:

$$f = f \; (\; r \; , \; r_r \; , \; r_{cb} \;) \qquad\qquad (2.24)$$

$$\partial f/\partial r < 0, \quad \partial f/\partial r_r > 0, \quad \partial f/\partial r_{cb} > 0$$

---

[16] The relationship employed here is simply the multiplier relationship developed earlier, generalized to account for additional money aggregates and financial assets. (See Papademos and Modigliani, 1990.)

$$MJ = \mu_j(\ r\ ,\ r_d\ ,\ r_t\ ,\ r_r\ ,\ r_{cb}\ ;\ Y\ ;\ z_d\ ,\ z_t\ )$$
$$M0 \quad (\ J\ =\ 1,2\ ) \tag{2.25}$$

The remaining interest rates may or may not be exogenous depending on the regulatory structure, although r, r_t and Y are viewed as endogenous in most models. The approach then goes on to analyse the impact of the endogenous interest rates on the multipliers. The total impact of the interest rates will depend crucially on the interaction of these rates with the rates of return on bank liabilities. The institutional atmosphere, and nature, of these relationships will determine the sign of the total interest-rate effect.

This story of money creation, however, is broadly similar to the classical case whereby monetary expansion is achieved by the Central Bank inserting reserves into the banking system. The banking system then responds in a deterministic manner and expands deposits by a certain multiple. The important extension is that the portfolio behaviour of individuals and banks in creating deposits is going to be significantly affected by variations in rates of return - the most important being the market rate, r. The interaction, then, of the public's demand for assets and the profit motives of the banking system, through a multiplier framework, is the basis of the Keynesian story regarding money creation. An expansionary monetary policy which creates an expansion in the supply of the bank's primary liabilities, $M0$, then leaves the bank with an excess desired quantity of free reserves. Assuming $r > r_r$, banks would seek to acquire a greater share of earning assets, which would have the supplementary effect of increasing investment. At the same time, banks would try to induce the public to hold this increased quantity of MJ (e.g. $J = 2$), which could be achieved by raising the time deposit rate, r_t (and thus r_l). As the public holds the increased deposits generated by bank credit funded investments, the quantity of banks' liabilities undergoes another increase, which stimulates another round of increasing credit, investment and deposits. The multiplied expansion of the monetary aggregate occurs until the additional increment in deposits falls to zero. The initial increase in base money, then, has an expansionary effect on the economy because it increases the liquidity of the banking sector, changing relative rates of return on assets, thereby encouraging portfolio shifts and ultimately investment. Again, the Central Bank can predict this portfolio behaviour and control the money stock, implying that movements in this exogenously determined money supply will be the prime determinant of movements in national income.

WEAKNESSES OF THE MULTIPLIER APPROACH

Whereas the monetarist and Keynesian approaches to the money supply do have significant differences, they share some similarities and this holds true of the approaches' respective weaknesses:

1. The first of the fundamental weaknesses of these multiplier approaches is that they rely on *ad hoc* (usually fixed coefficient) financial ratios in describing the bank's and non-bank's, portfolio behaviour. In so much as the Lucas (1976) critique holds, and the systematic behaviour of individual actions will not be invariant to the actions of the policy authority, an approach which assumes relative constancy of parameters will misspecify the true dynamic behaviour of the system's response to monetary policy action. Such an approach is not able to model (or even theoretically describe) in any consistent manner the effect of changing regulatory structures - deregulation or liberalization - on the transmission mechanism of money and income.

2. A second weakness revolves around the lack of a true, in-depth, theoretical understanding of the effects of bank behaviour on the money creation process in these approaches. Even in its portfolio balance incarnation, the multiplier approach does not have an explicit specification of how banks behave, and how this behaviour interacts with credit demand and the regulatory framework to create money.
   The omission leaves this transmission story with theoretical holes. In the story told above, banks need to increase the time deposit rate to induce the public to hold the larger supply of $M2$. However, such a response would reduce investment and credit demand, causing disequilibrium in the money market. Furthermore, there is no behavioural method by which the public has a choice to hold the increment in bank deposits. The resulting transmission mechanism looks incomplete, guilty of telling only part of the story. In not specifying the method by which banks deal with credit demands, how credit demands come about, and how such behaviour is affected by the regulatory system, the policy story told by these approaches is inadequate, incomplete and inconsistent.

3. A final weakness is the assumption of money's (at least weak-form) exogeneity which theoretically postulates a unidirectional causal effect flowing from money to national income. The assumed exogeneity, and the assumed ultimate controllability of the money stock by the monetary

authority, has led to a theoretical paradigm which focuses purely on the asset side (or bank liability side) of money creation. Demand for money, in the form of 'credit' money needed by the productive and consuming sectors, plays no effective role in the process of money creation. The effects on the behaviour of this sector's credit demand, engendered by various policy stances, and alternative policy targets, does not play a part in the story told by these approaches. In other words, credit demand arising from the creation of the "independent" income variable has no part in these theories of the money-creation process. Again, these approaches are guilty of telling only part of the story.

A New Paradigm?

Responding to these inefficiencies, a recognition has emerged that a better understanding of the monetary transmission mechanism, and of the fundamental behaviour and institutional factors that determine the relative effectiveness of alternative monetary controls, is required. Such an approach would incorporate the following concerns:

1. A recognition that the individual characteristics of financial systems, the specific structure of financial markets and institutions in a given country, and the related behavioural characteristics of market participants, have a great impact on the efficacy of specific monetary targets and policy tools. Hence, an understanding of the institutional framework in which monetary policy is being undertaken is required. Such a concern is particularly relevant when looking at developing country monetary economics, as existing market imperfections will play a large role in determining how monetary tools work.
2. A concern that a theoretical framework must be developed which goes beyond the conventional monetary theory with its focus on the role of narrow money aggregates as the major determinant of nominal income. Given the wide spectrum of monetary and credit aggregates which are suitable as potential targets and indicators of policy, a framework must specifically recognize that different adjustment processes and dynamics arise when the Central Bank controls various broad money and credit aggregates. Also, depending on the institutional setting, the quantities of alternative policy targets can be expected to influence the actions of lenders and borrowers in a more systematic and effective way, and thus the consequent spending behaviour of firms and households.
3. An understanding that a theoretical framework is needed to link

aggregate nominal output to alternative intermediate targets and instruments of monetary policy on the appropriate specification of the economy's financial structure. Of utmost importance here is a focus on the interaction of the credit market with the goods market, and specifically on the behavioural and stochastic factors which go into determining the demand for credit by productive enterprises. It is a recognition, in the end, that aggregate income factors affect money creation, and thus money should be 'endogenized' with respect to y, p and r.

To sum up briefly, the conclusion to emerge implies that what is needed is a model of bank behaviour which describes the determinants of the supply of deposits by banks, as well as their demand for earning assets and free reserves. Any model of bank behaviour, however, must be combined with behavioural descriptions of the process through which the non-bank public's demand for bank deposits and credit arise. The combination of both aspects gives a complete model of the money market, capable of telling a dynamic story of the creation of the money supply and the determination of any endogenous interest rates. What is needed, then, is a macroeconomic model with a financial structure.

THE POST-KEYNESIAN MONETARY POSITION

Before proceeding to a discussion of a post-Keynesian monetary model, the debate would be enlivened by a venture into the theoretical history behind post-Keynesian thought.[17] The term 'post-Keynesian' has been applied to the body of theory associated with economists such as Nicholas Kaldor, Basil J. Moore and Sydney Weintraub. Most post-Keynesian literature relies on a selective reading of Keynes's *Treatise on Money* (1930), and grew largely out of the 'banking school' aligned with Thomas Tooke (1844) and Gunnar Myrdal (1939). The central premises of the post-Keynesian approach are: (1) An assumption that the money supply is endogenous, responding to the credit needs of the economy. This assumption is consistent with the 'reverse-causality' hypothesis linking prior changes in

---

[17] At this juncture, it is possible to take two distinct routes to the destination. There is a route through the industrial heartland of models of the banking firm and analysis of liability management. There is also the seaside scenic route through the theoretical history of post-Keynesian thought. The latter route was unashamedly chosen.

nominal income to changes in the money supply. (2) The importance of profit expectations and cost-push factors in causing changing credit needs, which have the effect of calling forth monetary validation. (3) The independent ability of the financial system, for varied institutional reasons, to fulfil the demand for credit and create money.

An early statement outlining the argument for an endogenous money supply vis-a-vis nominal income is found in Myrdal's (1939) 'banking principle'.[18] Myrdal's observation was that bankers, 'who are in closest contact with the means of payment', have consistently maintained that the amount of means of payment would obediently reflect the needs for exchange. Any changes in the price level and in the quantity of money are both determined simultaneously by factors exogenous to the means of payment proper - namely aggregate economic activity. The intuitive rationale was that those changes in aggregate economic activity which alter the credit needs of industrial firms alter the amount of credit created by the banking system and, by extension, change the money supply. The story centres on the time lag inherent in a modern economy between the act of production and the receipt of income. In a modern economy production costs are generally incurred, and paid, before the receipt of any sales revenue. Now, consider an economy in a stationary state. Hence, any present costs would exactly duplicate past costs. Any present proceeds from past production runs, and sales, would be sufficient to finance current costs. No outside finance would be required by the firm and no credit would be created. However, if an autonomous increase in costs occurred during a production period where goods in process and employment are both constant, businesses would be required to seek (more) bank finance. Business firms here would borrow on the *expectation* that higher future sales revenue could finance these higher production costs. The nature of economic activity, therefore, calls forth more credit money which profit-oriented banks, or near banks, automatically provide on demand (see Moore, 1988, ch.15).[19] The radical contribution of Myrdal was this insight

---

[18]The banking school proper was most closely aligned with Thomas Tooke. Tooke's contribution was in arguing that money and prices moved together because prices cause money creation (see Laidler, 1991).

[19]Credit money should be distinguished from commodity money and fiat money. Commodity money is a physical asset (e.g. gold) with an independent supply function based on production cost, and whoever controls production controls supply. Fiat money is a liability of the government and thus is directly under control of the monetary authorities, although it is tied up with deficit spending. Credit money combines the financial claims making up the

that exogenous increases in the demand for credit money will trigger accommodating responses in the money supply. The fundamental interdependence between the money supply and money demand functions thus implies that the exogeneity of the former must be denied. The supply of credit money, then, is a demand-determined quantity.

The insight of Myrdal's 'banking principle' was seized on by Joan Robinson (1970) who used it to reinterpret the quantity theory of money. Robinson argued that the causality between money and nominal income should be reversed from its classical direction, and that the equation of exchange should be read with a causal arrow as such: $MV \Leftarrow PY$. Robinson argued that read in this way, 'with the dependent variable on the left and the independent variable on the right, although rather vague, it would not have been silly' (p.251). Illustrating reverse-causation, Robinson argued that an increase in PY from one time period to another would be due to an increase in economic activity (output or employment), or due to cost-push pressure on the general price level. If, following an increase in PY, the quantity of money had not increased, then the increase would be found in the velocity of circulation. Changes in the money supply and changes in velocity were then viewed as substitutes (Kaldor, 1982). If the velocity of circulation and, by extension, the credit multiplier seemed stable, it was only because the stock of money was unstable.

The story so far told, however, has a black box in that there is no explanation of how exogenous increases in nominal income arise and are transmitted to money creation. That is, by what mechanism is an increase in credit demand transcribed into changes in the quantity of money? To fill this black box, the post-Keynesian transmission mechanism relies fundamentally on a cost-push story - especially, but not exclusively, wage-push factors. Wage-push is viewed as particularly important as wages are a price entering practically all cost functions and the greater part of consumer demand functions. Movements in wage rates will affect practically all prices, and hence unemployment, given the demand for money. Building the insight of wage-push into a simple model was carried out by Weintraub (1978). He begins with a log-linear price equation (2.26) whereby prices are determined by some constant mark-up, b, over unit labour costs, w/a (where w is the average nominal wage and a is the average productivity of employed labour $a = q/n$). Once relative increases

total liabilities of all financial institutions issuing transactions deposits. Credit money is endogenous, as increased demand for bank credit is translated into changes in the supply of credit, which in turn may call forth changes in the quantity of money (Moore, 1988).

in the nominal money wage begin to outstrip the average productivity of labour ($w > a$) due to collective bargaining positions, prices will begin to rise by a stable and predetermined mark-up over labour costs. Equation (2.27) is a log-linear variant of the equation of exchange where y is *nominal* income ($p+q=y=m+v$) and (2.26) is substituted in. Taking the time derivatives and assuming constant b, n and v, gives equation (2.28) which implies changes in income due to changes in labour costs will be transmitted fully to changes in the money supply. If real output and employment are to be maintained in the face of rising labour costs, the supply of money must increase. Thus, a government fearing the political costs of unemployment would ensure that monetary policy would accommodate these credit needs.

Such a model could be made more general to account for other exogenous increases in the demand for money - from Keynesian 'animal spirits', to foreign price shocks (oil), to government policy shocks (interest rates).[20]

Table 2.7 Weintraub's simple model with wage-push

$$p = b\ (w/a) \qquad a = q/n \qquad\qquad (2.26)$$

$$y = p + q = b + w + n = m + v \qquad\qquad (2.27)$$

$$\dot{m}/m = \dot{y}/y = \dot{w}/w \qquad\qquad (2.28)$$

In specifying a money supply story capable of demonstrating how demand for credit money actually brings forth money creation, the post-Keynesians relied on telling a story establishing the independent ability of the financial system to create credit. The earliest theory stressed the importance of Central Bank accommodation of credit needs, arguing that monetary authorities were required to provide an elastic supply of credit to the banks.

[20] A question arises as to whether a monetary cause of inflation exists, given that a stock of demand-determined money can never be in excess. Moore addresses this and argues that while excess demand inflation may exist, it is not caused by an excess supply of money but rather by the too rapid creation of credit money. The policy implication is that the government must try to control the rate at which credit comes into existence.

Here, the story is that a higher level of deposits is created by bank lending to meet credit demands. The increment in deposits requires additional reserves in support, which the Central Bank as lender of last resort cannot refuse to provide in the form of note issuing, open market operations, or through lending on the discount window at a penal rate (Kaldor, 1982). If Central Banks were to refuse to provide discount facilities to commercial banks, they would be jeopardizing the solvency of the banking system. Given the contagious nature of financial instability, a solvency crisis could precipitate a liquidity crisis and could spread to challenge the general well-being of the financial system. Thus, the Central Bank was required to provide reserves to back up lending undertaken by the banking system. The Central Bank was then providing an elastic supply of money - a horizontal money supply line in interest-money space. The implication for interest rate determination is that interest rates will be set at a constant mark-up over the prime cost of funds - the discount rate at the Central Bank. Thus, the monetary authorities control the price at which credit is extended, and in so doing leave the quantity of money to be demand determined.[21]

Minsky's Theory of Financial Instability

Minsky (1982) builds these insights into a complete theory of financial instability whereby firms caught in a trap of Ponzi finance necessarily call forth an endogenous money supply. Minsky distinguishes between hedge, speculative and Ponzi financial postures by firms. Hedge finance characterizes a position where expected gross profits exceed payment commitments and thus is financially safe. Speculative finance is a position where expected gross profit may be less, for some period of time, than payment commitments. Refinancing will be available to meet any acquired shortfall in those deficit periods. Ponzi finance is a position whereby an unexpected increase in the rate of interest applying to 'refinance loans' serves to keep the sum of total payment commitments chronically above projected future cash flows. An exogenous shock may push hedge into speculative and speculative into Ponzi positions. Any firm caught in the

---

[21]It was not unusual, here, for post-Keynesians to argue that the supportive responsibilities of Central Banks rank high above their stabilization functions: 'The central and most basic monetary obligation of any monetary authority is to provide and maintain orderly conditions in financial markets and in the commercial bank system in particular.'(Moore, 1988, p.217).

Ponzi finance trap is forced periodically to take out additional short-term payment commitments (loans) incurred at higher and higher interest rates. In order for the firm to meet the rising interest payments, in excess of gross profits, it must allow its outstanding debt to grow, even if no new income-yielding assets are acquired. Ponzi finance is a double bind of increasing costs - both those due to increases in the short-term rate of interest and those due to the forced increase in the size of outstanding debt overtime.

The distinction between the three financial postures is an elastic, dynamic concept in which firms are able to traverse the boundaries in a rather short time depending on financial conditions. Minsky recognized that a shift in Central Bank policy, for example from targeting the interest rates to targeting the monetary base in an effort to combat inflation, resulting in a large increase across the spectrum of interest rates, could push firms into Ponzi financing. The ensuing excessive credit expansion inevitably leads to a credit crunch, at which point the viability of the whole financial system is threatened because of the cumulative bankruptcies which the structuring of credit layering entails. As in the previous story, the Central Bank has no option but to stem the systematic panic by injecting whatever amount of reserves necessary to restore the solvency and tranquillity of the financial system. A similar scenario would occur for an exogenous shock (e.g. oil price shock) which systematically increased the cost incurred by all firms and caused an increase in the amount of bank finance required.

The case for complete Central Bank accommodation in order to avoid systematic financial distress, although insightful, does not provide a comprehensive story of money creation. The main shortfall of this approach is its inability to account for periods of Central Bank non-accommodation which do not result in financial crisis. Thus, few post-Keynesians would dogmatically adhere to the position that the Central Bank must always accommodate desired reserves to avoid financial crisis.[22] Rather, it would be agreed that the story is significant in cases of extreme liquidity shortage, for which recent historical precedents can be found.

---

[22]Jao (1989) argues that the level of Central Bank accommodation will be dependent on conditions in the economy. Accordingly, the Central Bank will be more accommodating of the banking system's demand for reserves and liquidity if the economy is not fully employed and the inflation rate remains moderate. Sargent and Wallace (1982) stress the role of fiscal policy and Central Bank non-independence from the government deficit. If a Central Bank must accommodate government spending plans and must create fiat to do so, then the supply of money is endogenous, responding to the credit needs of the government deficit - this is a regime of fiscal dominance.

Recent Debates in Post-Keynesian Monetary Theory

A recent debate in post-Keynesain monetary theory has emerged which can be seen as continuing to develop a comprehensive story of endogenous money creation. Two strains of thought have been identifed in this debate - the 'accommodative endogeneity' (alternatively 'reserve price constraint') position and the 'structuralist endogeneity' (alternatively 'reserve quantity constraint') position (Pollin, 1991; Moore, 1991). Although theoretical differences are present between the two groups, both positions are firmly rooted in the post-Keynesian tradition and have the endogenous nature of money as the theoretical building block. Thus, both groups agree that loans create deposits and that the supply of credit money should be viewed as endogenously determined. The disagreement between the two is more on the precise nature of endogeneity.

Accommodative endogeneity
The first school, the more 'horizontal' of the two, is the accommodationist group most closely aligned with Moore. Palley (1991) summarizes the position as consisting of two central tenets: (i) the short-term cost of funds is pegged by the Central Bank and banks then act as mark-up pricers making loans that carry a fixed mark-up over costs, and (ii) the loan supply schedule is horizontally sloped at this price and thus the level of bank lending is determined by the level of (creditworthy) loan demand.

A discussion of Moore's (1991) exposition will provide more insight into these two premises. Moore begins with the contention that Central Banks can and do administer the level of short-term interest rates on a day-to-day basis. The monetary authorities do not peg the interest rate over a long time period. Rather, the authorities continually respond to changing economic conditions in an attempt to move key macroeconomic variables towards their preferred target values. The magnitude of the changes in interest rates in respect of changing economic conditions is then the Central Bank's reaction function. Since economies do not move along a full employment, balanced growth path, Central Banks will always retain recourse to the reaction function and some degree of discretion in their interest-rate policy. Thus, Moore concludes that 'Interest rates are an autonomous policy instrument. Their level depends on how Central Banks choose to respond. It all depends (Moore, 1991, p.46)'.

Moore goes on to argue that market forces do play a role in the determination of long-term interest rates - a position held in common with the structuralists. The reason is that whereas short-term rates are administered by the authorities in response to current and expected deviations of market outcomes from preferred positions, long-term rates are based on expectations of future short-term rates. The generation of such expectations is based around the interaction between the authorities and the financial markets. The key for Moore is that the authorities always retain a considerable 'degree of freedom' as to the level at which they set short-term interest rates and that long-term rates are then determined by the market.

The second proposition of the accommodationist school is the contention that once the interest rate is set in a market period by the Central Bank, the loan supply schedule is horizontal at that price. The intuition behind this position is that for the Central Bank to maintain its short-term interest-rate position in the market period, it must accommodate the lending extended at that price, or change its interest-rate target. Open market operations are then used by the Central Bank to maintain the interest rate position targeted. Moore does acknowledge that individual banks are unable to borrow unlimited funds at the discount window at subsidized rates, due both to administrative controls set by the authorities and to 'frown' costs incurred by over-borrowing at the discount window. However, the individual banks are able to borrow unlimited funds at the market rate - in the inter-bank markets, by issuing certificates of deposits, selling securities, and the like. Thus, the individual bank is a price-taker and is faced with a horizontal supply of funds at the short-term interest rate. By extension, the supply of credit at the mark-up rate is also horizontal in the market period. Thus, from the individual bank's point of view, additional funds from any source whatsoever are exactly equivalent to funds directly borrowed from the Central Bank in meeting reserve requirements. The key is that reserve requirements are fulfilled. From the system point of view, though, only borrowing from the discount window adds to the total supply of reserves. As long as the Central Bank is committed to defending the short-term interest-rate target, the required reserves needed to validate the total amount of credit extended by the banks will be made available to the system. The supply schedule for credit will then be horizontal at that interest rate.[23]

The transmission mechanism then between the exogenous policy tool, the short-term interest rate and economic activity is through the typical Keynesian cost-push nexus. The endogenous rise in the interest rate will cause a fall in investment. The reduction in investment comes from the

---

[23]It will be argued in subsequent chapters that due to the particular institutional features of most developing countries, the accommodationists' views on endogeneity take on particular relevance.

destruction of income caused by the higher interest payments which are incurred by indebted firms and households. The reduction in investment will have a multiplier - accelerator effect (negative) on output and employment, thus washing out the increased demand for money by reducing nominal income to below its original level. The important insight here is that the exogenous increase in interest rates requires a reduction in credit money demand which can only be managed by a reduction in income.

In addition to the reduction in credit demand from a reduction in income, banks will find that the creditworthy demand for credit will have decreased from the adverse selection effect of higher interest rates. Thus, although the loan schedule is horizontal at the new interest rate, banks will have faced a degree of credit 'price rationing'. For the accommodationist school, the contraction of credit in the system is achieved purely through the price-rationing mechanism of interest rates.

Structural Endogeneity

The second school is the 'structural endogeneity' position associated with authors such as Wray (1992) and Pollin (1991). The structural endogeneity position also may be summarized as having two premises: (i) the interest rate is determined through an interaction of the financial markets and the monetary authority, and (ii) the loan supply schedule is positively sloped, reflecting increasing marginal cost for funds on the market.

To understand the structuralist position more intuitively, consider the contention that Central Banks operate under a set of constraints which limit their ability to pursue accommodative monetary policy. It is reasonable to argue that whilst most Central Banks recognize the contractionary dangers of quantity restrictions, pressures generated from within the financial edifice (the 'market's sentiments') have led to a growing consensus among Central Banks that combating the inflationary dangers associated with monetary ease must be a first priority. Thus, Central Banks are likely to try to quantity-constrain lending.

The structuralists then argue that the Central Bank's efforts to control the growth of non-borrowed reserves through open market restrictiveness does indeed exert significant quantity constraints on reserve availability. Both the administrative restrictions and frown costs on discount window borrowing are real and effective constraints on lending activities. Thus, Central Banks can choose to restrict the growth of non-borrowed reserves. If they do, the banks must find additional reserves. Additional reserves, though not necessarily a fully adequate supply, are found within the financial structure itself - usually from innovative liability management and borrowing in the inter-bank market.

The banks then are having recourse to the wholesale markets to diversify their credit sources in such a way as to enhance their ability to equate the demands for funds with the supply. This liability management will go a considerable way to providing the reserves demanded through 'lend first, find reserves later' banking practices. The result of this liability management is that the banks now find themselves in a position whereby: (a) a given volume of reserves will support more liability-managed type deposits and (b) a given volume of demand deposits will support more bank loans to businesses. That is, in successfully using liability management, banks can generate additional effective reserves by increasing the velocity of circulation. The ability to increase the velocity of circulation provides the banks with a highly elastic supply of reserves.

If and when the money markets can not generate an adequate reserves supply by increasing velocity, a liquidity shortage will then emerge. Intermediaries will be forced to call in loans and sell assets to meet their reserve needs. The costs associated with such portfolio shifts for banks will make lending prohibitive by putting upward pressure on interest rates and reducing the creation of new loans. It is in such a situation that credit crunches arise and may lead to the Ponzi situations as outlined by Minsky.

Palley (1991) provides a simple model to illustrate the second premise in the structuralists' argument. Palley postulates a group of profit-maximizing banks which have n alternative assets and m alternative sources of funds. Given standard assumptions concerning decreasing marginal revenue and increasing marginal cost, the banks will profit maximize to the condition that $MR_1 = MR_n = MC_1 = MC_m$. Given this profit-maximizing condition, Palley considers an increase in loan demand. The result of an increased loan demand is that banks are now faced with increasing marginal revenue associated with lending. Banks will seek to lend more. The banks need to fund the lending and in general have three sources to draw on - the discount window, attracting funds from the non-bank public, and the wholesale market. As the *MC* for each source of funds is increasing, the banking system must pay more to obtain additional funds. Thus, for each additional loan extended, a higher interest rate must be forthcoming. The aggregate loan supply schedule must then be positively sloped - in disagreement with the accommodationists more horizontal view.

Into such a framework, the structuralists can then introduce financial innovation. For the structuralists, the role that financial innovation has to play is that it allows banks to fulfil the role of generating required reserves not otherwise forthcoming from the Central Bank. As such, financial innovation is a profit-maximizing response to counter upward interest-rate pressure. That is, successful financial innovation is an attempt to reduce the marginal cost associated with attracting new funds. Thus, the upward-sloping loan supply schedule provides the stimulus for financial innovation.

At this point, the key differences between the accommodationist and structuralist position have emerged. First, the interest rate for the structuralists is not an exogenous policy tool but is determined by the interaction between the authorities and the market. Second, by pushing up the costs of funds, the structuralists' quantity rationing leads to an aggregate loan schedule which has a positive slope. Thus, the central disagreement between the two groups concerns the interest rate elasticity of the credit supply function. Accommodationists see a perfectly elastic supply of reserves at the interest-rate the monetary authorities choose to peg. Structuralists see a highly, but not perfectly, elastic supply of reserves. The difference is one of magnitude. Indeed, it is the case that certain policy assumptions can render the two groups observationally equivalent. If the inter-bank market is pegged by the Central Bank or if the Central Bank targets borrowed reserves with a fixed discount rate, the marginal cost of funds would be constant. As a result, banks will exclusively finance additional lending from this source and the supply function of reserves (and, by extension, loans) will be horizontal (Palley, 1991).

So despite some non-trivial differences between the two groups, the central theme of an endogenous money supply is maintained. It is important to note in summation that for post-Keynesian analysis the endogeneity of the money supply arises from the loans creating deposits nexus. Thus, the money supply is endogenous regardless of the exact monetary and exchange rate regimes in place. While post-Keynesians may still differ and some points of contention still exist, the broad agreement on these central points of theory is most definitely maintained.

A Macroeconomic Model with a Simple Financial Structure

The implications of a demand-determined endogenous money supply is that any theoretical model aiming to analyse the effects of monetary policy must account for the determinants of credit demand. A basic model illustrative of this is found in Papademos and Modigliani (1990), who combine a standard Keynesian model with a simple financial structure.[24] The model

---

[24]The model chosen for reasons of brevity and simplicity does not fully account for the behaviour of the banking system, although key behavioural features implied in the transmission mechanism are present. For a full model of money supply based around banking behaviour

has two sectors: a private non-bank sector and a banking sector.

Table 2.8: A macroeconomic model with a simple financial structure

---

Part A

$$S = S(Y), \quad I = I(r,r_t), \quad S(Y) = I(Y) \qquad \text{(S1-S3)}$$

$$M1^d = PL1(r, r_d, r_t, Y) \qquad \text{(S4)}$$

$$M1^s = M1 \qquad \text{(S5)}$$

$$M1^d = M1^s \qquad \text{(S6)}$$

$$P = \bar{P} \qquad \text{(S7)}$$

Part B

$$\Delta L^d = PB(r, r_d, Y) \qquad \text{(S8)}$$

$$\Delta M2^d = PL2(r, r_d, r_t, Y) \qquad \text{(S9)}$$

$$PS + \Delta L^d = PI + \Delta M2^d \qquad \text{(S10)}$$

$$\Delta M2 = \Delta L \qquad \text{(S11)}$$

and credit demand, see Arestis (1988) and Arestis and Driver (1988). Neither paper solves the models for analytical solutions (being empirical models), thereby limiting their applicability to a theoretical discussion.

$$\Delta L^{d} = \Delta L \tag{S12}$$

$$\Delta M2^{d} = \Delta M2 \tag{S13}$$

$$(a)\ r_{d} = \bar{r}_{d}, \qquad (b)\ r_{t} = f(r) \tag{S14}$$

The non-bank sector can hold three assets: physical capital, K, narrow money, $M1$, and savings and time deposits, T. Likewise, the system also has three real interest rates: the rate on bank loans, r, the rate on demand deposits, r_{d}, and the rate on time and savings deposits, r_{t}.

Part A of the model outlines the basic Keynesian model, with system equations S1-S3 providing the commodity market equilibrium. The notable feature here is that investment, I, responds directly to interest rates whereas savings is a fixed proportion, s, to income. The implication is that any changes in the interest rate will be transmitted through changes in investment to the rest of the economy. S4 is a demand for narrow money function which is specified in familiar portfolio balance terms, with $PL1$ being the level of nominal credit. S5 is a money supply function where it is assumed, in a decidedly un-post-Keynesian manner, that the money supply can be 'exogenously' controlled unless the Central Bank chooses to control the supply of other financial assets or fixes the level of interest rates.[25] S6 is the money market equilibrium condition and S7 is a price determination equation.

Part B of the model specifies the economy's financial structure, apart from the money market. S8 specifies the demand for borrowing, S9 the demand for bank liabilities, S10 the budget constraint of the non-bank sector, S11 the bank sector budget constraint, S12 the loan market equilibrium, S13 the deposit market equilibrium, and S14 the interest rate determination.

The demand for bank loans reflects the behaviour of deficit units which borrow to finance their holdings of real capital and money. The flow demand for this sector's borrowing can then be thought of as representing

---

[25] For accommodationists such as Moore, the Central Bank always fixes the level of interest rates, as that is the main exogenous policy tool. The present model could be adapted to make it more accommodationist.

the difference between investment and savings plus the change in the holdings of real money balances of the deficit units.

$$\Delta L^d = PB(r, Y)$$
$$= P[I_d(r) - S_d(Y) + \Delta L1_d(r, Y)] \qquad (2.29)$$

where:

$$\partial B/\partial r < 0 \ , \ \partial B/\partial Y \lessgtr 0 \ if \ dS_d /dY \lessgtr \partial \Delta L1_d /\partial Y$$

and the subscript d is used to denote deficit spending units. The demand for bank loans is then a decreasing function of the interest rate, as a rise in the rate leads to an unambiguous decrease in borrowing and investment by deficit units. The income effect is intuitively ambiguous as a higher income can either increase savings and enhance the capacity for self-finance (positive), or increase the demand for real money balances and therefore the demand for borrowing (negative).

The budget constraint of the non-bank sector (S10) yields the flow demand for total liabilities of the banking system (S9) which can be thought of as the excess of saving over investment of surplus units plus the change in the money balances of deficit units. The demand for total bank liabilities is an increasing function of income, but it is ambiguous *vis-a-vis* the interest rate.

$$\Delta M2^d = PL2(r, r_t, Y)$$
$$= P[S_s(Y) - I_s(r_t) + \Delta L1_d(r, Y)] \qquad (2.30)$$

where:

$$\partial L2/\partial Y > 0 \ , \ \partial L2/\partial r \gtrless 0 \ if \ | \ dI_s /d_r \ | \gtrless | \ \partial \Delta L1_d /\partial r \ |$$

A positive interest-rate effect will occur if the interest-rate sensitivity of investment by surplus units (subscript s) is greater than the interest sensitivity of the demand for money by deficit units (subscript d). The rationale here is that the increased (broad) money holdings of surplus units engaged in portfolio readjustment, will outweigh the fall in broad money holdings of deficit units created by the ensuing reduction in loans.

The authors go on to close the model (see p.465) and use it to illustrate the workings of a post-Keynesian transmission mechanism. They begin by considering a case where the monetary authorities endeavour to control the supply of bank credit through reserve requirements against loans. Assuming the yield on reserves is lower than the loan rate, and abstracting from the effects of uncertainty on reserve management, profit maximization by banks implies that the quantity of bank credit is given by $L=R/z$, where R is the supply of reserves controlled by the Central Bank and z is the reserve ratio against bank credit. Thus, the system is closed by replacing ΔL on the right-hand side of (S12) by the following.

$$\Delta \bar{L} = \Delta \bar{R}/z$$

Substituting (2.29) in (S12) and maintaining the assumption that the price level is constant, yields the equilibrium condition for the bank credit market:

$$B(r, Y) = \bar{B} = \Delta \bar{L}/\bar{P} \qquad (2.31)$$

The mechanism whereby the monetary authorities allow banks to increase lending is by a reduction in required reserves. The resulting increase in excess reserves induces banks to try and expand loans. To do so, the banks are constrained by the demand for loans by deficit sectors (2.29) and must induce an expansion of investment and, ergo, credit demand by lowering the lending rate. The associated expansion of investment allows productive enterprise to generate more income and greater savings, which helps fund the increased investment. Here, relaxing their policy stance the monetary authorities *allow* a change in real income to occur by allowing the supply of bank credit to change. The money market plays only an indirect role by influencing the demand for credit by deficit units. At the new equilibrium, the supply of money is determined by the quantity demanded given the equilibrium levels of Y and r. The key, though, is that investment (or credit demand) drives the system, ultimately creating the savings necessary to finance the initial increment in investment. The causality is reversed - changes in national income (investment) cause changes in the money supply.

When the Central Bank implicitly imposes a limit on the supply of broad money ($M2$), the transmission mechanism will flow through the budget constraint of the banking sector (S11). As a result of the authorities pursuing a monetary aggregate as a target an additional equilibrium condition must be satisfied:

$$L2(r, \ Y) \ = \ \overline{\Delta M2}/\overline{P} \ = \ \overline{\Delta L}/\overline{P} \qquad\qquad (2.32)$$

The determination of nominal income under a regime of targeting the total amount of bank liabilities is best understood by examining adjustment in the credit market. The reason for this is that bank liabilities can only be created, or destroyed, by the initiative of banks acting in the process of expanding or contracting loans. Thus, to expand $M2$, banks must induce demand by lowering their lending rate, to induce an expansion of investment and thereby income. It is this subsequent rise in income, increasing savings, which stimulates the growth in demand for $M2$ by a quantity greater than the decrease originally generated by the fall in loan and time deposit rates. The subsequent increase in savings and money demand restores equilibrium in the market for total bank liabilities. Hence, an increase in the stock of broad money is expansionary, not because of a vague notion of liquidity, but because it is the unavoidable accompaniment with the process of credit expansion. The key is the credit expansion and the resulting rises in investment, income and saving which yield a positive relation between the stock of broad money and national income. To put it slightly differently, an expansionary monetary policy is only effective if it creates income (through credit expansion), whilst a contractionary policy is only successful if it destroys income. The causality is from changes in income to changes in money.

SUMMARY

This chapter sought to discuss the traditional approaches to the money supply and to highlight the shortcomings of these approaches. The conclusions that emerged were that the typical exogenous, fixed-coefficient, asset-oriented approaches to the money supply do not: (1) account explicitly for the behaviour of banks or their institutional surroundings, or (2) account for the fundamental importance of credit demand to the transmission mechanism between national income and money. By failing to deal with either of these concerns, the approaches fail to provide a story of the proper dynamic adjustment processes at work when the Central Bank attempts to control various financial and monetary aggregates in the economy.

It was then argued that a more post-Keynesian viewpoint, one which takes account of the importance of credit demand by explicitly reversing the causation between national income and money as well as explicitly detailing the institutional behavioural characteristics of banking firms, provides a more comprehensive story of money creation.

The implication for the remainder of this book is that any development monetary economics which seeks to account for the relevant transmission mechanism between national income (and thus growth) and money, must be able to account for the specific institutional characteristics of financial systems in developing countries, and must account for the determinants of credit demand.   Such a post-Keynesian approach to the money supply is particularly relevant to periods of financial liberalization, whereby the institutional processes undergo a structural change as the authorities seek to change the mechanisms of monetary policy.   The particular dynamic adjustment response to such a liberalization policy will be misunderstood by any fixed-coefficient approach, and thus requires a broader institutionally based paradigm.

APPENDIX 2: MATHEMATICAL SOLUTIONS

Money-Multiplier Approach

(2.9) into (2.8) yields:

$$H = hD + zD \text{ or } D = H (h + z)^{-1} \qquad (2.8')$$

Substituting above and (2.9) into (2.10) yields

$$M = H (h+z)^{-1} + h (H (h+z)^{-1}) \qquad (2.11')$$

or:

$$M = H \left(\frac{1+h}{h+z}\right)$$

Keynes's Liquidity Preference with Flexible Prices

Set equilibrium as (2.14) and (2.12) to derive:

$$m + u_{ms} = p + \alpha y + \beta I + u_{md}$$

Substitute in (2.13) and (2.15) into above to yield:

$$m + u_{ms} = p + \alpha(\bar{y}+\epsilon_y) + \beta (\bar{r}+\epsilon_r) + \beta (p^*_{t+1} - p)$$

Solving through for p yields:

$$p + \beta (p^*_{t+1} - p) = m - \alpha\bar{y} - \beta\bar{r} + \epsilon_p$$

where:

$$\epsilon_p = u_{ms} - u_{md} - \beta\epsilon_r - \alpha\epsilon_y$$

Setting:

$$\bar{v}(\bar{y},\bar{r}) = -\beta\bar{r} + (1-\alpha) \bar{y}$$

gives:

$$p + \beta (p^*_{t+1} - p) = m + \bar{v}(\bar{y}, \bar{r}) - \bar{y} + \epsilon_p$$

Keynes's Liquidity Preference with Fixed Wages

Substituting (2.20), (2.18), (2.19) into (2.17) yields:

$$m + u_{ms} = \bar{p} + \alpha \left[\bar{y} + c(y-\bar{y}) + d(r-\bar{r}) + u_d + u_y \right] + \beta(r) + u_{md}$$

Solving through for y yields:

$$\alpha c y = m + u_m - \bar{p} - \alpha\bar{y} + \alpha c\bar{y} - \alpha d \ (r-\bar{r}) - \alpha(u_d + u_y) - \beta r$$

or:

$$y = \bar{y} + \mu(m-\bar{p}) + \mu(\bar{v}-\bar{y}) + \epsilon_d$$

where:

$$\mu = (\alpha c)^{-1}; \quad \bar{m} = \bar{p} + \bar{y} - \bar{v}$$

$$\bar{v} = - (\alpha d + \beta)r + (1-\alpha)\bar{y}; \quad u_m = u_{md} - u_{ms}$$

$$\epsilon_d = (-d\bar{r} - u_d - u_y)c^{-1} - \mu u_m$$

3. Financial Repression and Liberalization

INTRODUCTION

The preceding chapter looked at the development of the theory of money supply and the debate over the nature of the transmission mechanism linking money to nominal income. The next two chapters seek to look at these subjects again, but this time seek to apply the concepts and critiques developed above to the framework of development monetary economics. As the subject matter which has dominated development monetary economics has been concern over the effects of a program of financial liberalization, these chapters will look at the monetary transmission mechanism as developed in financial liberalization theory. The same themes regarding the nature of money supply will emerge, with the important provisos that: (1) the majority of theoretical models discussed explicitly model the effects of monetary policy changes on economic growth, and (2) the institutional structures accounted for differ, at times, from those discussed earlier.

The present chapter seeks to outline and assess the theories of 'financial repression' and 'financial liberalization'. In doing so, it will involve a perhaps unholy alliance of employing both descriptive anecdotes and theoretical models in order to provide a clearer intuitive picture of the evolution of the debate. The following chapter will look at the neo-structuralist critique of liberalization theory and the neo-classical response to that critique.

TOBIN AND THE THEORY OF 'FINANCIAL REPRESSION'

Theoretical Foundations

The story begins in the 1960s and early 1970s with the elimination of colonial empires and the creation of independent developing countries. The intellectual climate at this time was one where government intervention was seen as a possible antidote to perceived market failures, and resulted in policy advice which was broadly interventionist. The framework which represented the formalization of these ideas into a coherent theoretical framework was based largely around Tobin's (1965) seminal paper 'Money and Economic Growth'.[1] Tobin extended a Solow model to include money and analysed the effects of monetary policy on the steady-state growth rate of the economy. Employing the standard neo-classical market clearing assumptions and assuming physical savings and investment are continuously equilibrated, Tobin builds a two-asset portfolio choice model. In the model, growth is dependent on capital deepening, defined as an increase in the capital-labour ratio, k. Capital deepening occurs due to individuals' portfolio allocation between the competing assets of physical capital and real money balances. The precise allocation of individual wealth amongst these assets (assuming gross substitutability) will depend on the relative yields of assets and on the tastes of asset holders. The lower the yield on money relative to the marginal productivity of capital (or the return on capital), the greater the amount of real capital that will be held in individuals' portfolios. Such capital deepening leads to consequently higher economic growth.

Tobin's formal analysis begins by introducing money, as government fiat, into a non-monetary economy. The effect of introducing this 'new' asset is to lower the steady-state level of capital accumulation, as in a non-monetary economy all savings are necessarily held in physical capital. The introduction of money means some savings will go into the holding of real money balances to satisfy precautionary and speculative demand. The only way for the government to offset this is to provide new money to absorb the savings now going into real balances. The way to do this is to continuously run a deficit financed by the issue of new money.

Incorporating this into a formal model, Tobin defines y as the output per unit of capital, which will correspond to an equilibrium value of capital

---

[1]Tobin was not the first to look at the role of money in development. Schumpeter (1911, 1935) highlighted the importance of bank credit in the financing of entrepreneurial innovations and the importance of this to economic growth. Gerschenkron (1962) advocated 'universal banking' so that the banking system may serve as the prime source of both capital and entrepreneurship in countries who are late comers to economic development. From this Patrick (1966) distinguished between the 'demand-following' and 'supply-leading' phenomena and sought to classify experiences of development into the appropriate category. Goldsmith (1969) set out to empirically quantify these lessons by constructing a 'Financial Interrelations Ratio' (FIR) which measured the value of financial assets to national wealth. Goldsmith found in general, that the FIR tends to increase with the real economy. For a summary, see Jao (1985).

intensity, k; w is defined as being the "warranted" rate of growth of capital stock[2]; d as the deficit per unit of capital; and $m(k,r)$ as the required amount of money per unit of capital in equilibrium, which is a positive function of the policy set return on money, r. Assuming the government purchases goods and services at a fraction of national income, g, then disposable income is $Y_d = y(1-g) + d$. The disposable income identity allows the derivation of an aggregate supply equation (3.1) which is a version of a standard savings-investment equality condition. The government deficits steady-state value (3.2) will be given by the equilibrium value of money ($m(k,r)$) and the equilibrium or warranted growth rate of capital stock ($w(k,r)$). The reason for this is that any government-induced additions to wealth (deficit spending) must be held either as money or as capital in individuals' portfolios. Substituting (3.2) into (3.1) and solving for $w(k,r)$ yields the equilibrium condition for the warranted growth rate of capital (3.3).[3]

The conclusion to be drawn from the equilibrium condition is that an increase in the warranted rate of capital accumulation requires an increase in the propensity to save, s, but a reduction in the propensity to hold money as an asset, m. That is, an economy must save, but in the form of physical capital, and not money balances. The policy rub is that if savings are so great that capital intensity is increasing, the yield on capital must fall with the decrease in the marginal productivity of capital. Given a constant nominal yield on money (exogenous r), a portfolio shift into money balances will begin to occur which will reduce the growth rate of capital. The implication is that the stock of money per unit of capital must also rise to offset the portfolio shift into money balances and to lower the real return on holding those balances. The job of the policy maker is to engineer such an increase (a monetary deepening) so that capital deepening can proceed apace. Intuitively, an increase in the rate of growth of the nominal money supply, and by extension the steady-state rate of inflation, results in a higher steady-state capital-labour ratio by lowering the rate of return on real balances.

[2]Tobin defines the 'warranted' rate of capital growth, w, to be that rate consistent with a given level of savings and investment per year, per unit of existing capital stock. If w is greater than the natural rate of growth of the labour stock, n, capital deepening will occur. In equilibrium, diminishing returns to capital will ensure that $w=n$.

[3]See Appendix 3 for full mathematical derivation.

Table 3.1: Tobin's monetary model of economic growth

$$S = s(y(1-g) + d) = d + w(k,r) \qquad (3.1)$$

$$d = m(k,r)w \qquad (3.2)$$

$$w(k,r) = \frac{sy(k)(1-g)}{1+(1-s)m(k,r)} \qquad (3.3)$$

The transmission mechanism between the money supply and national income is determined here by the fact that money enters as government spending, and thus directly creates disposable income. The additional income must then be allocated between the holding of real balances and physical capital, and such a decision will be influenced by competing rates of return. The job of the policy maker is to encourage asset holders to choose physical capital. As money enters purely as fiat, the foundation of Tobin's model is an exogenous money supply. The creation of this money supply causes a change in national income by instantaneously increasing disposable income in the first instance, and increasing investment through capital deepening in the second. Money loses its strict neutrality in the model since the equilibrium growth rate, even in the long run, is no longer independent of changes in the money supply.

The major weakness of Tobin's model is the assumption of the existence of only fiat money, which limits the relevance of the model to economies characterized by credit money. Fry (1988) demonstrates, by discussing Lee (1980) and Sidrauski's (1966) extensions of Tobin, that the above results are completely reversed by substituting inside (credit) money for outside (fiat) money, and inflation hedges for productive capital in households' portfolios. The assuming away of credit money also implies the redundancy of any specification of the behavioural characteristics of financial markets and the determinants of credit demand. The transmission mechanism between the money supply and nominal income is broadly Keynesian, but it is loosely specified and misses the fundamental characteristics of money in a credit economy. Thus even as a first approximation, the Tobin model is severely limited.

The Tobin model is important, however, in that it formalized the views that: (1) an inflationary policy is conducive to economic growth in so much as it stimulates investment, and (2) the return on money must be sufficiently lower than the return on capital (MP_k) for investment and capital accumulation to occur.

Policy Formulation: the Legacy of Theory.

Congruent with this academic climate, there was a widespread recourse in developing economies to expansionary fiscal and monetary policy - the latter through the maintenance of low interest-rate regimes.[4] Often, these policies were taken in conjunction with broader development policy goals formulated by the government weighing up political concerns with economic viability. The intellectual and policy environment at this time was characterized by an optimistic view of the role of the government in development, as illustrated by credence lent to the 'big-push' arguments. The broad development policies formulated at this time had very specific industrial goals in which the government was expected to play a crucial role in bringing the goals to fruition. The development of these policy goals was often motivated by concerns about 'market failure' and 'infant industries'.[5]

The market failure in financial markets was, in general, due to the inadequacy of the existing financial environment to provide long-term credit, or to provide for an adequate sharing of risks amongst financial institutions and industry (Cho and Khatkhate, 1989). Additionally, the oligopolistic banking structures meant that any market-determined rates of interest would have a component of rent-seeking in their determination. The result of the market failures was that a gap had opened up between social rates of return

[4]Often, Keynes's 'liquidity trap' is invoked as a justification of expansionary monetary policy and low interest-rate policies. The notion of a liquidity trap covers a scenario in which an excessive liquidity preference by wealth holders, due to the vagaries of economic life, makes necessary too high an interest rate to permit investment. To alleviate the trap, an expansionary monetary policy would reduce the interest rate and, at the same time, satisfy the increase in liquidity preference. The ideas are too peripheral to the main body of Keynes's work to be applied as standard policy prescription.

[5]Stern (1989) provides a taxonomy of reasons for purported market failure in developing countries. The reasons, including monopolistic/oligopolistic elements, increasing returns to scale, and informational problems, are all seen as posing potential difficulty for the establishment or maintenance of equilibrium and the efficient allocation of resources. Governments reacted, in general, by direct involvement in the market, often administering the allocative and pricing functions of markets.

and private returns on investment, implying a sub-optimal level of investment would be undertaken unless government intervention could equalize those rates of return by providing an appropriate subsidy. The rationale for government subsidy was bolstered by the 'infant industry' arguments, which argued that developing industries must be allowed to prosper in a "hot-house" of protection and subsidy until they are developed enough to compete in their own right. Thus, an interest-rate ceiling providing low nominal interest rates, paid and received by banks, would provide a subsidy to industry capable of equating social and private rates of return.

The scope and role of government, however, was not limited to the provision of subsidy. Government's role in industrialization was perceived to be much broader and led to more direct intervention in the credit market. In order to induce enough investment and lending to satisfy their particular policy goals, governments took to allocating credit to preferred sectors through the use of controls and incentives to the commercial banking system (Fry, 1993b). The controls frequently took the form of requirements that banks should allocate a specific proportion of their loan portfolios to favoured industrial sectors. Incentives were along the lines of implicit (or explicit) loan guarantees on loans extended in conjunction with policy aims, and access to rediscounting facilities at favourable rates. The resulting patterns of credit extension were such that policy-favoured firms and industries often received an elastic supply of credit to meet any financial requirements they might have. Thus, the resulting policy structure was such that the government took an active role in setting the price of credit and in determining the allocation of credit.[6]

The expansionary fiscal policies undertaken also provided a rationale for low nominal interest rates, as governments in developing countries are perpetually short of resources due to their narrow tax base and lack of expertise in tax administration (Cho and Khatkhate, 1989). The resulting deficits had to be financed either from the financial markets or the Central Bank. In so far as they were financed from domestic financial markets, low nominal rates provided the government with access to cheap finance. Central Bank accommodation took the forms of directly supplying finance (seigniorage), giving special incentives to financial institutions to hold government debt through tax incentives, and the use of government

---

[6]Fry (1993b) lists subsidized loans, differential rediscount rates, direct budgetary surplus, credit floors, credit ceilings and the reliance on specialized financial institutions as elements of directed credit programs.

liabilities to fulfil liquidity/capital requirements. The Cental Bank accommodation of government spending, when combined with credit pressures arising from the objectives of development policy, led inevitably to inflationary pressure. In order to maintain a modicum of monetary control in the face of such broad accommodation, the Central Banks had to resort to direct quantitative limits on private sector borrowing and steep reserve requirements on banks (Leite and Sundararajan, 1990). The result of both these policies was to squeeze dry lending to sectors outside of the scope of development policy, leading to a large proportion of private sector credit demand being rationed. The broad financial policy was then one where the government, by the use of direct controls on the financial sector attempted to control the price, quantity and allocation of credit.

Weaknesses of Government Intervention: Identifying Repression

Institutional weaknesses began appearing, however, in both the industrial and financial sectors of many developing countries. These institutional fissures were seen as having an adverse impact on economic growth (Dooley and Mathieson, 1987). Too often the regulatory controls were an excuse for a government to run riot with the Central Bank's printing press. The resulting excessive inflation distorted all economic relationships in the economy, increased uncertainty and discouraged development. Large elements of corruption and poor planning by governments resulted in poorly performing investments and an industrial base structurally flawed. Specific to the financial sector, inefficiencies became apparent in:

1. Resource Mobilization. The policies of low, and often negative, real interest rates provided no incentives to savers, creating a current bias towards consumption and reducing savings to sub-optimal levels. The problem increased the reliance of financial institutions on the government and created additional demand-pull inflationary pressure.
2. Credit Allocation. The portfolio restrictions placed on banks meant credit was allocated on the basis of political and non-economic rationale. The elastic supply of subsidized credit to firms favoured by government policy meant firms lacked a discipline to use credit efficiently or effectively, and led to the misuse of resources. Inefficient investments were also feasible at below market interest rates and were undertaken at the expense of projects within firms being credit rationed.
3. Banking Activity. The large amount of government intervention in the financial markets increased the reliance of banks on policy direction. Banks were not required to acquire loan appraisal skills as they often

relied on government loan guarantees in extending credit. Problems of asymmetric information were not effectively surmounted and banks were left with portfolios that were severely weakened by non-performing loans.

The policy structure of government intervention in all aspects of the credit market was identified as the cause of the growing distortions, erosion and ultimate atrophy of financial systems. This policy structure was identified and labelled 'financial repression' in the seminal books by McKinnon (1973) and Shaw (1973). The McKinnon and Shaw papers signalled a change in the intellectual climate which was characterized by growing distrust of government-intervention, treated as 'government failure', and growing belief in the ability of the market to allocate resources optimally. The McKinnon and Shaw case for 'financial liberalization', or the freeing of the financial markets from the regulatory shackles, has become the main theoretical basis for financial sector analysis and policy over the last two decades.

McKINNON AND SHAW AND THE NEO-CLASSICAL SCHOOL[7]

The case for financial liberalization does touch on most aspects of developing country financial markets, but the greatest venom has been saved for the policy of interest-rate ceilings which frequently resulted in highly negative real interest rates. The primary policy prescription arising from McKinnon and Shaw's work is the general freeing and raising of institutional interest rates and/or a reduction in the rate of inflation. It would appear the two policies are treated as identical, both policies increasing the real rate of interest and thereby increasing the savings rate, the funds available for investment and, eventually, the rate of economic growth.[8]

---

[7]Although the McKinnon-Shaw models do differ from traditional neo-classical and monetarist models, they share the same theoretical foundations (money exogeneity, efficient markets), policy prescriptions and general spirit as the neo-classical school. The literature is generally classified as neo-classical, see Fry (1987).

[8]A consistent feature of liberalization literature is the positive relation between an increase in deposit rates and the growth rate (Fry, 1993b). The predominant inflation-growth trade-off whereby anti-inflationary increases in interest rates tend to be growth reducing, is noticeable by its absence.

Theoretical Foundation: McKinnon

The first theoretical pillar in the house of financial liberalization is the premise that interest rates have a positive relationship with economic growth. The contribution of McKinnon and Shaw is to provide a theory linking increases in interest rates to increments in output.

The formal analysis of McKinnon adopts the assumption that all economic units are confined to self-finance and that in these countries, indivisibilities in investment have an important role to play. The first assumption drives McKinnon's model by implying that any potential investor must have accumulated all the money balances necessary for investment prior to undertaking the project. A higher real deposit rate of interest makes the opportunity cost of saving real balances to invest lower, and hence acts as an impetus for firms wanting to finance investment projects. Rather than money and capital being substitutes, as they would be in Tobin's portfolio approach, money and capital are seen as inherent complements. This complementarity is expressed in a demand equation for real balances (M/P):

$$M/P = L(\ Y,\ I/Y,\ d-\pi^{*})\quad ;\quad \frac{\delta(M/P)}{\delta(I/Y)} > 0 \qquad (3.4)$$

where Y is real GNP, I is the investment term, and $d-\pi^{*}$ is the real interest rate. Complementarity between real money balances and investment appears in the positive partial derivative. In the McKinnon model, the conditions of money supply have a first-order impact on decisions to save and invest, which are taken to be part of the same decision. McKinnon shares with Tobin the assumption of a purely fiat money stock created through government debt which is necessarily exogenous. In employing purely exogenous fiat money, McKinnon follows the implication of a world without credit money, but in changing initial assumptions regarding the relationship of money and income is able to interject on Tobin's portfolio approach, stand it on its head, and emerge with a neo-classical-monetarist policy prescription. The implicit assumption behind the approach is that money and capital are two completely distinct goods arriving in the economy through independent production functions - money being provided through government expenditure. As no borrowing exists in a fiat world, again there is no need to supply a mechanism through which the process of producing capital calls forth the money needed to finance its creation. If the first assumption of McKinnon is to be altered and credit money is introduced, the unusual assumption that in any one period the business sector must be a net saver rather than net debtor, would be needed at least for the complementarity thesis to hold. As in Tobin's model, the absence of credit money represents a substantial weakness in the hypothesis, even as a first approximation.

Theoretical Foundations: Shaw

Shaw's formal theoretical contribution is not based on the stringent assumption of a fiat money world, focusing instead on the role financial intermediaries have to play in development. A case for financial liberalization, in terms of increasing interest rates, arises mainly from expanding the amount of financial intermediation occurring between savers and investors.   By increasing the returns offered to savers, financial intermediaries' capacity to lend is increased and the banks are able to allocate this larger volume of investment funds. The increase in investment funds leads to, or causes, an increase in the quantity of investment. Shaw argues that the real cost of borrowing to the investor decreases and the average efficiency of investment is raised, because banks can now reap economies of scale in risk diversification, lending, operational efficiency and information costs.   The arguments contained in Shaw's model have become known collectively as the debt-intermediation view (DIV) and are summarized in the following money demand equation

$$M/P = F(\ Y,\ \gamma,\ d - \pi^*)\qquad ;\qquad \frac{\delta M/P}{\delta d - \pi^*} > 0 \qquad (3.5)$$

where γ is a vector of opportunity costs in real terms of holding money. The view essentially expects that the yields on all forms of wealth, especially money, will have a positive effect on the savings rate, and therefore investment.

Shaw's model relies on neo-classical market-clearing assumptions, specifically the assumption that the rate of interest functions in an equilibrating manner to ensure equality between the supply and demand of loanable funds in the financial markets. Given efficient financial markets in Shaw's world, the decision to reduce consumption and increase savings does not reduce demand but, rather, alters its composition from consumption towards investment expenditure. Investment is constrained by the lack of savings entering the financial intermediaries, and this constrains growth. Given a constant, equilibrium money supply, the goal of the policy maker is to increase the demand for real money balances (broadly conceived) and thereby increase the supply of loanable funds, investment and economic growth. Hence, it is the holding of real money balances which brings forth investment and growth. Saving is then the primary engine for investment and growth.

The primary weakness of Shaw's model is the absence of any behavioural mechanism specifying the workings of the banking system. In terms of what financial liberalization tries to address - fragmented, distressed, oligopolistic, rationed credit markets - it seems awkward that the primary adjustment mechanism is firmly rooted in assumptions requiring efficient and competitive markets. However, as a first approximation, Shaw's theoretical construct remains more intuitively plausible than McKinnon's.

THEORETICAL REFINEMENTS: ADVANCES ON THE ESSENTIAL THEORY

Subsequent extensions of the McKinnon-Shaw hypothesis seek to explore more rigorously the concepts of financial liberalization, and define more explicitly the workings of the transmission mechanism between monetary policy and economic growth (national income).

Kapur's Model of Liberalization

Central premise explored: a financial liberalization enhances growth by improving the quantity of investment.

Kapur (1976) presents a model that illustrates the primary relation in liberalization theory that an increase in interest rates is growth enhancing because it increases the quantity of investment funds and, therefore, investment.

Table 3.2: Kapur's model of liberalization policy

$$\dot{K} = \frac{1}{1-\alpha} \ [\mu q \frac{M}{P} - \pi\theta(1-\alpha)K] \qquad (3.6)$$

$$\frac{\hat{M}}{P} = Ye^{-a(\pi^* - d)} \qquad ;a>0 \qquad (3.7)$$

$$\frac{\dot{K}}{K} = \frac{\dot{Y}}{Y} = \gamma = \mu \frac{\sigma q}{(1-\alpha)} e^{-W} - \pi\theta \qquad (3.8)$$

$$\mu + \dot{W} = \pi + \gamma \qquad (3.9)$$

$$\pi = h(\frac{M}{PY} - \frac{\hat{M}}{PY}) + \pi^* \qquad (3.10)$$
$$= h(e^{-W} - e^{-\hat{W}}) + \pi^* \; ; h>0$$

$$\dot{W} = -\mu(1 - \frac{\sigma q}{1-\alpha} e^{-W}) + (1 - \theta)\pi^* \qquad (3.11)$$
$$+ (1-\theta)h[e^{-W} - e^{-a(\pi^* - d)}]$$

$$\frac{d\pi^*}{dt} = \beta(\pi - \pi^*) = \beta h[e^{-W} - e^{-a(\pi^* - d)}] \qquad (3.12)$$

$$\dot{W} = 0 = \frac{d\pi^*}{dt} \qquad (3.13)$$

The intuitive rationale for this is found in Shaw's debt-intermediation view. That is, higher interest rates increase the level of savings, thus expanding the banking sector and thereby causing an increase in the quantity of investment.

Kapur also looks at competing stabilization programs and argues that stabilization through an initial increase in the average nominal interest rate paid on money holdings, has significantly more favourable short-run effects on real output than does stabilization through an initial reduction in the rate of money expansion. Occupying a central position in Kapur's transmission mechanism is the working-capital nexus which links bank financing to aggregate supply. The importance of working-capital is used to explain both the initial downturn in real output historically characterizing attempts at price stabilization, and the subsequent expansion of real output as inflationary expectations recede and the real stock of money increases.

Kapur's formal model begins with the simplifying assumption that all bank credit is used to finance the holding of working capital. The total usage of working capital at any given time will be $(1-\alpha)K(t)$, where $K(t)$ is the total flow of utilized capital and α is the proportion used for fixed capital. Of this, it is assumed a fixed fraction, θ, is required to be financed through bank lending, and the remainder to be replaced through retained earnings. A part of the increase in bank lending will be used to fund increments in real working capital, and a portion will be used to meet the increased cost of working-capital replacement as a result of a rise in the price level P $\theta(1-\alpha)K$.

Building in the above considerations, Kapur derives an equation for the change in the capital stock (3.6) where

$$\mu q \ \frac{M}{P} = \frac{\dot{L}}{P}; \quad \pi = \frac{\dot{P}}{p}; \quad \mu = \frac{\dot{M}}{M} = \frac{\dot{L}}{L}$$

The equation states that increments in the capital stock will be equal to the excess of the increase in real bank lending over the increase in the nominal cost of replacing the bank finance component of worn-out working capital. Equation (3.7) is the money demand equation for desired real balances, which is an exponential function of the expected return on deposits $(d-\pi^*)$.

Letting γ, be the economy's growth rate, dividing (3.6) by K and substituting in the production function, $Y=\sigma K$, gives the growth equation (3.8) where $e^{-W}=1/V=M/PY$ from the dynamic logarithmic formulation of the quantity equation in (3.9) $(W=\log V)$. The result is an implicit equation in a single unknown, the growth rate of national income, γ. The presence of the exponential function allows Kapur to demonstrate that there exists a unique positive value of μ which maximizes the resulting value of γ, assuming the deposit rate, d, is fixed. To increase μ beyond this equilibrium level leads to a reduction in the values of γ. Kapur argues that regions above the equilibrium value of μ correspond to a financially repressed region and that to return to the higher steady-state solution of γ requires a reduction in μ, the rate of money creation. The intuition is that a higher than equilibrium rate of monetary growth will be inflationary. This domestic inflation requires that a greater proportion of bank financing must go to finance increases in the nominal value of working capital, $\pi\theta$. As more money goes to finance increases in working capital bills caused by inflation, less real credit is available for financing capital stock accumulation. As the size of the real banking sector decreases, then so does the rate of capital accumulation and, by extension, the rate of growth. Money here is not neutral as the rate of monetary creation has a monotonic impact on the steady-state value of growth and thus national income. Money in this regard displays strong-form exogeneity via national income.[9] The key insight Kapur provides is that a monetary disequilibrium is inimical to economic growth and capital formulation.

Kapur's Dynamic Formulation: Competing Policy Options

Turning to short-run dynamics, Kapur begins by defining the inflation rate, π, as a function of deviations from monetary equilibrium relative to the aggregate supply of goods and an expectations term (3.10). Substituting (3.10) and (3.8) into (3.9) gives (3.11). (3.12) is a variant of Cagan's adaptive expectations formulation such that changes in inflationary expectations are based on deviations of actual from expected inflation. An equilibrium condition is imposed in (3.13) which requires velocity (W) to be constant and perfect foresight in expectations. (3.11)-(3.13) then represent the self-contained dynamic system which is used as the basis to analyse the effects of two competing policies - an increase in the deposit rate, d, and a decrease in the rate of monetary expansion, μ.

Beginning with a steady-state, Kapur introduces an upward shift in d. The increase in the interest rate succeeds in producing an instantaneous downward shift in inflation.[10] The reason for the instantaneous decline is that the change in d creates an immediate increase in desired real money

---

[9]The monotonic relationship between γ and μ implies that investment can be increased indefinitely, even exceeding the value of output through indefinite expansion in μ. Fry (1988, p.36) criticizes this non-neutrality on the basis that it lacks a behavioural savings function or supply constraint which would determine where the extra finance would come from. Fry 'salvages' this part of the model by rewriting (3.10) so that it no longer provides any relationship between μ and γ, and thereby restores money's neutrality in the theoretical framework.

[10]Kapur defines $d=q(l-z)$ where l is the loan rate and z is the costs of the monetary system, defined to be a constant fraction, z, of the money supply. This requires that a change in d causes a change in l, a fairly reasonable assumption. Kapur, however, does not take any such cost increases into account in the adjustment phase of a new policy.

balances by asset holders. The immediate reduction in inflation causes expected inflation to be larger than actual inflation, leading to a readjustment downwards of inflationary expectations, π^*. The readjustment of inflationary expectations downwards creates a new lower equilibrium rate of inflation. However, the initial large reduction in inflation is offset by a falling velocity, W (3.11), which increases the ratio of money to output. Therefore the initial reduction in inflation overshoots its new reduced equilibrium level and it takes an increase in W to stimulate π to converge back to its long-term level.

Since π registers an instantaneous downward jump, γ registers an instantaneous upward jump assuming a constant μ. This can occur because the initial increase in d has no instantaneous effect on the net flow of real bank credit but, by decreasing inflation, it decreases the cost of replacing worn-out capital. Hence the amount of investment finance going to finance increments in capital stock increases, and so by extension does economic growth. Additionally, the fall in W implies an increase in the real size of the banking system relative to output, stimulating a further increase in the net flow of bank credit. Thus increasing d has favourable effects on both π and γ, in both the short and long run.

Kapur also analyses the effect of an exogenous decrease in the rate of growth of the money supply, μ. The decrease in μ has no instantaneous impact on π (3.10), but it does cause an increase in velocity, W, which implies a fall in the real supply of money and thus a decrease in expected inflation. The two factors jointly produce an excess demand for money (broad), and therefore engineer a reduction in π. The reduction in μ, however, causes an instantaneous reduction in growth, γ, by decreasing the net flow of real bank credit due to the initial increase in W.[11] Eventually, W begins to decrease as the real size of the banking system, relative to output, begins to increase. The fall in W begins once π has fallen sufficiently. The subsequent fall in W allows γ to increase beyond its initial equilibrium value to come to rest at a new, higher steady-state value. The initial fall in growth, however, implies that the reduction in μ has more adverse effects on the economy than a comparative increase in d.

The key feature in the transmission mechanism between monetary policy and growth in Kapur's model is the neo-classical mechanism of the holding

---

[11]An implication of the negative relation between velocity and growth is that in quantity theory based models, increases in velocity are due to changes in P and Y not being matched by a change in M. A policy implication would be that any non-accommodating stance by the Central Bank which serves to increase velocity is necessarily growth reducing.

of real money balances. Changes in *d* exert an impact on growth by increasing the demand for real balances and the size of the banking sector, thereby stimulating a concomitant increase in the flow of bank credit. After this initial period, monetary authorities can then proceed to gradually reduce the rate of monetary expansion as inflationary expectations decline. In doing so the flow of real bank credit need not decline during the stabilization process and the short-run squeeze on working capital and real output can be avoided. The policy prescription from this is that an interest rate liberalization, resulting in an increase in the nominal deposit rate, is unambiguously growth-promoting by increasing the quantity of investment.

The primary weakness of Kapur's model is the fundamental independence of the interest rate, *d*, and the rate of creation of the money supply, μ. Such independence only makes sense in a system of exogenous money. Thus, although the main link between policy and growth is the working-capital nexus, changes in *d* are not seen as having any effect on the demand for working capital.[12] Specifically, changes in *d* which must, by Kapur's assumption, cause changes in *l*, are seen as causing an instantaneous reduction in π. The model and policy story told, therefore, do not account for any increased cost effects arising from the increased cost to finance working-capital payments. Thus, although it is possible that an increase in the real size of the banking sector occurs, it is also possible that increased financial requirements for working capital may be greater than the increment in real credit. In this case, the new steady-state growth rate would be below its original equilibrium level.

Additionally, even if an initial cost-push effect was allowed in the model, the impact would be only on π, through *W*, and not on μ, given the government wishes to keep μ constant (from the assumption of exogenous money). The model, thus, has the theoretical quirk that while μ is defined to be the rate of change of bank lending (equivalent here to the money supply) it cannot change in response to a change in *d* and *l* - the price of that lending. The invariance of the rate of change in the money supply to changes in the price of credit is explained by the assumption of strong form exogenous money and perfect government control of the money supply. The exogeneity of the money supply then allows the peculiarity that changes

---

[12]A reason suggested as to why a broad-ranging liberalization may produce an increase in the competitive free market equilibrium deposit rate without affecting the loan rate, is that a reduction in intermediation spreads may occur if reserve requirements are reduced (or alternatively, if competitive interest rates are paid on required reserves). The increase in deposit rates then comes from the reduced costs of intermediation (Fry, 1993b; Snowden, 1987). Such a result requires a highly competitive banking industry.

in d and μ are seen as distinctly different policy options. The government, thus, has the ability to engineer an immediate reduction in μ, presumably by forcing the banks to reduce the rate of their lending regardless of credit demand. As the drop in μ has no instantaneous impact on π, the demand for working capital must be assumed to remain unchanged. Hence, lending behaviour by the banking system must be assumed to react directly to the will of the monetary authority. No behavioural specification is present in the model, however, of how policy induces such behaviour by the financial system.

Galbis's Model of Investment Efficiency

Central premise explored: a financial liberalization enhances growth by improving the quality of investment.
Galbis (1977) illustrates a second primary tenet of the financial liberalization school, that high interest rates are growth promoting even if total real savings are interest inelastic, because they bring about an improvement in the quality of the capital stock. Intuitively, the improvement in the quality of the capital stock is due to the rationing function of higher interest rates on investment demand. Under financial repression, it was assumed that inefficient and low yielding investments could be undertaken due to the effective subsidy granted to them by low nominal interest rates. The financing of such investments implies that higher yielding investment projects are crowded out of the official credit markets, and are thus often not undertaken. A policy which eliminated the subsidy, by raising nominal interest rates, was advocated in order to ration out the lower yielding investments and improve the allocation of resources in the financial system.

Table 3.3: Galbis's model of investment efficiency

$$Y = Y_1 + Y_2 = r_1 K_1 + w_1 L_1 + r_2 K_2 + w_2 L_2 \tag{3.14}$$

$$I_1 = H_1 (r_1, d - \pi^*) Y_1$$
$$; \quad \frac{\partial H_1}{\partial r_1} > 0 ; \quad \frac{\partial H_1}{\partial (d - \pi^*)} < 0 \tag{3.15}$$

$$S_1 = I_1 + \frac{d(M_1/P)}{dt} \tag{3.16}$$

$$I^s_2 = S_2 + \frac{d(M1/P)}{dt} = \frac{d(M2/P)^s}{dt} \tag{3.17}$$

$$I^D_2 = H_2 \ (r_2, \ l-\pi^*) \ Y_2$$
$$; \ \frac{\partial H_2}{\partial r_2} > 0 \ ; \ \frac{\partial H_2}{\partial (d-\pi^*)} < 0 \tag{3.18}$$

$$\frac{d(M_2/P)^D}{dt} = \beta I^D_2 \tag{3.19}$$

$$\frac{dM^s_2}{dt} = \frac{d\bar{M}^s_2}{dt} \tag{3.20}$$

$$(\frac{d(M_2/P)^D}{dt})_A = \beta H_2 \ (r_2, \ (l-\pi^*)_A) \ Y_2 \tag{3.21}$$

Galbis demonstrates the increasing efficiency of investment with a two-sector model incorporating a traditional sector with capital investment yielding a low rate of return, r_1, and a modern sector with a higher yielding rate of return on capital investment, r_2.[13] The process of income growth

---

[13]The justification of this assumption is that developing economies are fragmented economies where the coexistence of old and modern technologies, with different degrees of efficiency in using scarce physical and human resources, result in wide disparities in the rates of return of different investments (see Galbis, 1977).

(3.14) is seen as one occurring due to both an increase in inputs and a redistribution of inputs toward the more advanced technologies. Assuming capital is fully employed, an increase in K_2 at the expense of K_1, leaving K constant, would imply an increase in Y since the change in the structure of capital would be associated with the higher returns available in sector 2. Employing the basic Keynesian aggregate expenditure and savings functions, Galbis derives an investment function (3.15) for sector 1, assuming that all sector 1 investment is self-financed and credit rationed. Sector 1 individuals, however, can save in the form of bank deposits as an alternative to investing in physical capital.[14]

The savings-investment decision by the traditional sector is then given by the identity (3.16) which makes their savings equal to their investment plus the accumulation of bank deposits in real terms by this sector. Assuming a competitive banking system, the accumulation of bank deposits by sector 1 frees resources which can be used for investment in sector 2. The supply of investible resources for sector 2 is given by (3.17) which is equal to their non-consumed output, plus the accumulation of bank deposits by the traditional sector. Sector 2 are constrained to invest their whole savings in the form of physical goods, and thereby keeping no savings of their own in the form of financial assets. The decision to invest by this sector is then a function of the rate of return on capital and the real rate of interest on loans (3.18). In this equation, Galbis maintains that it is crucial for the return on capital, r_2, to be rather large compared to the real loan rate, $l-\pi^*$. Taking a simple incremental demand for financial assets by individuals in sector 2 (3.19) and assuming an exogenous money supply (3.20) completes the framework from which Galbis proceeds to analyse the effects of policy on the transfer of resources from one sector to another.

Galbis begins by assuming the monetary authorities set real interest rates at $(l-\pi^*)_a$, an "acceptable" level of real rates which is lower than their equilibrium level. The consequences of the lower real rate are that:

1. Sector 1 will not put money into bank accounts as they foresee higher returns from their own self-financed investment. The result is that relatively lower yielding sector 1 investments will be taken out at the expense of higher yielding sector 2 investments. The economy thus suffers a reduction in the rate of growth with a concomitant loss of individual income. Individuals in sector 1 lose income as they undertake

---

[14]The approach is very similar to Tobin, with individuals choosing between two competing assets, bank deposits and physical capital.

investments with returns lower than the equilibrium rate of return on bank deposits. Individuals in sector 2 lose income as they undertake fewer of the higher yielding investments, and the resulting decrease in producer surplus is lost to the whole society.[15]

2. The resulting disequilibria between the real supply of, and demand for, investible resources leads to financial instability which will tend to exacerbate the initial effects from the imposed control on interest rates. Assuming entrepreneurs in sector 2 are allowed to satisfy their demand for loans at the prevailing borrowing cost, provides relation (3.21). Here, financial disequilibria result due to the excess demand for loans putting pressure on the banks to raise their lending rates, which is prevented.   As a result, the demand for investible resources remains larger than the supply of investible resources, as credit demand is not reduced (through l) and deposit mobilization is not increased (through d). Additionally, this excess demand for investible resources tends to drive the price level upward.   The resulting inflation further aggravates directly the potential disequilibria by reducing the real rates of interest on financial assets and reducing the level of real money balances. Hence, unless there is a credit restriction (ceiling) that brings back the effective demand to the effective supply, at the prevailing real rates of interest on financial assets, the system will not by itself have a tendency towards equilibrium.

A Theoretical Black Box: a Gap in Galbis's Reasoning

A question does here arise, how does excess demand for investibles cause such inflation to occur? Given that the nominal interest rate is fixed, so that the real rate of interest must be falling, and bank lending is seen to be implicitly constrained by the size of their deposits, what mechanism allows the price to rise if the money supply is exogenously controlled?   A neo-classical answer would be that changes in velocity would accommodate changes in the price level. However, credit restrictions would exacerbate and not solve a velocity problem. This would tend to suggest that a gap in neo-classical reasoning exists, stemming from the assumption of an exogenous money supply, that has not satisfactorily been resolved.

In further assessing Galbis's model, another major weakness is the

---

[15]Burkett and Vogel (1992) use similar reasoning to restate McKinnon's complementarity hypothesis as a complementarity between attractive financial assets and the quality of investment.

simplicity of the envisaged monetary transmission mechanism. A change in deposit rates is seen as merely involving portfolio shifts of savings from physical capital to bank deposits (for sector 1) which then can be used in technologies with higher returns in sector 2. Given its simplicity, Galbis's model may work as a first approximation but it misses a whole web of financial interrelations which could affect the growth path of the economy. For instance, from (3.14) it would appear that a movement of resources from K_1 to K_2 would, ceteris paribus, increase the marginal productivity of K_1 (r_1) while decreasing the MP_{K2} (r_2), which would suggest that the rates of return from the two sectors would eventually equalize. Once the rates equalized, any further movement of capital from the sectors would be growth and income reducing. The transfer of resources also carries with it the implicit assumption that labour is fully mobile. If labour is not fully mobile, as the MP_{K1} rises the MP_{L1} must fall, and with it comes a decrease in the wage rate for this sector. Thus, in the absence of full labour mobility, the welfare gains in Galbis's model are more likely to be concentrated in one sector, with the poorest individuals in the traditional sector constrained to losses in their welfare.

Galbis does illustrate, however, the important point that institutional credit ceilings are a second-best policy for countries having a rigid structure of interest rates on financial assets. Credit ceilings allow a modicum of price stability in the face of excess demand and the resulting price level stability ensures real rates of interest are as high as they can be, given the restriction on nominal rates. The optimal policy from Galbis is, however, to allow interest rates to rise to the level at which the supply and demand for investibles is equal, thereby eliminating the need for rationing controls and ensuring that the full income gains from the transfer of resources are realized. Any financial liberalization which involves the freeing of deposit rates and the elimination of quantitative controls on credit is, therefore, essentially a movement from a form of direct monetary control to more indirect methods of monetary control.

The Mathieson Open-Economy Model of Liberalization

Central premise explored: a financial liberalization is best conducted by a rapid reform program in which changes to the regulatory regime occur simultaneously. As a result, internal and external policy changes must be co-ordinated together to facilitate adjustment.
The policy mix of financial liberalization generally calls for a 'big bang' of liberalization in which deposit and loan rates undergo large, discrete changes and the financial system is freed from the majority of repressive policies.

The rationale for this is that the adjustment period is over rapidly and 'political' factors do not have time to mobilize resistance to the process of reform. Economic justification relies on neo-classical ideas concerning the working of free markets and the efficient functioning of price signals. The simultaneity of reforms implies that the liberalization program is often done in a framework that includes the open economy. Mathieson (1979) extends the financial liberalization literature to an open-economy case in order to look at the impact of capital flows on stabilization and financial reform. The Mathieson model demonstrates the potential interdependency between financial liberalization and exchange-rate policy in a comprehensive program of stabilization. Intuitively, the interdependence occurs because a program of financial liberalization will have at its heart a desire to increase the supply of investible funds. The increase in the domestic rate of interest in an open economy will lead to a capital inflow, which will initially increase the supply of savings. The capital inflow, however, will put upward pressure on the exchange rate which will reduce the country's competitiveness in trade. As the balance of payments worsens, expectations of a future depreciation will arise and stimulate a capital outflow, reducing the supply of investibles. As a result, exchange-rate policy must be co-ordinated to offset the potentially insalubrious effects of capital inflows on the balance of trade. The Mathieson model is of interest as it sets out a rigorous theoretical framework from which the IMF programs of stabilization in the 1980s drew heavily and which characterized the majority of attempts at financial liberalization.

In opening up the economy to capital flows, Mathieson first specifies an inflation rate (3.22) which includes both a domestic price term, P, and an imported goods price term, XP_f, where X is the exchange rate and P_f is the world price level. Approaching inflation in a demand-pull framework (based on the excess demand for goods), income and expectations are included in the function. Credit market equilibrium is also affected by the removal of capital controls, as capital movements can now alter the supply of deposits to the banking system and hence the supply of loans. The deposit-income ratio (3.23) will thus be determined by portfolio allocations amongst domestic assets and foreign assets.

Assuming standard portfolio behaviour by asset holders, the relative rates of return on the competing assets will determine the demand for deposits. The only innovation here is that the real yield on foreign assets will equal the expected real foreign interest rate plus the anticipated capital gain generated by a depreciation of the exchange rate (x^*).

Table 3.4: The Mathieson open-economy model

$$\pi = \dot{P}/P = \psi(XP_f - P + Y + \pi^* + Y_f) \qquad (3.22)$$

$$\frac{D}{PY} = f(r_d - \pi^*, r_f + x^* - \pi^*);$$

$$\frac{\partial f}{\partial(r_d - \pi^*)} = f_1 > 0 ; \qquad \frac{\partial f}{\partial(r_f + x^* - \pi^*)} = f_2 < 0 \qquad (3.23)$$

$$L = (1 - k) D \qquad (3.24)$$

$$H = DC + XR \qquad (3.25)$$

$$\gamma = \dot{K}/K = s(r_k - r_l) + \alpha\pi + (1 - \alpha x))\sigma; \\ s' > 0; \quad s'' < 0 \qquad (3.26)$$

The level of deposits will then determine credit market equilibrium by (3.24) which makes the stock of loans, L, respond deterministically to the nominal supply of bank loans, $(1-k)D$, where k is the required reserve ratio on deposits.[16]   The money market condition is the traditional neo-classical open economy identity (3.25) whereby base money, H, is equal to the stock of domestic credit, DC, and the value of foreign reserves XR, with X the exchange rate and R the stock of reserves.   A by-product of the open-economy extension is that under fixed or managed exchange rates, base

[16]A common feature of repressed financial systems in developing countries is the prevalence of high-reserve requirements on bank deposits. High reserve requirements are usually needed as an aspect of monetary control in these economies, as heavy government borrowing and lending to priority sectors puts large upward pressure on monetary aggregates. Calls to reform the financial system often focus on this 'pernicious' feature of financial systems. For example, see Fry (1988) and Dooley and Mathieson (1987).

money becomes endogenous.[17]   The source of endogeneity for the money supply are the private sector portfolio decisions (3.23). Portfolio adjustment will generate a balance of payments deficit (surplus) whenever domestic credit is growing more (less) rapidly than the demand for nominal money. The authorities can therefore use domestic credit to influence the balance of payments even though they cannot control the rate of monetary growth. The endogeneity of the money supply thus does not apply to the domestic component of the money supply which is still viewed as exogenous. Rather, the money supply is endogenous because of a foreign component to the money supply which is not directly under the control of the authorities.

The growth rate of real income, γ, in the model (3.26) is determined by the investment decisions of firms.   The investment decisions of firms depends on the marginal productivity of capital, $MP_K = r_K$, the loan rate r_l, the rate of increase of the price level, π, and the expected rate of depreciation of the exchange rate, x^*.

Given these conditions, the authorities seek to rectify an assumed situation of repression and disequilibrium by undertaking a program of stabilization and reform. Mathieson specifies an optimal control problem for policy makers who seek to limit deviations from target growth and inflation levels.[18]   After specifying further subsidiary conditions regarding the determination of interest rates, Mathieson then solves the system by a linear approximation of this system around its steady-state equilibrium and uses the model to analyse the optimal policy mix.

The optimal policy mix is implemented in two phases. During the initial phase, the program consists of increases in the loan and deposit rates, a depreciation of the exchange rate below its long-run equilibrium level, and

---

[17]Base money becomes endogenous when pursuing a fixed exchange-rate target, as international movements of capital require the authorities to alter their holdings of reserves in order to meet their target. Capital inflow (outflow) swells (reduces) the demand for domestic currency, putting upward (downward) pressure on the exchange rate. To maintain the exchange rate, the authorities must supply (demand) domestic currency to the markets and acquire (sell) foreign reserves. Thus, the stock of base money responds to the international flow of capital.

[18]Fry (1988) criticizes this feature of Mathieson's model, arguing instead that the effective loan rate is actually likely to be above, rather than below, its competitive market equilibrium level under conditions of repression. The argument is that loan-rate ceilings are always evaded - for example by compensating balances requirements - so that the effective loan rates are higher than their equilibrium loan rates. Thus, a higher real deposit rate lowers the effective real loan rate by increasing the resources in the banking sector. The lower effective loan rate stimulates investment in this sector which increases overall efficiency of investment by curtailing some of the worst public sector excesses.

a decline in the rate of growth of the domestic component of base money. The working mechanism of the policy mix begins by removing the initial shortage of real working capital through an increase in the deposit rate, so that the deposit-income ratio can rise to equal its long-run equilibrium level. The increase in deposits allows an expansion of loans through (3.24) which alleviates the shortage of working-capital finance. Since the deposit-income ratio is sensitive to expected real yields on domestic and foreign assets, the interest rate and exchange rate must be co-ordinated from the outset. An initial over-depreciation of the exchange rate will lower the expected rate of depreciation in the near future, thereby reducing the yield on foreign assets and stimulating a substitution towards domestic assets. The increase in foreign savings implies that although the increase in r_d may well establish a nominal deposit rate above its long-run value, the real deposit rate may be below its steady-state value.[19] The real deposit rate will be kept below its long-run value because foreign savings will replace some of the domestic savings which would need to be mobilized to maintain the deposit-income ratio in equilibrium. Although current-period inflation is higher due to the cost-push effect of the devaluation, the increase in nominal interest rates and the lower rate of expected depreciation will also allow a lower real interest rate to persist.

The over-depreciation of the exchange rate will also improve the trade balance by improving domestic competitiveness, thereby leading to an increase in the domestic money supply.[20] If the increase in demand for nominal money, due to the increase in deposit rates, falls short of the increment in the supply of money from the open-economy sources, an initial discrete decrease in the domestic component of base money will be required to maintain price stability. Regardless of the size of the initial reduction in the money supply, the rate of growth of the domestic component must decline sharply if any improvements in the balance of payments are to be sustained. The model demonstrates a logical inconsistency at this point. The problem is that for the liberalization to be successful, the amount of

[19]Mathieson views the depreciation of the exchange rate and the increase in deposit rates as substitute policies. The larger the initial exchange rate adjustment, the smaller the necessary initial increase in the interest rate.

[20]Mathieson draws some mammoth conclusions about the effects of depreciation. The possible contractionary effects of devaluation are well understood and expressed in the structuralist literature, which builds a case largely around the negative effects on imported input prices and foreign debt servicing. See, for instance, Lizondo and Montiel (1989), Solimano (1986) and Katseli (1983).

demand deposits held must increase. However, for the liberalization to be sustainable, the amount of domestic money must decrease. The two goals are incompatible. If the amount of domestic deposits increases, the supply of money, by definition, must increase as well. Mathieson is arguing that the Central Bank should essentially be sterilizing all capital inflows.

The second phase of the liberalization program involves a gradual appreciation of the exchange rate, gradual reductions in the nominal loan and deposit rates and a gradual increase in the rate of growth of the domestic component of base money. The trade surplus and the expansion of output in the initial phase will then put upward pressure on the exchange rate, pushing it back to its long-run equilibrium level. The initial increase in aggregate supply responding to competitive advantages, and the subsequent reduction in demand for foreign goods (inputs), begin to reduce domestic inflation. Falling inflation further reduces inflationary expectations and allows a reduction in nominal deposit and loan rates. Real deposit rates will rise, provided the fall in inflation is greater than the fall in nominal rates. Once portfolio equilibrium is reached, capital inflow will cease, implying that real interest rates will need to rise to their long-run values to maintain the steady-state deposit-income ratio. As foreign savings are no longer entering the economy, the domestic component of the money supply can be allowed to increase gradually to maintain the equilibrium deposit-income ratio. The higher real deposit rates will ensure increased demand for domestic money matches the increased supply. The economy then comes to rest at its newer, higher steady-state level of growth.

The optimal stabilization policy mix can then be summed up as 'a phase of gradual changes in policy instruments, including an initial phase of discrete (and potentially large) changes in policy instruments. These discrete changes are a vital part of the adjustment program because they create inflation and exchange rate expectations consistent with the authorities stabilization program' (Mathieson, 1979, p.472). The Mathieson model is interesting because it lends theoretical credence to the policy mix which has formed the bedrock of the majority of IMF-supported stabilization policies.

GENERAL WEAKNESSES OF THE NEO-CLASSICAL APPROACH

The particular weaknesses of the Mathieson model are demonstrative of the general weaknesses that are inherent in the liberalization literature. The main elements of contention stem from the assumption of an exogenous (domestic) money supply:

1. The assumption of an exogenous money supply implies changes in the rate of interest will have no direct effect on the money supply. Money may retain its strict neutrality, or it may have an impact on growth levels, γ, but since changes in d have no effect on the money supply (due to exogenous control), there is no first-round effect on γ. Rather, changes in d only cause a favourable impact on growth by stimulating portfolio shifts amongst assets. If these portfolio shifts increase the amount of bank deposits held, the increase in investible funds will stimulate a greater quantity of aggregate investment.[21] No immediate effects on the real economy occur, *per se*. However, if the money supply endogenously reacts to changes in the real economy, changes in d (and therefore l) would have an immediate cost-push effect - an instantaneous increase in inflation - which would call forth higher credit demand and an increase in the money supply. The initial increase in money supply would thus have implications for the dynamic paths of all state variables in the subsequent period. The presence of a cost-push effect highlights another defect of the neo-classical models, namely the specification of the inflation equations follows the typical monetarist formulation that inflation is always a phenomenon of excess demand for goods (and therefore from Walras's law, due to the excess supply of money).[22] In none of these models are cost-push effects considered, which is a substantial theoretical weakness in analytical models assessing the effects of discrete changes in a highly significant input price - the price of credit. The conditions of aggregate supply, and by extension economic growth, will depend on the price of the necessary inputs into that process. Credit is a crucial input, and by changing the conditions of supply a direct and immediate impact on aggregate supply will be felt. Such concerns are noticeable only by their absence in the neo-classical approach.

---

[21]This approach is consistent with the neutrality of money. It is not money which stimulates the increase in growth but the holding of real balances.

[22]Fry (1988) demonstrates this point in his empirical model by formulating an inflation equation which is determined proximately by the rate of change in nominal money supply and the determinants of real money demand. Fry argues that: 'Provided any feedback from inflation to money supply growth occurs with a lag, the model is recursive. In such cases, changes in nominal money can be treated as exogenous for the purposes of estimating inflation.' (p.59).

2. In assuming exogenous money, no mechanism is specified through which the government can engineer changes in the money supply. In assuming $\mu \Rightarrow \pi\gamma$ ($M \Rightarrow PY$), no impact on the vector of national income occurs until the change in M occurs. Implicit in this approach is a simple multiplier framework in which base money is related to broad money through a deterministic relation. For instance, Mathieson assumes that $L=(1-k)D$, such that loans respond as a set fraction of deposits. Changes in monetary policy tools only affect asset demand for money. In general, however, the very method by which the government effects changes in M must necessarily affect national income - the government can only change the money supply by affecting credit demand, conditions in the real sector and the behaviour of the financial system. The process of monetary control is a dynamic relationship centring around both the supply and demand for bank credit. By ignoring any possible credit demand, or aggregate supply effects, liberalization theorists are guilty of telling only part of the story, and in doing so miss many of the inter-relations that could alter and reverse the dynamic movements of the state variables. Hence, on a purely conceptual level, their stories regarding the time path of the key variables - Y, M, P - are suspect and incomplete.

3. The exogenous money assumption causes some additional theoretical difficulty. An implicit assumption in all these models is that investment in developing economies is unduly constrained by the level of savings entering the official financial markets. Savings in official financial markets is measured by a broad monetary aggregate ($M2$) which is assumed to be exogenously created by the monetary authority. Surely, if the level of investment is sub-optimal, the problem of finance is a problem of money and exogenous money is no problem here? The case for financial liberalization is one which has as its centre point the necessity of an expansion in the size of the banking sector. With an assumption of an exogenous money supply, the question to be asked is: why bother? It would seem that the government, through its own volition, could expand the size of the banking sector since it controls the expansion of the money supply. The government could then use the interest rate to ensure money demand is large enough to equal any increases in the money supply it wishes to engineer.

A more general criticism is levelled at the underlying assumptions of neo-classical market clearing and the efficiency of markets. The essence of the liberalization literature is to address the problem of 'government' failure in the market place. In doing so, there is a general presumption that the elimination of such government failure will allow the market to allocate resources efficiently. The intellectual framework was, therefore, one which saw 'government' and 'market' failure as two mutually exclusive phenomena. However, in developing countries, the reason for most initial government intervention in the market is as a response to the perception of market failure. To perceive that the subsequent intervention which in itself is seen as a failure, actually removed these underlying problems with the functioning of markets, takes a substantial leap of faith. Rather, it would be safer to assume the coexistence of market and government failure side by side in an economy suffering financial repression, and seek policy solutions based on this understanding. The liberalization literature appears to be based on a flawed understanding of what constitutes the full problem in developing economies and only focuses on one part of the problem. The inherent flaws in the financial markets, which McKinnon and Shaw catalogued, represent significant barriers to the functioning of markets and significantly limit the freedom such markets should be allowed. In liberalization literature, no place exists for intelligent government intervention to alleviate the failings of markets, and this must be considered a substantial weakness.

SUMMARY

This chapter has aimed to provide a theorist's travelogue of the early days of the financial debate, beginning with the growth models of Tobin and progressing on to the body of literature emerging from the original McKinnon-Shaw models. Representative models illustrating the basic tenets of the financial liberalization school have been presented and discussed. The main tenet which emerged was that an optimal program of financial liberalization, characterized by a 'big bang' deregulation of interest rates, was growth enhancing as it improved the quantity and quality of investment. Additionally, the McKinnon-Shaw approach identified existing weaknesses in financial markets and how government obstructionism was limiting prospects for growth.

Along the way, critical appraisal of the individual models has been included which focused primarily on one of the common assumptions running through these models - the assumption of an exogenous money supply. It has been argued that the assumption of exogenous money is a serious theoretical flaw to the approach and limits the general applicability of these models' conclusions. Specifically, the assumption of exogenous money glosses over, or ignores, many aspects of the transmission mechanism between money and the variables of national income which could alter the time paths of these key variables.

The travelogue was also interrupted at times by policy snapshots giving some idea of the context in which these theories were presented. The travelogue, in this sense, was limited in its nature as it sought to cover the debate as it stood to the end of the 1970s. The 1980s held great importance for ideas on financial liberalization because: (1) the debt crisis and subsequent importance of IMF conditional lending made it vitally important to come to a greater understanding about the effects of programs of financial liberalization, and (2) the neo-structuralist critique of the McKinnon-Shaw paradigm brought new concerns to the attention of theorists and policy-makers. It is these issues on which attention is focused in the following chapter.

APPENDIX 3: MATHEMATICAL SOLUTIONS

Tobin's Model

$$S(y(1\text{-}g)+d)=d+w \qquad (3a.1)$$

$$d=m(k,r)w \qquad (3a.2)$$

Substituting (3a.2) into (3a.1) gives:

$$S(y(k)(1\text{-}g)+m(k,r)w) \;=\; m(k,r)w+w(k,r)$$
$$Sy(k)(1\text{-}g)=m(k,r)w+w(k,r)\text{-}sm(k,r)w$$
$$Sy(k)(1\text{-}g)=w(k,r)(m(k,r)+1\text{-}sm(k,r))$$

$$w(k,r) \;=\; \frac{Sy(k)(1\text{-}g)}{1 \,+\, (1\text{-}s)m(k,r)} \qquad \textbf{(3A.3)}$$

Kapur's Model

Deriving first conclusions:

$$\frac{\dot{K}}{K} \;=\; \frac{\mu q\ M/P}{(1-\alpha)K} \;-\; \frac{\pi(\theta)(1-\alpha)K}{(1-\alpha)K}$$

Multiply first term on RHS by Y/Y to yield:

$$\frac{\dot{K}}{K} \;=\; \mu\ \frac{qY}{(1-\alpha)K}\ \frac{M}{PY} \;-\; \pi\theta$$

Substitute $Y/K=\sigma$, $e^{-w}=M/PY$ to give:

$$\frac{\dot{K}}{K} \;=\; \mu\ \frac{\sigma q}{(1-\alpha)}e^{-w} \;-\; \pi\theta$$

Deriving the second conclusion: (3.08), (3.10) into (3.11) gives:

$$\mu \,+\, \dot{W} \,=\, h(e^{-w}-e^{-\bar{w}}) \,+\, \pi^{*} \,+\, \mu\frac{\sigma q}{(1-\alpha)}\,e^{-w} \,-\, \theta h(e^{-w}-e^{-\bar{w}}) \,-\, \theta\pi^{*}$$

$$\dot{W} = -\mu + \mu \frac{\sigma q}{(1-\alpha)} e^{-w} + (1-\theta)\pi^* + (1-\theta)h(e^{-w} - e^{-\bar{w}})$$

Substituting in:

$$\bar{W} = \frac{\bar{M}}{PY} = e^{-a(\pi^* - d)}$$

gives:

$$\dot{W} = -\mu \left(1 + \mu \frac{\sigma q}{(1-\alpha)} e^{-w}\right) + (1-\theta)\pi^* + (1-\theta)h(e^{-w} - e^{-a(\pi^* - d)})$$

4. The New-Structuralists and Beyond

INTRODUCTION

For developing countries, the experience of the early eighties was coloured by the debt problems brought about by high world interest rates and the onset of world-wide recession. With the accumulation of debt and the consequential difficulty in raising capital from world equity markets, many developing countries were forced to look for concessional loans from supranational institutions such as the IMF in order to meet their international payment obligations. The IMF and World Bank, in general, made the granting of such loans conditional on the adoption of broad-based reform packages which often had financial liberalization as a large element. Such stabilization programs frequently called for the freeing of interest rates, sharp reductions in government budget deficits, reductions in the rate of growth of wages and the money supply, a contraction of nominal credit and a stiff devaluation of the exchange rate (Greenaway and Morrissey,1992). Countries not undergoing Fund-supported stabilization also tended to get policy advice stressing the need for financial reform, due to a technocratic atmosphere which accepted the McKinnon-Shaw prescriptions as orthodoxy.

As a result several countries, including the Pacific Basin developing countries of Korea, Indonesia, Malaysia and the Philippines, embarked on financial reforms with varying degrees of intensity. The experiences and results of financial liberalization in these countries have been mixed, but more often than not have made matters worse in the short run. New bank lending often continued to go to non-viable, unproductive projects and, as a result, bad debts grew rapidly. Many businesses and banks suffered a deterioration of their financial positions and became insolvent or suffered bankruptcy, resulting in systematic financial crisis. To alleviate the resulting financial distress, governments intervened in the market and often reintroduced facets of the policies originally thought to be causing the repression (Cho and Khatkhate, 1989; Diaz-Alejandro, 1985).[1]

A profound disillusionment grew with these rapid periods of financial liberalization, and led to a theoretical and practical reaction against the current orthodoxy. In general, it was felt that either the financial liberalization literature missed out on particular features relevant to the transmission mechanism of policy in developing economies, or that the perceived failure of liberalization was due to other extraneous reasons. The present chapter seeks to discuss these developments by first assessing the new-structuralist formal critique of liberalization literature and then looking at the neo-classical response to that critique and the perceived failings of liberalization programs.

THE NEW-STRUCTURALIST CRITIQUE

In response to the broadly perceived failure of financial liberalization to deliver benefits to the financial sector, a group of theorists associated with van Wijnbergen, Taylor and Buffie, began to analyse the particular institutional structure of developing economies' financial systems. The result was a critique which emphasized two distinct features of those systems which were seen as altering the way monetary policy affects the real economy.[2]

The New-Structuralists and the Unofficial Money Market

First central tenet: the unofficial or curb market is more efficient than the official market. A financial liberalization which enlarges the size of the official sector at the expense of the unofficial market reduces the real amount of credit and is therefore inimical to growth.
The first element of the new-structuralist critique focuses on the importance of the role played by the 'curb' or unofficial money market (UMM) which

---

[1]Diaz-Alejandro (1985) looked at the Latin-American financial reforms of the late 1970s, early 1980s, and concluded that for Chile 'bankruptcies, financial distress and confusion delay recovery beyond what would be necessary to achieve real adjustment to the new international terms of trade, capital market realities and expectations of growth in the international economy.' (p.17).

[2]The theoretical body is labelled new-structuralist because although they share some broad theoretical similarities, they differ significantly from traditional Latin-American structuralists (Lim, 1987).

coexists alongside the regulated, official sector in a financially repressed economy.[3] By explicitly recognizing the UMM, the new-structuralists claim they are able to provide a better description of the institutional characteristics of developing economies than do McKinnon and Shaw. The UMM is the informal market where loan suppliers, and demanders, transact freely at interest rates not subject to control by the authority. The importance of the UMM to the transmission mechanism of policy, is approached by the new structuralists using a credit multiplier framework. The thrust of the critique is that reserve requirements represent a leakage from the process of financial intermediation in official markets. The UMM operates without reserve requirements and all of the savings which are allocated to the UMM are efficiently intermediated into investment. The UMM, thus, has a larger credit multiplier than does the official market by virtue of it providing one-to-one intermediation, whilst commercial banks are constrained to providing one-to-$(1-k)$ intermediation, where k is the required reserve ratio.[4] In this respect, UMM financing is not analytically distinct from direct financing through an efficient equity market. A liberalization process which draws funds from this efficient UMM into the constrained regulated markets, will decrease the supply of real credit available to businesses by causing a reduction in the economy's effective credit multiplier.[5] The reduction in net financing causes a reduction in aggregate supply, and thus is consistent with a growth-reducing adjustment period (Taylor, 1983).

[3]The existence of official and regulated markets alongside each other is often referred to as 'financial dualism'.

[4]The Mathieson and Kapur models incorporate this type of mechanism where loans are related to deposits by $L=(1-k)D$. The new-structuralists were not questioning the validity of the theoretical approach used by the neo-classical school, only questioning the validity of the conclusions.

[5]Van Wijnbergen (1985) uses a macroeconomic model with Korean data to estimate the effects of a change in deposit rates. The results reported are that time deposits are closer substitutes to curb market loans than to $M1$. Mcleod (1991), however, utilizing a broad section of firm-level case studies, finds banks are often at a competitive disadvantage in mobilizing savings and lending in certain areas, and thus such portfolio effects are not likely to be dominant. Leite and Sundararajan (1990) argue that portfolio substitution is most likely to come from the hoarding of goods, which would then increase aggregate supply.

The Working-Capital Cost-Push Link

Second central tenet: a working-capital cost-push effect from a change in real interest rates will impose a contractionary adjustment period on a program of financial liberalization.

The second element is the importance of working-capital cost-push effects in providing a link between the financial and real sectors of the economy. Working capital, which is needed to finance payments to inputs (labour and raw materials) prior to the receipt of sales, is generally financed in developing countries by recourse to bank and UMM credit. The persistent need for working capital, and hence a debt contract, implies that the cost of credit, or the real interest rate, is a significant component of input costs. Assuming Kaleckian mark-up pricing rules gives an immediate cost-push effect on prices of any increase in the rate of interest (van Wijnbergen, 1982; Lim, 1987). The new-structuralists retain their focus on the UMM by attributing the relevant cost of credit to be the UMM rate, as the UMM is seen as the dominant supplier of working capital funds. The story told is that tight monetary policies lead to expensive credit, pushing firms into the UMM, driving up UMM interest rates and leading to an increase in input costs. The effect of mark-up pricing stimulates inflation, whilst at the same time reducing output below that obtained from the demand- reducing effects of restraint. Thus, monetary restraint, or abrupt increases in the interest rate, causes an added supply-side shock aspect which tends to make such policies stagflationary in a developing country context. The adjustment period during which the working-capital cost-push effect is present is assumed to be fairly short term due to the short maturity of most credit in these countries. The supply shock is, thus, of a transitory nature and is worked out of the system quickly. The demand-restraining impact is seen to be more persistent, initially reducing aggregate demand (investment) which in turn increases unemployment, and then gradually easing real wage pressure and inflation. A typical response to a one-off tightening of monetary policy would then be an inverted U-shaped path for the inflation rate, initially accelerating, and then tapering off once the aggregate demand effects begin to dominate (van Wijnbergen, 1982).

The impacts of these two additional features were built into formal theoretical models which illustrated the stagflationary bias of the tight monetary policies which accompanied stabilization and financial reform.

Buffie's Model of Financial Repression

Buffie (1984) explicitly builds the UMM and working-capital cost-push effects into a model which is characteristic of new-structuralist literature. Buffie begins with a CES production function (4.1) where w is the nominal wage rate, r_{umm} the curb market rate of interest, l labour, and σ the elasticity of substitution. Total labour costs, and therefore labour demand, are influenced by the UMM rate due to the lag between payments to labour and receipts from sales. The UMM rate is relevant due to financial repression, which implies that the official markets trade at below market interest rates and do not clear. Fluctuations in the UMM rate are then the mechanism which allows the residual credit demands of firms to be met and the credit market to clear. Buffie assumes wide-spread credit rationing, implying that the UMM rate is the dominant cost for financing, therefore influencing labour demand and overall production.

Table 4.1: Buffie's new-structuralist model of financial liberalization

$$l = \bar{\alpha} \, Y \, [w \, \frac{(1 + r_{UMM})}{P}]^{-\sigma} \qquad (4.1)$$

$$\frac{D}{P} = f^{D} \, (r_{D}, \, r_{UMM}, \, Y) \, W \qquad (4.2)$$

$$\frac{B_{UMM}}{P} = f^{B} \, (r_{D}, \, r_{UMM}, \, Y) \, W \qquad (4.3)$$

$$\frac{eF}{P} = f^{F} \, (r_{D}, \, r_{UMM}, \, Y) \, W \qquad (4.4)$$

$$W = \frac{M + eF}{P} \qquad (4.5)$$

$$B = (1-k) \, D \qquad\qquad (4.6)$$

$$B + B_{UMM} = wl \qquad\qquad (4.7)$$

$$\dot{w} = q\dot{P} \qquad\qquad (4.8)$$

The financial system is represented by equations (4.2)-(4.7) and employs the standard asset-stock portfolio choice models. Households allocate personal wealth, W, amongst four competing assets: demand deposits (D) currency (C) loans to the UMM (B_{UMM}) and foreign bonds, (F)(with e being the exchange rate). Using Walras's law allows the elimination of the equilibrium condition for the currency market, giving the three remaining asset conditions (4.2)-(4.4). The share of each asset in total wealth depends upon competing rates of return and real income.[6] All assets are gross substitutes, but due to the absence of an equity market real capital does not constitute a competing asset for any of the financial assets. Total private sector wealth, W, is given in (4.5) as the real sum of stocks of high-powered money, M, and foreign bonds.

Since interest rates are controlled by the government, the commercial banking system is assumed to passively accept the amount of demand deposits supplied to it as a result of portfolio decisions. The supply of bank loans, B, is then strictly determined in (4.6) by the amount of deposits and the required reserve ratio, k. Equilibrium in the financial markets occurs through the fluctuation of the curb market rate in (4.7) which functions to

---

[6]Van Wijnbergen (1982) disagrees and in his broadly similar model assumes credit market loans are inferior goods that have negative wealth responses. Mcleod (1991) supports this by arguing that as individual income increases, recourse to the UMM decreases and people become integrated into the official markets.

equate the demand and supply of loanable funds. The comparative statics model is then closed with equation (4.8) which determines the extent to which increases in the price level feed back to wages - assumed to be a constant proportion, q.

Buffie goes on to solve the system (see Buffie, p.311) and analyse the effects of a program of financial liberalization, captured as an increase in r_D, the deposit rate. The initial increase in r_D expands the supply of bank credit, but is not seen as necessarily increasing the total supply of loanable funds. When r_D is raised, households undertake instantaneous portfolio substitution from the remaining assets - currency, foreign bonds and loans to the UMM - in favour of demand deposits. Portfolio shifts out of currency and foreign bonds increases aggregate loan supply by decreasing the currency-deposit ratio and, therefore, expanding the size of the money multiplier. Portfolio substitution occurring at the expense of loans to the UMM, however, reduces the size of the money multiplier due to the resulting leakage into reserve requirements. The result is an ambiguous response to the initial change in interest-rate policy. However, the total supply of credit will decrease if UMM loans constitute a larger share of total loanable funds, and if there is a higher elasticity of substitution between loans to the UMM and deposits than *vis-a-vis* the other assets and deposits. The success of financial liberalization, then, hinges on the empirical question of whether demand deposits are closer substitutes for currency and foreign bonds than UMM loans. Buffie recognizes though that even if the net response is negative in the short run, a strong savings response may sufficiently increase the stock of wealth to offset the unfavourable substitution effects tending to contract aggregate loan supply. Thus, the negative effects arising from substitution out of the UMM are likely to have only transitory effects.

Buffie then analyses a more dynamic response by allowing the increase in r_D to cause a sharp increase in r_{UMM}. The initial effect of this rise in r_{UMM} is a reduction in employment and output through the working capital nexus of (4.1). Additionally, a possible contraction in individuals' expenditure may occur if savings are increased via greater holdings of UMM loans and deposits. The savings effect improves the balance of payments (current account) by reducing domestic expenditures on imports. However, the negative output effect worsens the trade balance by reducing the export capacity of the economy. Providing the savings rate is not extraordinarily sensitive to r_{UMM} and σ is not negligible, the output effect of (4.1) dominates the savings effect of (4.3). The ensuing payments deficit further reduces the available stock of financial wealth through a depreciation of the exchange rate (4.5). The reduction in wealth reduces actual asset holdings below desired levels, further driving up r_{UMM} and leading to a repetition of the above process. However assuming the stability of the adjustment path, implies that the savings effect must eventually begin to dominate the output effect. Once this powerful savings effect comes into play, it produces a current-account surplus. The progression of current-account surpluses eventually raises the real stock of wealth sufficiently, through appreciation of the exchange rate, to overcome the adverse substitution effects which have been contracting loan supply.[7]　As the stock of real wealth grows, this will reduce r_{UMM}, allowing positive output effects to be realized. Thus, the increase in savings from the liberalization will eventually allow positive output gains to be realized and will push the economy to a more favourable position. However, the new-structuralist contribution lies in pointing out that during the transition period, r_{UMM}, and hence unemployment, will be higher everywhere than in the initial equilibrium.

Extensions to the General Critique

Taylor (1983) expands on this story by introducing an element of cumulative causality. Taylor's approach allows for the positive savings response to an increase in real interest rates through the real wealth effect, as in Buffie's model, regardless of whether the inter-portfolio substitution occurs at the expense of loans to the UMM. However, if the initial effect is to decrease the total supply of funds to the business sector, inflation will surge because aggregate supply will decrease by more than aggregate demand. A period of rapid inflation reduces international competitiveness, and in so doing further decreases profits and investment, thereby causing a fall in the rate of economic growth. The reduction in economic growth may produce a smaller amount of wealth, despite an increase in the savings rate, than would have existed had there been no increase in the time deposit rate. The cumulative effects then stay with the economy and lower the trajectory of the country's growth path. In the medium term the reduction in net wealth reduces aggregate demand, lowering the inflation rate and thereby causing real wages to rise, given a lagged wage response. An increase in real wages causes a reduction in employment, thus decreasing economic growth as entrepreneurs suffer from squeezed profits.

---

[7]Buffie allows for the opposite outcome whereby strong substitution effects dominate relative to the savings effect. Such adverse substitution is aggravated by a series of payments deficits lowering the aggregate stock of real wealth.

The Transmission Mechanism

The key to the transmission mechanism for the new-structuralists to link increases in interest rates to the real economy is the portfolio substitution out of UMM loans which leads to a reduction in the total amount of loanable funds.[8] The shortage of loanable funds pushes interest rates in the UMM upwards, causing an inflationary and growth-reducing adjustment period. Accompanying this supply-side shock are the traditional aggregate demand reducing effects of higher interest rates on investment demand. Cumulative causal effects may appear which cause a downward spiral and a reduction of growth potential in the economy. Fundamentally however, the critique rests on the initial negative response of total credit to an increase in interest rates following liberalization. All it would take to rebuff the critique would be a demonstration that the expansion of the official sector would reduce credit rationing, allowing firms the chance to satisfy credit demand at a lower (market) interest rate. If such were the case, the central themes of the new-structuralists' critique vanish. Hence, there must be an initial negative total credit response which pushes up the dominant rate of interest. In turn, the negative credit effect rests on the assumption that most substitution is out of UMM loans and that the UMM allocates loanable funds more efficiently, thereby having a larger multiplier. The importance of this aspect is due to the implicit assumption of an exogenous money stock which is subsequently divided into three separate assets. The percentage of the money stock allocated to each asset, by changing the size of the money multipliers, determines the amount of credit and output in the system. The causation runs from an exogenous change in M, multiplied through the credit system, to a change in Y and economic growth. The size of the multiplier thus determines the net impact of policy changes.

WEAKNESSES OF THE NEW-STRUCTURALIST CRITIQUE

The new-structuralist critique has been subject to certain criticism, which

---

[8] In general, this has led proponents of liberalization to discount the importance of the savings mobilization response to an increase in interest rates. For Collier and Mayer (1989), liberalization's importance stems from the 'presumption that informal curb markets are unlikely to be the most appropriate medium for allocating financial resources'. Rather, the gains from liberalization are improvements in efficiency from replacing informal with well-organized markets.

exposes serious flaws in the theoretical foundations of the approach. Owen and Solis-Fallas (1989) attack the new-structuralist's characterization of the UMM as a perfectly efficient competitive market achieving 100% intermediation of high-powered money from lender to borrower. The UMM's greater efficiency means the quantity of credit must decline in response to portfolio moves largely at the expense of UMM loans and not the other 'unproductive' assets. Drawing from the largely descriptive material of the UMM which has emerged, Owen and Solis-Fallas find this a questionable assumption to make. The picture of the UMM which emerges is of a highly localized, segmented market, which can only provide short-term loans, and suffers from inefficiencies in intermediation. Participant lenders in the UMM are quasi-monopolistic, occupying small-scale, spatially defined sub-markets which preclude substantial opportunities for providing maturity transformation of funds or achieving economies of scale in administrative and risk-pooling activities. The UMM exists, rather, due to its ability to overcome problems of asymmetric information at the local level and the ability of UMM agents to resort to supra-legal methods of loan recovery. As a result, the average UMM loan may be subject to lower transaction and information costs than the average bank loan, but the overall system-wide efficiency of these fragmented informal markets is very low (Llanto, 1990).

Modifying the typical new-structuralist portfolio choice model to allow for greater efficiency in the banking system than the UMM, implies that an increase in the quantity of time deposits would be unambiguously growth inducing. Given greater efficiency in the bank market and stable asset market equilibrium, the term deposit rate will have a standard negative relation to the inflation rate whilst, at the same time, being expansionary due to the positive effect on the quantity of working capital. Owen and Solis-Fallas then go on to argue, correctly, that if the initial contractionary effects do not occur, the beneficial effects of financial deepening and higher savings rates in the medium and long runs are much more likely to occur.

The criticism gets to the heart of the new-structuralist theory by exposing at its core a misconception of the institutional workings of the UMM. The misconception is further carried over to the ideas about how the UMM effects the size of the money multiplier. The existence of a multiplied effect on deposits intermediated through the banking system is a result of having bank liabilities act as a means of payment. In functioning as a payments system, the official market's liquidity-creating capacity benefits from having funds redeposited with it from the loans it extends, and these can then be on-lent to new customers. Since UMM institutions act purely as an intermediary between primary savers and actual investors, its liabilities are not used for payment and it does not benefit from redeposits (Bhaduri, 1989). The UMM's ability to create liquidity is constrained to be equal to, and no more than, the initial amount of deposits. The credit multiplier of the UMM is thus unitary, and the amount of credit expanded can never be more than the quantity of initial funds - not the case for a banking system functioning on fractional reserves. A consequence of this is that any substitution which increases the deposit-money ratio will increase the size of the multiplier and, in so doing, the total amount of credit in the system. The micro-foundation of the new-structuralist model appears then to be fundamentally flawed, and is capable of producing McKinnon-Shaw policy results upon modification of those assumptions.

Kapur (1990) also takes the new-structuralists to task for their treatment of required reserves. Kapur points out that reserves have a productive function in that they enable banks to meet cash demands in excess of concurrent cash flows. The desirability of this liquidity, as an aspect of a financial asset, is that it allows asset holders to meet unexpected contingencies. Thus, the banking sector is able to mobilize a greater quantity of resources than the UMM because it allows asset holders to minimize their holdings of money balances for transactions. An expansion of the official sector then allows a greater quantity of savings to be used productively. The UMM, on the other hand, is seen to have a 'comparative advantage' in the provision of higher yielding, but illiquid, deposit instruments.

Additionally, the new-structuralist theoretical basis suffers from those weaknesses which plague the portfolio approach to modelling the effects of changes in monetary policy. Namely it lacks any behavioural story for the commercial banking sector, which is assumed to react passively to the amount of deposits that households may wish to allocate given a government set interest rate. Burkett (1986) points out that even with controlled interest rates, banks may compete on non-price grounds for deposits.[9] The behaviour of banks, and their response to any such changes in interest rates or operating environment, will then have a significant impact on what effects the policy ultimately has in the economy. In developing countries, banking behaviour is also largely affected by the actions of government and the focus of policy goals (Germidis, 1990). To discount the behaviour of banks and

---

[9]Burkett (1986) argues that a profit-maximizing bank in a financially repressed economy will be forced to substitute explicit interest-rate payments for implicit interest-rate payments in the form of providing guaranteed credit lines, subsidized loans or bribes. The net effect of an interest-rate ceiling, given this substitution, is to increase the marginal interest rate cost, provided savers prefer explicit to implicit payments.

government as being purely passive obscures some important aspects of the transmission mechanism linking policy to the real sector. As a result, the new-structuralists cannot explicitly account for the presence of the widespread bank failure which often follows a financial liberalization.

A further failing of the critique is the lack of any specification of credit demand, and how such credit demand is able to impact on money creation. In not specifying any such linkage, a theoretical black box is exposed whereby an inflationary period is able to accompany a reduction in the net size of bank credit. In specifying a negative credit response to higher interest rates, there appears to be no source whereby increases in inflation, due to cost-push, can be immediately accommodated. The new-structuralist theoretical reason for higher inflation is that the reduction in aggregate supply is greater than the corresponding reduction in aggregate demand. However, this does not provide a reason for an instantaneous increase in inflation which is consistent with the earlier assumption of mark-up pricing. Mark-up pricing does not imply a reduction in aggregate supply without some further assumptions about price elasticity and the impact of total revenue effects on investment demand. Moreover, the transitory reduction in real wages implied by the inflation should help offset the contractionary effect of the rise in interest rates, mitigating the aggregate supply response. The inherent problem here is that the high-powered money stock is an exogenous quantity to be divided amongst competing assets to determine the amount of credit in the system. In being ultimately exogenous, the theoretical framework supplies no outlet for changes in credit demand to influence the supply of money, and thereby provide a source of accommodation for higher prices. In not envisaging a positive credit response to higher interest rates, the importance of cost-push effects on the adjustment process, which is a significant theoretical objection, unfortunately becomes devalued.

The internal ambiguity and above weaknesses of the new-structuralists' critique has largely undermined the important issues which the critique sought to address and highlight. The importance of accounting for the UMM in theoretical descriptions of developing country financial markets and the importance of interest rate cost-push effects, however, should not be denied.

THE NEO-CLASSICAL RESPONSE TO THE DIFFICULTIES OF FINANCIAL LIBERALIZATION

Although the new-structuralist critique ultimately lacked authority, the proponents of financial liberalization were still troubled by the fact that so many experiences with financial liberalization ended in financial instability. The response of proponents was to maintain emphasis on the benign nature of financial liberalization, but to stress that any failure was due to the presence of adverse factors which supervened in the process. The primarily descriptive response found lessons in the experience of liberalization which suggested the preconditions and atmosphere in which liberalization could be successful, but it did not fundamentally question the logic of the reforms. McKinnon's (1989) restatement on the financial liberalization paradigm illustrated this viewpoint succinctly: 'Finance and trade liberalization, with borrowing and lending at substantial rates of interest made possible by a stable price level, is not easy and is full of potential pitfalls. Nevertheless, it remains the only game in town as far as successful development is concerned.' McKinnon continues, however, that he is now 'more inclined to emphasize the pitfalls'(p.53). Enthusiasm for putting countries through a 'big bang' of liberalization also began to wane, with earlier proponents, such as Mathieson, becoming wary enough to suggest 'financial reforms should be phased in gradually to protect the domestic financial system during transition' (Dooley and Mathieson, 1987, p.33). However, not all neo-classical writers agree. Leite and Sundararajan (1990) argue that a gradual approach to liberalization may introduce distortions of its own and raise the question of political sustainability of the process. The broad idea is that as time goes on the political will to implement the reforms wanes - perhaps after they have received their concessional loans - and thus it is better to do it all at once whilst hearts do not beat faint.

Stiglitz and Weiss Model of Imperfect Information

Despite the above disagreements, the proponents of liberalization have developed a body of theory to explain the reasons for financial liberalization's failings, which is steeped in the 'control' or 'informational' theories of financial intermediation most closely associated with Stiglitz and Weiss (1981). The importance of the Stiglitz and Weiss theory is that it demonstrates that an equilibrium loan market rate may be characterized by credit rationing. The theoretical reason for this is that the interest rate a bank charges tends to sort out potential borrowers (adverse selection) as well as affect the actions of borrowers (moral hazard). Adverse selection and moral hazard are the results of severe asymmetric informational problems that result in banks not being able to truly and adequately define the risk characteristics of their borrowers.[10] In not being able to choose between borrowers on the basis of true risk, the banks push the lending rate up to compensate, which has the unanticipated effect of causing a deterioration in the creditworthiness of borrowers. The reasons for this are two fold. First, the borrowers who are deterred from borrowing by the high cost of capital may be precisely the borrowers to whom the bank could most profitably lend because they are safe borrowers (adverse selection). Intuitively, as the rate of interest rises above a critical value, the only borrowers willing to borrow are those with little intention of paying back the higher charges. Second, if borrowers have a choice of projects, they will tend to favour projects with higher probability of default when the interest rate is increased (moral hazard) (Cho, 1986). Intuitively, this is because a riskier project has a higher rate of return in good outcomes, and a lower one in poor outcomes.

Table 4.2: Stiglitz and Weiss asymmetric information model

$$P(R,r) = \min [R + C; B(1+r)] \tag{4.9}$$

$$\pi(r,\theta^*) = \int_0^\infty \max [R-(r+1)B; -C] \, dF \, R,\theta^*) = 0 \tag{4.10}$$

$$\frac{d\theta^*}{dr} = \frac{B \int_{(1+r)B-C}^{\infty} dF(R, \theta^*)}{\frac{\partial \pi}{\partial \theta}} > 0 \tag{4.11}$$

[10] Asymmetric information in this case is defined as the situation where borrowers have greater information about their own default risk than do banks (Villanueva and Mirakhor, 1990). Llanto (1990) argues that the production of such information for banks is very costly and thus banks will seek to minimize the associated costs.

Stiglitz and Weiss's formal model illustrates these points. The model begins with the assumption that the bank can identify groups of projects on the basis of mean returns, but that it cannot ascertain the riskiness of a project due to asymmetric information. Each project which requires funding has a distribution of gross payoffs, $F(R,\theta)$, where F is the probability distribution, R is the mean gross return, and θ is a measure of riskiness - a greater θ corresponding to greater risk.   The borrower receives a fixed amount of loan, B, at an interest rate, r, and only defaults on this loan if the project's return, R, plus the collateral, C, is insufficient to meet the debt obligation. The return to the bank undertaking the loan (4.9) is either the contracted amount $(B(1+r))$ or the maximum amount the borrower can repay $(R+C)$.

Stiglitz and Weiss go on to illustrate that for a given interest rate, r, there will exist a critical value of θ, θ^*, such that a firm will undertake a loan contract if, and only if, $\theta > \theta^*$. The value for θ for which the borrower's expected profits (π) are zero satisfies (4.10). Differentiating (4.10) yields (4.11) which indicates that the critical value of risk, θ, increases as the rate of interest increases. The reason for this is that an increase in the cost of credit causes the least risky borrowers to judge credit as too expensive given their expected returns, and thus drop out of the market.   Only riskier borrowers with higher expected returns (in good states) will be left, and thus the creditworthiness of the pool of borrowers applying for loans from the banks will have deteriorated sharply. As the expected return on a bank loan is a decreasing function of the riskiness of the loan, an increase in r which triggers such adverse selection will coincide with a deterioration of the bank's expected profitability. Since the rate of returns to the bank is not a monotonic function of r, a banking system in a competitive equilibrium will display interest rates below the 'Walrasian market clearing' rate and exhibit credit rationing.[11]

An implication that these insights hold for financial liberalization is that it illustrates how certain institutional features characterizing developing countries conspire to make problems of asymmetric information a binding constraint to liberalization. The problem is that a financial liberalization which causes a rapid increase in the rate of interest will elicit a deterioration in the loan portfolios of banks. Not only will the loan portfolios deteriorate,

---

[11]Stiglitz and Weiss (1981) define credit rationing as a situation in which an identifiable group of individuals in the population are unable to obtain loans at any interest rate, with a given supply of credit, even though with a larger equilibrium supply of credit they would be able to borrow.

but there is no guarantee that existing credit rationing will be alleviated as banks will still be plagued by asymmetric information. If banks are not accustomed to competitive behaviour, their behaviour in a liberalized regime will push up interest rates above their prudent levels causing an increase in mean risk levels of projects, thereby worsening banks portfolios and endangering the stability of the financial system. The key here is that large increases in interest rates from liberalization is the culprit for ensuing financial instability.

Macroeconomic Stability and Financial Liberalization

In this approach, an important accomplice is seen to be the inconsistent macroeconomic policies, particularly fiscal policies, which run counter to the direction of financial reform. In general, large fiscal imbalances are seen as especially troublesome given the difficulty in offsetting the adverse inflationary effects of large-scale deficits (Dooley and Mathieson, 1987; Snowden, 1987). A large fiscal deficit implies the inevitability of an inflationary environment due to recourse by the government to raising revenue through the inflation tax. The problems that such high and variable inflation rates pose for liberalization programs are that they require larger, and more variable, increases in nominal interest rates to accomplish the goals of reform. However, higher and more variable interest rates further exacerbate the adverse selection and moral hazard problems that are seen to be the main reasons for market failure in developing financial markets.[12] Additionally, in a period of macroeconomic instability, the change in the price of goods and factors of production leads to increased variance and positive covariances in project returns. All projects then suffer increasingly variable returns, and are all jointly affected adversely by the uncertainty wrought by poor macroeconomic performance. Owing to this higher variance in project returns, the bank's optimal lending rate should be reduced further, with a concomitant increase in credit rationing. The large actual increase in interest rates following liberalization worsens the moral hazard process and exaggerates the deterioration in the borrowing pool (Villanueva and Mirakhor, 1990). Thus, when asymmetric informational problems are binding, liberalization could actually worsen the banks' portfolios and make the financial system more susceptible to economy-wide

---

[12]McKinnon (1989) also recognizes this by pointing out that there is a limit to which interest rates can rise without stimulating undue adverse selection and moral hazard problems. Further discussion is found in Cho (1986) and Stiglitz (1989).

adverse shocks.[13]   The deterioration of banks' portfolios given macroeconomic instability, is then provided as a compelling theoretical reason for the occurrence of financial crisis in the wake of financial liberalization.

The problem with the Stiglitz and Weiss model as an explanation for the periods of financial distress following liberalization, is that the deterioration of banks' portfolios in this model would not be immediate. It would take a substantial time gap for the higher interest rates to feed through the adverse selection nexus to significantly deteriorate banks' portfolios. Banks would need to be exposed to an operating atmosphere of excessively high interest rates for a prolonged period for their portfolios to significantly corrupt. However, this is not the case as most banks in these countries have poor portfolios prior to liberalization. The problem firms in the post-liberalization environment are precisely those firms which were the recipients of credit at 'repressed' interest-rate levels. As an explanation of the rapid slide into financial disarray accompanying liberalization, the Stiglitz and Weiss theory is not overtly applicable. However, it does highlight problems of prolonged periods of liberalization and the difficulty of liberalizing in an atmosphere of macroeconomic instability. As McKinnon (1989) stresses, 'full liberalization of banks during a high and variable inflation is not warranted....These problems with prudential control over bank loans portfolios become magnified in stressful periods when the Central Bank is trying to impose tight monetary control in order to disinflate successfully'(p.49).

De Grauwe (1987) supplements this approach by finding that high and variable rates of inflation encourage the excessive accumulation of debt through moral hazard. As inflation represents a net transfer of resources from lenders to borrowers, the incentive to take on debt increases for those in the most inflationary sectors of the economy, in order to maximize the scale of this transfer. The excessive debt accumulation leaves the financial system vulnerable to a sudden turnaround in relative prices. When such a turnaround happens, projects undertaken with large debt exposure are driven into bankruptcy with knock-on effects throughout the financial system. A strong debt deflation then occurs. The de Grauwe story provides a good intuitive explanation of why a liberalization following on the heels of a prolonged inflationary period may lead to a rapid debt deflation.

---

[13]Cho (1986) argues that equity finance is free from adverse selection and moral hazard effects and thus the fostering of equity markets must be necessary as part of a comprehensive liberalization strategy.

The upshot of these issues is that macroeconomic stability, especially price stability, is seen as a necessary pre-condition for the implementation of a successful financial liberalization strategy.   A stable macroeconomic environment will reduce the extent of the ensuing interest-rate rise, and thus minimizes the resulting adverse selection/moral hazard problems for banks' portfolios.   Macroeconomic stability will also have a favourable impact on the risk-sharing relationship between bank and borrower.   In general, for banks to enter into and maintain risk-sharing contracts with borrowers, they must have a degree of certainty about the range of future opportunity cost of funds.   Macroeconomic instability which creates uncertainty about the future cost of funds introduces instability and undermines the willingness of banks to engage in long-term risk-sharing contracts (Villanueva and Mirakhor, 1990).   The key to such stability is fiscal responsibility, which implies a broad reduction in the level of government spending.   Thus, the failure of financial liberalization was seen to be due to the inconsistency of other macroeconomic policies with the goals of reform.   For financial liberalizers, this implied the reforms were not flawed but that the implementation was flawed.   The key to successful reform would be to initially achieve macroeconomic (price) stability before proceeding to financial reform.[14]

Regulation and Supervision: Another Pre-condition

The problems of adverse selection and moral hazard are seen to be additionally worrisome when they interact with the absence of a prudent and efficient regulatory and supervisory apparatus. The lack of adequate supervision is seen to allow the problems of moral hazard and adverse selection to fully exacerbate the problems associated with a financial liberalization. If liberalization proceeds in an atmosphere of weak bank supervision, including inadequate provision for loan losses, and the provision by the monetary authority of unconditional deposit insurance, then banks will not be dissuaded from engaging in moral hazards. Banks will have an incentive to charge high interest rates and provide high risk loans due to the banks profiting from an unfair bet against the government. The reason is that due to the government's function as lender of last resort, banks can keep higher profits in good times without having to pay the full

---

[14]A slight problem here was that financial liberalization was originally envisaged as an aspect of stabilization. Now, financial liberalization could only be seen to proceed apace once stabilization had been achieved.

costs in bad times. Such a scenario serves to create a risk-taking banking climate where banks take undue risks in order to maximize their profits in states of good outcome. Such moral hazard is further exacerbated if the borrowing company is linked to the bank through a large holding company.[15] By engaging in such moral hazard, the risk characteristics of the financial systems' assets are worsened, and the stability of the system becomes more easily threatened with the occurrence of adverse shocks.

Supervisory policy, therefore, during a liberalization must be aimed to limit the banks' commitment of funds to risky enterprises, particularly to those enterprises linked to the institution via a holding company. Key elements in this prudent supervision would be the requirement of sufficient reserves against loan losses and the appropriate pricing of deposit insurance.[16] Such steps would seek to discourage and contain the risks associated with moral hazard. The implication is that adequate supervision and regulation are a necessary pre-condition for the success of financial liberalization. Dooley and Mathieson (1987) warn against the dangers of assuming that a supervisory framework exists, or that one will develop rapidly. At a minimum, the supervisory skills of the authorities will evolve with the financial system and will be tempered, most likely, with a degree of painful experience. In the absence of such a supervisory framework, and given the potential insolvency of non-bank enterprises under a market oriented system, 'special subsidies or purchases of shares by the government in such firms' may be necessary (p.33).[17] The problem of inadequate supervision runs very deep, however, as inadequate regulatory provisions are surely part of the failings of which repressed monetary regimes were guilty. As a result, prior to proposed liberalizations, most financial systems

---

[15]Such holding companies tend to be fairly ubiquitous in developing countries. Dooley and Mathieson (1987) point to the initial substantial cross-ownership of financial, industrial and commercial firms as a barrier to liberalization. They find that 'such groups may be ill-equipped to adjust quickly to a market-determined cost of credit, particularly if they have for a long time received favourable treatment under the previous regime' (p.33).

[16]Villanueva and Mirakhor (1990) argue that moral hazard in the banking system is a consequence of full and costless deposit insurance, implicit or explicit, and asymmetric information. De Grauwe (1987) argues that insured financial institutions will take on more extensive risks on their portfolios if they can be relatively sure that the government will bail them out in a crisis.

[17]This is at least a nod to the basic realization that government failure in the form of incompetence, negligence and corruption does not justify complete reliance on market processes (Collier and Mayer, 1989).

will suffer from the concentrated risks that are the result of deficient regulation. Thus, it is not so much that poor supervision contributed to the failure of attempted liberalization, but that liberalization was unwarranted in such a regulatory atmosphere.

A Proper Sequencing of Reform

Related issues dealing more specifically with macroeconomic concerns have also been exposed as serious handicaps to the ultimate success of financial liberalization policies. The first such issue is that there have been inherent flaws in the design and sequencing of the reforms. These flaws were associated with the simultaneous undertaking of liberalization in financial (both external and internal) and trade regimes. The tensions that were exposed were primarily due to the fact that goods and financial markets adjust at different speeds, and the real exchange-rate changes generated by an opening of the capital account make the integration of domestic and foreign goods markets much more difficult (Dooley and Mathieson, 1987). The basic story is that trade liberalization stimulates a reallocation of the factors of production away from the non-trade and import-substitution industries towards the export sector. As a result, imports and exports will increase but there will be an initial, temporary trade deficit due to the production lag as resources are transferred between sectors. In the absence of capital movements, this will lead to a depreciation of the currency which is desirable for its positive impact on export- and import-competing industries.[18]   A smoother adjustment process then follows if trade liberalization can precede a financial liberalization (de Grauwe, 1987). If both are undertaken simultaneously, the inflow of capital in response to the financial liberalization will cause an appreciation of the exchange rate. This appreciation will hinder the export- and import-substituting industries' competitiveness, undermining the reform process and increasing the adjustment costs paid by the economy.

Blejer and Sagari (1988) argue that there are other reasons for sequencing the liberalization of capital controls and interest rates. If capital controls are liberalized first (or simultaneously), only a few large borrowers will gain access to international borrowing due to informational problems, with the

---

[18]The simplistic argument is rife with many assumptions, particularly about the primarily positive effects of a devaluation. The potential contractionary effects of devaluation are well understood and the reader is directed to the relevant literature e.g. Lizondo and Montiel (1989) and Solimano (1986).

majority of financial players excluded. As only a small number of banks are competing, pricing by one bank will have a significant effect on the financial flows to the others. The few with international access can undertake monopolistic rent seeking, especially if large spreads exist between domestic and international interest rates, leading to undue concentration and monopolistic behaviour in the financial markets. The increased concentration is of added importance if foreign banks benefit primarily from the liberalization at the expense of domestic intermediaries. The conclusion is drawn that the monopolistic structure of the banking sector must be at least weakened by internal financial liberalization before external liberalization is contemplated by the authorities. The authors suggest allowing the 'domestic interest rate to be freely determined by market forces, as being the best way to reduce the monopolistic structure of financial markets' (Blejer and Sagari, 1988, p.31), but do not specify the mechanism by which this would work. It would seem that competitive pricing by financial institutions for deposits would still suffer from possible monopolistic behaviour by the most powerful banking institutions.

The general presumption, however, in the liberalization literature is that trade and financial liberalization programs are best conducted in autarky, and that the opening up of the economy to financial flows should be left until very last.[19]

Monetary Control in a Regulated Regime

Another issue is the difficulty of implementing and maintaining monetary control in the liberalized markets. The main issue here is that the shift to a market orientation changes the appropriateness of particular monetary aggregates, whilst simultaneously changing the tools available to the policy maker (Villaneuva, 1988). Liberalization of financial markets is a movement towards more indirect monetary control, whereby the monetary authorities attempt to use the appropriate instruments to indirectly influence the financial system in a way reflecting policy objectives. A key to the monetary authorities' success in accomplishing such goals is their ability to monitor and intervene in the money markets to stabilize and influence

---

[19]Leite and Sundararajan (1990) also suggest that authorities might have to sequence the liberalization of non-bank institutions, private banks and state-owned banks depending on the regulatory and institutional features. The rationale seems questionable as any groups which benefit from an early liberalization will be at a competitive advantage *vis-a-vis* those who are exposed late to liberalization. Such sequencing is likely to create severely disadvantaged institutions.

money market rates.   Money market rates are important in so far as they serve as the marginal cost of funds to banks.   If money markets are weak and ineffectual, the ability of the authorities to influence banks' marginal cost of funding is small, and this can lead to a tepid response of banks in their pricing practices.   As a result, banks can use the freedom of the liberalized market to develop large spreads between deposit and loan rates which may diverge excessively from world interest rates.   The resulting excessive and persistently high rates will frustrate the goals of policy makers, casting doubts on the validity and wisdom of liberalization (Leite and Sundararajan, 1990).

Thus, any liberalization process should preferably be preceded, or at least accompanied by, measures aimed at strengthening the money and inter-bank markets, and improving the effectiveness of monetary policy.   Such measures would include harmonizing the use of reserve requirements and open market operations, integration of the various aspects of financial markets (including formalizing the UMM), the homogenization of portfolio restrictions, reduction of selective credit programs, the development of secondary markets and the prudent introduction of competitive government bonds.   If not, the responsiveness of the banking system to policy manoeuvres by the Central Bank will be sluggish and the ability of the authorities to contain liquidity and monetary growth will have declined.

CONCLUSIONS FROM THE LESSONS OF LIBERALIZATION

To briefly synthesize the above, the broad consensus amongst the proponents of liberalization appears to be that the liberalization of interest rates is possible and desirable, given (i) a stable macroeconomic environment devoid of fiscal imbalance; (ii) a competitive financial market functioning in relative autarky with active money, bond and equity markets; (iii) the absence of informational deficiencies; and (iv) prudent supervisory and regulatory frameworks able to discourage excessive risk taking by financial institutions. Although none of these conditions seemingly apply to developing countries, there appears to be few other reasons why the liberalization of interest rates is not a viable policy. The essence of the literature is to say that financial liberalization did not succeed where institutional structures characterizing a repressed financial system were present.

The nature of the neo-classical response is important because it implicitly illustrates the underlying weaknesses of the traditional theoretical approach.

In pointing to institutional bottlenecks - problems of asymmetric information, monopolistic behaviour by the banking system, weak regulatory bodies - it demonstrates that the models of financial liberalization, which still survive as the theoretical underpinnings of much policy, are based on an inaccurate and incomplete picture of the institutional realities prevalent in developing countries. Specifically, by initially ignoring the starting points from which these economies begin reform, the proponents are left championing a policy prescription which will only work *once the institutional realities have changed.*[20]   Economics, and especially development economics, should be more concerned with that which it can do given present limits. Economics must be concerned with the art of the possible. A policy prescription requiring significant institutional change prior to implementation is of little immediate validity and worth. Rather, policy should be prescribed in recognition of the present institutional impediments.

A more fruitful approach is to build a theoretical paradigm which explicitly accounts for the present institutional structure, and use this to develop a better understanding of the transmission mechanism between financial policy and economic growth. Central to this will be a broader recognition of how the behaviour of the existing financial system influences the transmission mechanism of monetary policy. The value of the Stiglitz and Weiss theoretical insight lies in providing a behavioural (micro) framework of the banking firm and how such bank behaviour ultimately effects the working of monetary policy. It provides a graphic account of the importance of interactions between borrowers and bankers in influencing the workings of monetary policy and the transmission effects to the real economy.

The importance of such interactions on the effects of policy have been shown to be magnified when placed in a developing country context replete with imperfect, shallow financial markets characterized by severe informational deficiencies. The Stiglitz-Weiss insights do not offer a model of macroeconomic system response, nor tell a money supply story. Instead, the insights provide the microeconomic foundations from which macroeconomic models embodying such institutional concerns may be based. What is missing, then, is a theoretical paradigm which has an internal logic able to account for the experience and lessons from periods of financial liberalization.

---

[20] Proponents of liberalization have recognized this incongruity. Dooley and Mathieson (1987) state that 'the "typical" institutional arrangements that have marked developing countries may not be able to survive in an open and highly competitive international environment' (p. 34).

THE REVISED NEO-CLASSICAL VERSION: MONTIELS MODEL

The awareness that institutional concerns specific to the situation of developing countries are important for analysing policy response has become more apparent. The majority of the work done in this field, which is still in its infancy, has tended to apply a modified neo-classical approach to account for the theoretical insights given by, for instance, the new-structuralists. A model representative of this field is found in Montiel (1991). Montiel proceeds from the premise that 'an understanding of the nature of a financially repressed economy, and the way monetary policy works in this setting, is essential for predicting the effects of financial liberalization policy' (p.85). He builds a more broadly based model of monetary policy which captures in the transmission mechanism those effects occurring through the typical neo-classical and new-structuralist channels, as well as those through wealth effects which are induced by other movements in the economy. Specifically, the model includes those effects induced by the changes in the degree of financial repression, the black-market exchange-rate premium, inflationary expectations, and net foreign assets. The Montiel model considers a small open-economy portfolio balance model (with a commodity market). The economy consists of four sectors: households, the banking system, the Central Bank and the government. Montiel employs the standard monetarist short-run assumptions of full and instantaneous price flexibility, implying as a conjunct that the economy will be at full-employment. The real level of output is constant over the time frame of the analysis, with a vertical aggregate supply curve and full money neutrality.[21] Monetary policy changes are constrained to be limited in impact to shifting the economy's aggregate demand curve. It is assumed there is no market for government securities and the stock of physical capital is constant.

Rather than a formal discussion, the Montiel model will be informally described so that emphasis can be retained on the transmission mechanism derived in the paper.[22] In the model, Montiel assumes that households

---

[21]As a fundamental characteristic of development, *per se*, is increasing returns to scale, such full-employment assumptions are of dubious validity, particularly for a model aimed at presenting a more realistic view of institutional features.

[22]See Appendix 4 for a fuller exposition of the model.

allocate assets amongst competing assets, the most important being deposits, loans, loans to the UMM and foreign currency holdings. As households hold deposits, an increase in the deposit rate will lead to an increase in household wealth. Additionally, implicit subsidies and taxes are present in the financial system based on the level of financial repression in the economy. The intuition is that households with access to bank credit at the controlled rate, r_c, receive an implicit subsidy which is equal to the interest rate differential $(r_{umm}-r_c)$ multiplied by the amount of bank credit they receive. Those households which are net creditors to the banking system would then be paying an implicit tax. The present value of the implicit subsidy (tax) per unit of bank credit due to repression is a net addition (reduction) to household financial wealth. Since binding interest-rate ceilings imply $r_c \leq r_{umm}$, the rate of tax must be positive during a period of financial repression. The effects of financial repression on household wealth are then incorporated into a net wealth function. The net wealth effects of repression depend on whether the households are net creditors $(D\text{-}L>0)$ or net debtors $(D\text{-}L<0)$ to the banking system. If households are net creditors, an increase in the degree of financial repression reduces household wealth, since the implicit tax imposed by the interest rate ceilings on deposit exceeds the subsidy received by favoured borrowers.

Montiel solves the model and analyses the adjustment paths for changes in the monetary policy variables. For the present discussion, the most relevant policy tool is an increase in the administered interest rates, r_d, which is the essence of financial liberalization. In Montiel's partial equilibrium framework, an increase in r_d results initially in an excess supply of foreign exchange, as portfolio reallocation increases the funds in the domestic financial system at the expense of foreign asset holdings. As the level of deposits increases, bank lending will rise and household lending will fall due to portfolio substitution out of UMM loans. Invoking the new-structuralist arguments that since banks hold reserves whereas private lending agents do not, each unit moved out of UMM loans and into the regulated banking system decreases the net supply of loans. The system-wide response of loan supply will thus be ambiguous, determined by which assets in portfolios are closer substitutes to deposits. Montiel analyses a hypothetical 'currency substitution' case as being the most relevant for a developing country, and finds that the expansion of deposits would primarily be at the expense of foreign currency holdings, rather than loans to the UMM.[23] In this case, an

---

[23] A currency substitution case is one in which a foreign currency is held as a store of value and a means of payment in domestic asset holder's portfolios.

increase in r_d will result in an incipient excess asset demand for deposits, which in turn will push down the r_{umm}, due to the increase in net loan supply.

Apart from the portfolio effects, the change in administered interest rates will involve direct and indirect wealth effects. The direct wealth effect is due to the instantaneous increment in the value of the household's financial portfolio. The indirect effect operates through the reduction in the degree of financial repression. In the currency substitution case, the repression tax falls due to the corresponding reduction in market interest rates. Even when market interest rates rise, under certain limiting conditions their rise will be proportionately smaller than that of the controlled interest rates, so that the degree of financial repression will be reduced and generate positive wealth effects.[24] Essentially, the limiting condition is that the semi-elasticity of demand for deposits with regard to its own interest rate, r_d, does not greatly exceed the cross-semi-elasticity with regards to r_{umm}. The indirect effect, thus, comes from reducing the implicit tax on depositors, the size of which is determined by the differential on market and administered interest rates. Instigating financial liberalization, therefore, should stimulate unambiguous positive wealth effects for households.

Turning to aggregate demand effects, Montiel argues financial liberalization has an ambiguous effect on demand in principle. However, analysing the currency substitution case, the interest-rate effect is positive towards net bank credit in the system. The expansion of credit brings down market rates of interest, reducing the degree of financial repression and thereby increasing real private wealth. The positive wealth effect then generates a positive aggregate demand effect throughout the economy. The effects of the financial liberalization are then unambiguously expansionary.

In order to determine more precisely the effects of policies and to account for the additional, indirect (open-economy) channels through which adjustment effects may be transmitted, the model is represented and solved in a general equilibrium format (see Montiel, 1991, pp.100-103).

The general equilibrium effects of an increase in the controlled interest rate on aggregate demand are that it initially increases the steady-state stock of foreign assets and reduces the steady-state premium in the free (black) foreign exchange market. The implication is that the real exchange rate

---

[24]Lin and Chu (1989) estimate that for Taiwan, UMM rates respond in an inverted-U pattern to changes in administered rates, first increasing due to the initial reduction in credit, and then falling once the additional savings in the official market start generating a net increase in credit levels.

appreciates, which can only be brought about by a reduction in the domestic price level. The effect, then, must be contractionary on impact. The negative impact is due to the initial reduction in the black-market premium in the foreign exchange market, brought about by an increase in the relative attractiveness of holding assets in the form of deposits with domestic banks. The reduction in the premium, as the demand for foreign currency falls, represents a one-time reduction in wealth for households which hold foreign currency in their asset portfolios. The one-time reduction in wealth means that the initial effects of the increases in the administered interest rate are contractionary, but only when the effects of international capital movements are taken into account. The general equilibrium effects then demonstrate why the sequencing of liberalization is seen to be a prerequisite for success. Whether these general equilibrium repercussions are stronger than the positive partial equilibrium effects discussed earlier is dependent on the particular parameterization of the model.

The key channels through which changes in monetary policy are transmitted are still primarily the portfolio actions of asset holders. Households' portfolio reallocations in response to changes in relative rates of return generate either contractionary or expansionary impetus to aggregate demand which then feeds through to prices. Inflation is solely a demand-induced phenomenon, influenced by the portfolio decisions of investors. The causality in the system is characteristic of the monetarist theoretical paradigm and follows on directly from the implicit assumption of money neutrality. Into the monetarist story, Montiel builds the traditional neo-classical and new-structuralist channels, as well as the wealth effects which are assumed to arise out of the implicit financial repression tax levied on depositors. General equilibrium effects generated through black-market premiums and the net stock of foreign assets are also included and demonstrated to have potential negative effects on the adjustment paths.

Weaknesses of the Monetarist Approach - Montiel

The Montiel model is interesting in that it attempts to take stock of some of the theoretical insights into the behaviour of developing countries' financial markets that have advanced. The main weaknesses stem from the theoretical blinkers of the monetarist approach which impose a simplistic story on the process of money creation. The monetary story, which implicitly accepts an exogenous money supply, provides no true behavioural role for financial intermediaries and in doing so fails to utilize the insights provided, for example, from the Stiglitz and Weiss approach. In omitting a role for the behaviour of financial intermediaries, the framework is not able to shed light on or account for issues such as macroeconomic and financial instability. In the model, financial liberalization is unambiguously welfare enhancing, except when open-economy considerations are taken into account. The model, thus, still fails to grapple theoretically with most experiences of financial liberalization which were undertaken in relative autarky, via capital mobility and which still had contrary results.

Additionally, the neutrality of money in the model, which follows from the assumption of a vertical aggregate supply curve, rules out the impact that credit demand for productive purposes has on the creation of money. In omitting direct impacts on credit demand, the model is not able to account, even implicitly, for the cost-push mechanism that forms such a large part of the new-structuralist critique. It does appear that the model has included the 'wrong' or discredited aspect of the new-structuralist critique in the transmission mechanism. As inter-portfolio substitution effects do not fundamentally provide a channel through which adverse effects are most likely to rise, the positive welfare effects arising from liberalization in the model are not surprising. In not accounting for credit-demand effects, there is also no role to be played for capital accumulation as a result of credit being extended. Instead, the capital stock is assumed constant although capital accumulation is the *sine qua non* of economic development. The main effects and main channels through which financial liberalization works are thus conspicuous only by their absence.

Turning to another particular assumption, it seems odd that the only non-bank private sector actors are households. Households, in general, suffer almost complete credit rationing in a repressed financial system and thus should always be characterized as net creditors to the banking system (as Montiel assumes).[25] To this extent, wealth effects from reducing the level of financial liberalization should always be positive, as it coincides with a reduction in the implicit tax. The problem for such a characterization, however, is that the implicit tax for one sector (households) is an implicit subsidy for another sector. Any wealth increases in one sector from decreasing repression will be completely offset by wealth reductions in other sectors. In developing countries, the almost exclusive non-public beneficiaries of credit under directed credit schemes are firms. The wealth-enhancing effects for households will, then, only come at the expense of wealth reductions for firms. Households and firms, thus, differ substantially

---

[25]Interestingly, a positive correlation has been found between the credit rationing of households and savings levels. A financial liberalization which increases customer and mortgage finance is likely to reduce savings ratios (Jappelli and Pagano, 1991).

in their behavioural response to changes in the price and availability of credit. Such concerns are particularly relevant in a corporate environment of very highly leveraged firms which rely on bank credit for the bulk of their financial requirements (Sundararajan, 1985). This serious omission renders the Montiel model incapable of demonstrating how cost-push effects might arise and how such interaction would influence the working of monetary policy. The model is guilty of ignoring the primary channels through which a program of financial liberalization is likely to be adverse and contractionary.

The monetarist story is thus largely incomplete, unable to account for either the actual experiences of financial liberalization, or the theoretical insights which have been gained from such lessons.[26]

SUMMARY

The preceding discussion has endeavoured to follow the evolution of thought and understanding concerning the problems and complexities of financial liberalization. Implicitly, a recognition has begun to emerge that an unfettered financial system is the last thing most developing countries need. The problems of financial liberalization in the last decade have clearly demonstrated the inability of markets to correct, by themselves, the problems which a prolonged period of (mis-)intervention has wrought. This recognition has made proponents place several limiting constraints on the case for financial liberalization in the form of pre-conditions and sequencing. The pre-conditions amount to a requirement that the financial markets should act as a relatively perfect competitive market. In the absence of such complete markets, however, it is recognized that some form of government intervention, often seen to be limited and respecting of the imperfections in the markets, will be Pareto improving (Stiglitz, 1989, p.61).

A theoretical paradigm, though, has yet to emerge which in its own internal logic provides a role for intervention and an explanation for the failings of liberalization. Rather, traditional theoretical foundations are paid

---

[26]Fry (1993b) argues that recessionary effects of a stabilization program can be produced from an expectations-augmented Phillips curve. The logic is that following a liberalization, the reduction in actual inflation below expected levels increases the real wage, reducing employment and output. Once expectations have time to adjust, employment and output will increase back to the NAIRU. Such an approach is unconvincing in light of the upheaval in these countries' macroeconomies following such programs.

lip service to and developing countries which are able to undertake independent policy decisions have become increasingly pragmatic. Hence, what is needed is a rethink of developing country monetary policy which can provide an alternative paradigm explicitly accounting for the economy's starting points. This alternative paradigm can then be used to develop a sharper understanding of the transmission mechanism between policy and growth. Such a theoretical paradigm can build on the insights provided by the new-structuralists and the microeconomic foundations of Stiglitz and Weiss, to capture the experiences of development. Central to any such comprehensive approach would be an approach to the money supply capable of dealing with the interactions between bankers and borrowers and how such dynamics generate changes in the way monetary policy works. Post-Keynesian monetary economics, with its emphasis on policy in 'historical' time and institutional settings, seems the ideal candidate from where such an approach may arise. The following two chapters seek to apply post-Keynesian monetary economics specifically to the situation of developing countries.

APPENDIX 4: MONTIEL'S MODEL OF MONETARY POLICY

Montiel's model of monetary policy

$$\frac{D}{P} = L \ (r_{UMM}, \ rD, \ \hat{s}); \quad L_1, L_3 < 0; \ L_2 > 0 \qquad (4A.1)$$

$$\frac{C}{P} = (-)H \ (r_{UMM}, \ r_d, \ \hat{s}, \ \frac{A}{P}); \quad H_1 > 0, \ H_2, H_3 < 0, \ 0 < H_4 < 1 \quad (4A.2)$$

$$\frac{sf_p}{P} = F \ (r_{UMM}, \ r_d, \ \hat{s}, \ \frac{A}{P}); \ F_1, F_2 < 0, \ F_3 > 0, \ 0 < F_4 < 1 \qquad (4A.3)$$

$$c = c \ (r_{UMM} - \hat{P}, \ \frac{W}{P}); \quad c_1 < 0, \ c_2 > 0 \qquad (4A.4)$$

$$r = \frac{(r_{UMM} - r_c)}{r_l} \qquad (4A.5)$$

$$\frac{W}{P} = \frac{(1-r)(D-C) + sf_p}{P} \qquad (4A.6)$$

The Banking System

$$R + C = D + B \qquad (4A.7)$$

$$R = kD \qquad (4A.8)$$

$$r_c = \frac{r_d}{(1-k)} \qquad (4A.9)$$

The Central Bank

$$\bar{sf}_c = P_x \left(\frac{\bar{S}}{P}\right) \qquad (4A.10)$$

$$\bar{sf}_c + B = R \qquad (4A.11)$$

The Government

$$P_g = r_c B \qquad (4A.12)$$

The Commodity Market

$$\Omega = c \left(r_{UMM} - \dot{P}, \frac{W}{P}\right) + g + x\left(\frac{\bar{S}}{P}\right) - \bar{y} = 0 \qquad (4A.13)$$

The specific form of Montiel's model begins with the assumption that households allocate their wealth amongst five assets: domestic currency, bank deposits, D, curb market loans, foreign exchange, f_p, and bank credit, C. Equilibrium conditions in the currency market are eliminated using Walras's law and bank deposits and UMM loans are treated as a single asset by assuming perfect substitutability between them.

The theoretical rationale for combining the two is that this allows all rationing responses due to changes in bank credit to be restricted to, and analysed, within a single market. From these considerations, households' portfolio behaviour is captured by the remaining asset demand equations (4A.1)-(4A.3). Asset demand is influenced by the curb or "market" clearing rate of interest, r_{umm}, the deposit rate of interest, r_d, the expected rate of depreciation, s(hat), and the financial value of households' portfolios, A/P. All of these assets are assumed to be gross substitutes, and this is reflected in the signs of the first three partial derivatives. The partials must satisfy the adding-up constraints: (1) $L_i + H_i + F_i = 0$ where $i = 1, 2, 3.$, and (2) $H_4 + F_4 = 1$.

In addition to choosing the composition of their portfolios, households make consumption decisions, c, based on their net wealth, W/P, and the real interest rate (4A.4). The value of households' net wealth is seen to be influenced by the level of financial repression in the economy. The logic is that households with access to bank credit at the controlled rate, i_c, receive an implicit subsidy which is equal to the interest-rate differential $(r_{umm}-r_c)$ multiplied by the amount of bank credit they receive. Those households which are net creditors to the banking system would then be paying an implicit tax. The present value of the implicit subsidy (tax) per unit of bank credit due to repression, r, which is a net addition (reduction) to household financial wealth, is given in (4A.5). Since binding interest rate ceilings imply $i_c \leq i_{umm}$, r must be bound between zero and unity during a period of financial repression. The effects of financial repression on household wealth are incorporated into the net wealth function (4A.6). However, the net wealth effects of repression depend on whether the households are net creditors $(D-C>0)$ or net debtors $(D-C<0)$ of the banking system. If households are net creditors, an increase in the degree of financial repression, r, reduces household wealth, since the implicit tax imposed by the interest-rate ceilings on deposits exceeds the subsidy received by favoured borrowers.

The banking system and money supply story is the familiar simplistic neo-classical accounting identity framework (4A.7). Assets of the banking system - reserves at the Central Bank, R, and credit extended to households, C, - are held against their liabilities - deposits, D, and credit received from the Central Bank, B. The amount of reserves held will be determined by the reserve ratio, k, and the level of deposits (4A.8). The banks are assumed to operate according to a zero-profit condition (4A.9) under the constraints that reserves pay no interest but that interest is charged on credit from the Central Bank.[27]

The Central Bank pegs the official exchange rate at a value, s(bar), with foreign exchange reserves, f_c, being used to offset the trade balance which is a function of the real exchange rate. The stock of foreign exchange resources than evolves according to (4A.10). The Central Bank's balance sheet is given by (4A.11).

Real government spending on domestic goods, g, gives a government budget constraint (4A.12). The model abstracts from fiscal policy and thus has a peculiar feature that the government budget constraint is devoid of tax revenue. The model is closed by the equilibrium condition in the commodity market (4A.13) such that the goods market always clears.

---

[27]Zero-profit conditions follow directly from competitive marker assumptions. Again such assumptions serve to place large constraints on the validity of the model when dealing with monopolistic/oligopolistic markets not characterized by freedom of entry and exit.

Montiel then substitutes (4A.7) and (4A.11) into (4A.6) and rewrites the wealth equation as:

$$\frac{W}{P} = \frac{sf_p + \bar{s}f_c + r(B-R)}{P} \qquad (4A.6a)$$

which encapsulates the open-economy and repression tax effects on real household wealth. The conclusions of the model are then as presented in the body of the chapter.

5. An Alternative: An Application of Post-Keynesian Economics

INTRODUCTION

The previous chapters argued that there is a need for an alternative paradigm for the analysis of monetary policy in developing countries. Briefly restated, an alternative paradigm would be able to tell a more complete story of the money supply, explicitly accounting for institutional features of developing countries. Knowledge of these institutions would come from the vigorous observation of each individual economy's structures. Central to such an institutional approach is an inclusion of the producing, or 'real', economy's influence on the creation of money, through its interaction with the financial system. By providing a channel through which credit demand factors influence the supply of money, the approach can tell a much more comprehensive story concerning the functioning of monetary policy. The importance of real effects in the money supply process cannot be over-emphasized as the problems of development are consensually agreed to be problems of production (supply). As shortages of demand are usually not held to be an inherent bottleneck in the development process, it seems most peculiar that existing theories of monetary policy dwell almost exclusively on asset demand. The asset demand channel of the portfolio balance approach is capable of generating immediate changes only in aggregate demand. However, the impact of policy changes on the productive sector, occurring through the channels of credit demand, are going to be much more important in terms of their effect on any concerted effort for development. An approach which glosses over such costs is not likely to be fruitful or successful in its policy prescriptions. An alternative will be much more relevant to the situation of development and will enable the theorist to analyse those effects of monetary policy which are most likely to be binding for a developing country.

The current chapter seeks to move towards such an alternative theoretical view by applying the ideas of post-Keynesian economics to the study of monetary policy in developing countries. A primary task in such an application is to argue convincingly that money in a developing country should be theoretically treated as endogenous - responding to changes in the vector of national income. The reversal of traditional monetary causality, and the assumption of endogenous money, provides the theoretical stepping-stone from which a diverging paradigm may arise. The chapter will then provide an in-depth look at the institutional features of developing countries in which the endogeneity of the money supply will be argued. The ideas of endogeneity arise from analysing the behaviour of the banking system responding to credit demand from productive enterprises, and in doing so creating credit money.   If the money supply is theoretically endogenous, the workings of monetary policy through the financial institutions may lead to substantial side effects not accounted for by traditional monetary theory. Such an approach will thus be much more relevant in accounting for large monetary policy shifts, such as a financial liberalization.

Institutional Characteristics: Financial Systems under Repression

As a preliminary to the analysis, financial systems in developing countries are characterized by the existence of financial dualism.   Although the analytical framework applied is dualistic, separating organized from unorganized (UMM) market participants, it must be recognized that there exists a broad spectrum of financial intermediaries subject to varying amounts of regulatory control, and a broad spectrum of firms with varying access to financial markets. The dualistic divide includes, on the one side, large and complex commercial banks, state banks, finance houses and evolving stock markets which all fall under government regulation. Productive enterprises with access to the official credit market generally include large, and the largest middle-sized, state and privately-owned enterprises. These companies are able to appropriate the majority of credit and dominate the macroeconomic response of the economy to changes in monetary policy. The other side of the divide involves smaller, but still important intermediaries such as pawn brokers, loan houses and suppliers' credit which are all more-or-less free from government regulation on their lending activities.[1] Small firms, those financially unsophisticated, generally rely on this funding to finance any costs not met through retained income.

---

[1]For good summaries on the dualistic structure of financial markets and for descriptions of the curb or unorganized market, see Owen and Solis-Fallas (1989), Cole and Patrick (1986), Llanto (1990), Fernando (1988), Burkett (1986), Germidis (1990), Patalinghug (1987), Lee and Han (1990), Fischer (1989), and Mcleod (1991).

The presence of such financial dualism, the sectoral interaction and the specific institutional characteristics of each intermediary all impart a significant influence on the mobilization of resources, creation and allocation of credit money, the nature of money and the manner in which the financial system is able to respond to demand. It is likely that the importance of financial dualism increases the greater the level of financial repression, in that highly repressed official sectors tend to be the weakest, demonstrate the most severe credit rationing, and thus require a greater share of economic activity to be financed by the UMM (Cole and Patrick, 1986). With these points in mind, the following discussion will go on to look at the various participants active in the financial system of developing countries, on both the credit demand and supply sides.

CREDIT DEMAND: PRIVATE SECTOR FINANCING REQUIREMENTS

The genesis of credit demand emanating from the private sector is found in the certainty that production costs are regularly incurred and paid before any sales revenue is received. For an economy resting in a steady state such that it simply reproduced itself, current and past costs would be identical and present revenue from sales of past production would be sufficient to finance current costs (Moore, 1988). However, in an uncertain and dynamic environment, firms will not always be able to perceive correctly their working-capital requirements. First, there may be unexpected changes in a firm's cost structure, in terms of changes in the wage bill, input prices or tax payments. Second, there may be an unexpected change in a firm's received revenue, perhaps due to exogenous shocks to income. Both will succeed in changing a firm's working-capital requirements, giving rise to an alteration in credit demand. In general, the firm will attempt to smooth the impact of these cost or revenue shocks through borrowing. The ability of the firm to acquire credit will then determine its current-period productive behaviour. If credit is not forthcoming, the firm will need to take steps to reduce the size of its working-capital requirements. As monetary policy changes can alter both the cost structure and revenue prospects of firms, the impact of policy changes on desired and actual borrowing will ultimately alter the behaviour of productive firms.

In a growing and developing economy, increments in employment and output due to new investment will also be reflected in increased total costs and demand for credit. In general, any ambitious program for capital accumulation will require an additional source of finance. The excess amount of desired investment over retained earnings will give rise to credit demand. Subsequent to any new investment, the resulting increase of fixed capital in proportion to output suggests that firms will be above the minimum point on their (short-term) average cost curves. To exploit decreasing costs will require additional employment of new inputs, which succeeds in further raising firms' current financing requirements (Stern, 1989; Arida and Taylor, 1989).[2] If credit is not forthcoming, for either new investment or working capital, the firm will face a barrier to increasing its scale of production and to introducing modern technology (Sines, 1979).

In the expectation of receiving higher sales revenue in the future, the firm then enters into a debt contract to meet the higher production costs. Credit money is demanded in order to allow the future realization of expected higher revenue created by financing current production of higher valued inventories of goods. Production and financing decisions are, then, based on expectations of future income, largely independent of both present income streams and present savings. Thus, credit money is demanded either to finance the economic activity that firms wish to undertake, based on perceptions of the probability of likely favourable outcomes, or due to unexpected cost/revenue shocks. It is this generation of additional income, through investment spending and working capital, which gives rise to increments in the money supply.

Once the firm enters into a debt contract, future periods will find the firm making interest and amortization repayments. In undertaking this borrowing, the firm will need to balance its future income expectation (future expected repayment ability) against the future cost of credit. If the firm expects the future repayment costs to be low, due perhaps to negative real interest rates, the firm will have no incentive to minimize its credit demand or use its capital efficiently. Excess capacity may be created and left to lie idle, without any penalty being met by the firm, as the firm needs to generate only a small increment in repayment ability to meet its future repayment obligations.[3] However, if there is an unexpected deterioration of

---

[2] Both Arida and Taylor (1989) and Stern (1984), emphasize that increasing returns are a fundamental aspect of the process of development. The intuitive explanation for decreasing average costs is the heavy investment in fixed capital as a proportion of total GNP.

[3] The expectation of paying on debt contracts with negative real interest rates causes the firm to increase its current-period borrowing requirement (Fry, 1993b). As such contracts carry a subsidy, the firms are maximizing their receipt of subsidy by maximizing the amount they

repayment ability or a change in the cost of credit, the need to meet repayment obligations could increase the firm's future demand for finance. Thus, current-period borrowing behaviour can also succeed in altering future credit demands.

A peculiar characteristic of firms in developing countries is their almost exclusive reliance on debt finance. Loans from the banking system have largely been used as a substitute for stock issues (equity) and the flow of foreign savings has been primarily in the form of debt, rather than equity (Sundararajan, 1985).[4] Sundararajan develops a debt-equity choice model for firms in developing countries. He argues that the cost of equity is higher than the cost of debt, due in part to a risk premium, and this is exaggerated in developing countries due to the repression of interest rates. Firms then acting optimally will increase the debt-equity ratios to balance the benefits of additional subsidized credit from banks with the associated costs of the increased riskiness of additional investment. Further reasons for high debt reliance in developing countries include the fragility of equity markets, the lack of suitable accounting practices and the desire of entrepreneurs to maintain corporate secrecy (Snowden, 1987). Given this reliance on credit, and the lack of substitutes for external finance, firms will be very sensitive to changes in the flow and price of credit. Anything which alters the banks' ability to create credit will, by extension, succeed in altering the behaviour of industrial firms.

Firms, then, rely on banks for financing their desired investments, working capital and interest or amortization repayment obligations. The decision to invest logically precedes a firm's decision to borrow. Firm behaviour, in turn, will be influenced by the type of credit contract that is offered. The exact quantity of money created by the dualistic financial system in response to these demands, and the relative importance of each type of intermediary, will be dependent on the institutional structure

borrow. Indebtedness is then an appropriate response to negative real interest rates.

[4]In the literature, reliance of firms on debt finance in developing countries has been analysed using a firm life-cycle approach. The argument is that in the early years, firms lack reputation to raise equity and are thus heavily reliant on bank finance. As an economy and its firms mature, bank finance dwindles in importance relative to security markets (Collier and Mayer, 1989; Mcleod, 1991).

present.[5]

CREDIT DEMAND: PUBLIC SECTOR BORROWING REQUIREMENTS

An ubiquitous borrower in developing economies is the government sector, which is interpreted broadly enough to include the array of publicly owned enterprises. Government's credit-money demand in the development process occupies a unique position as the public sector often prescribes for itself a particular responsibility in the attainment of growth. Governments in developing countries will tend to spend a larger proportion of their budget on capital formation, but will also be faced with priority spending on goods as diverse as health, education, military and poverty relief (Ahmed and Stern, 1989). The final consumption basket that government spending ultimately acquires will be determined by the political priority ascribed to the three types of goods they purchase.[6]

The first area of government expenditure comprises the flow of 'free' public services to households and businesses - public goods, transfer payments and goods which may carry an ethical justification for state provision (e.g. education and health). The spending is undertaken to reap the future benefit streams accruing to increased quality of life and/or to reap benefits associated with other policy criteria.

The second type of expenditure is infrastructure spending for the economy, which tends to be concentrated on large-scale projects - for example, building roads, pipelines, irrigation facilities. The implicit rationale for spending on infrastructure is its positive impact on the marginal productivity of private capital. Infrastructure enters into the production function as a

---

[5]From this discussion some potential sources of money demand are possibly absent, notably money demand for conspicuous consumption and the demand for speculative balances which are likely to be dominant in a hyper-inflationary economy. Hyper-inflationary situations apart, government intervention in financial markets has served to discourage lending for consumption in most developing countries.

[6]The make-up of government budgets in terms of fund allocation have been analysed in models of endogenous public choice. Such models frequently employ game theoretic concepts whereby policy is determined amongst competing agents achieving an equilibrium solution through movements along reaction functions. Ahmed and Stern (1989) advocate the use of an analytical model where the welfare of households is the central policy criterion as the one most relevant to development situations.

gross complement to private capital, and may thus encourage higher levels of private investment (Todaro, 1989). The government engages in infrastructural spending in the expectation of reaping a future stream of productive benefits (income and thus tax revenue), realized by the provision of inputs into productive processes.

The final area of budget expenditure in developing countries is on public investments which are close substitutes for potential private projects. The government undertakes the spending either due to an assumed market failure - lack of private capital, potential monopoly - or due to more politically based considerations. Where such substitutability arises between public and private projects, an expansion of government expenditure amounts to an increase in total capital stock. However, with diminishing marginal returns, the productivity of capital for a given quantity of private capital must decrease as the level of state capital increases, which may suggest crowding out (Barro, 1989). Given the small capital base of most developing economies, though, it is unlikely that these economies will be affected substantially by diminishing returns. Public investment will then not have much adverse effect on private investment and should, *a priori*, have a positive effect on national investment and growth. The possible dynamic role for government expenditure, however, in the process of development has been obscured perhaps by the often poor quality of government spending.

The forms of government spending share two characteristics. First, by its very nature government expenditure is income creating.[7] In terms of the first two goods, the expenditure creates income for those providing the service and the infrastructure with no direct consumable productive benefit accruing in the same period. Income is created in the expectation that a future, but uncertain, stream of productive benefits will occur at an unknown point. For the last good, income is created as a direct result of a productive process. Therefore, the expenditure is providing the goods which will in part help satisfy the aggregate demand that the income creation is forming. The amount of domestic income which is created by government expenditure will be inversely related to the amount of imported inputs (important in both infrastructure and investment spending) employed in

---

[7]Viewing government expenditure as an income-creating process provides an intuitive reason for the inflationary consequences of deficits. For example, the eponymous 'white elephant' projects (e.g. Bauer, 1984) in developing countries are income-creating projects, although they are inherently unproductive, and thus stimulate an increment in aggregate demand. The inherent unproductiveness of such goods, by not providing a future stream of aggregate supply, implies such spending will be potentially inflationary.

government projects.   If the propensity to import in these projects is substantial, the domestic income spill-overs will be reduced.

Financing Government Spending

Secondly, all government spending must be financed. As a policy choice, governments in developing countries must strike a balance between tax and non-tax revenue, which will reflect financing options and constraints. The government will rely on tax revenue to the extent it is able to exploit the taxable capacity of the economy. Tax capacity reflects both the ability of individuals to pay and the ability of the government to collect tax. Difficulties in exploiting the taxable capacity due to administrative problems have led to a focus on 'tax handles', or simple and easily administered methods and instruments of tax collection. Tax handles try to minimize tax enforcement costs and maximize tax coverage. As a result, tax handles tend to be indirect (sales or export taxes) so that indirect taxation provides a far higher fraction of revenue in developing countries than in developed countries (Ahmed and Stern, 1989).[8] Regardless of the tax framework chosen, developing country governments will face practical problems (maladministration, large enforcement costs) and social problems (tax avoidance, black economy) in exploiting the current tax base (Alm, Bahl and Murray, 1991).

As a result, the key feeling in developing countries is that there are 'too few sources of revenues and too many demands for expenditure' (Ahmed and Stern, 1989, p.1010).   Thus, the cost of expenditures will usually be met only partially through taxation and profits of state-owned enterprises. The extent to which government spending will exceed current expected income (the public sector borrowing requirement) will be based on a mix of perceived current need, the expected future revenue generating consequences of current expenditures, and the amount of 'excess' spending the government expects to repay.   If a large proportion of the borrowing requirement is financed by borrowing from the Central Bank (the printing of money), the inflationary potential of this spending may serve to decrease the real quantity of government debt.   As the expected future repayment obligations increase, the quantity of current spending over tax revenue will increase.

The entering into of a debt contract, based on current expectations, will

---

[8]Direct taxation such as income tax, is generally unimportant, being less than 2 per cent of GDP on average (Tanzi, 1987).

then create credit money to finance current expenditure.[9]   The government borrows on the joint expectations that the future social productive benefits acquired, and any seigniorage gains, will provide the required tax revenue to meet debt obligations entered into in the present.[10]   The government can enter into debt obligations by borrowing direct from the non-bank domestic private sector, from foreign sources, or from the monetary authority and commercial banks.   To the extent that financial markets exist and thrive in developing countries, borrowing in financial markets from non-institutional agents represents an alternative to taxation for accessing private sector resources.   Debt finance carries slightly different consequences for the macroeconomy than taxation as it is unlikely the two revenue instruments will display Ricardian equivalent characteristics.[11] In general, debt finance will generate non-Ricardian solutions in the sense that any given fiscal expansion through debt creation will support greater effective aggregate demand than an equivalent expansion through taxation (Ahmed and Stern, 1989).   The reason for this solution is that individuals in developing countries are unlikely to correctly perceive future tax loads, and unlikely to view future tax liabilities in the same terms as a current tax liability.   In financing deficits with this debt, the government can achieve an inter-generational transfer of resources from an assumedly more wealthy future generation to the present.   In not requiring the current-period consumption of individuals to be forgone, as would taxation, and by not entering into current household expectations, the potential demand-enhancing (and

[9]The government will create credit money only if, by entering into a debt contract, it borrows from the banking system.   If the Central Bank neutralizes the lending to fund the PSBR by reducing the flow of credit to the private sector, the effect on the money supply will be minimal.

[10]The analysis prescribes a general benevolence by the government which is often lacking in developing countries.   For more self-serving governments, borrowing is done for the enrichment of vested interest.   In this case, the myopia of the government starves the country of future ability and makes the repayment of debt obligations, particularly foreign debt, difficult.

[11]Ricardian equivalence suggests domestic borrowing is equivalent to taxation in terms of individual behaviour and welfare since individuals would realize that debt spending and future repayment entail taxation in the future.   Liquidity constraints, imperfect capital markets characterized by a divergence of personal and government interest rates, myopic consumers, and the distortionary effects of taxation are likely to cause divergence from Ricardian equivalent solutions (Ahmed and Stern, 1989; Crushore et al., 1990; Barro, 1989).

possibly inflationary) consequences of debt finance may be quite large. However, governments in developing countries are primarily constrained from exploiting the non-Ricardian gains of debt finance due to the shallowness and unsophistication of domestic financial markets (de Haan and Zelhorst, 1990). The governments are constrained by the lack of a developed and well-functioning mechanism - a developed secondary market for government bonds - to sell debt to the private sector. Additionally, governments must attach a competitive structure of interest rates to any debt instruments it wishes to sell in financial markets. As a result, debt finance may be a relatively high priced and unattractive financing method *vis-a-vis* the alternatives (Hutchison, 1986).

Foreign financing may prove more attractive, especially if such foreign capital flows include aid or concessionary loans. Foreign financing is attractive in as much as it delivers non-Ricardian benefits in terms of aggregate demand, although this is tempered to the extent foreign finance is used to purchase foreign goods (Hutchison, 1986).[12] That is, the import of inputs carries no direct domestic income-generating counterpart and thus no increments in aggregate demand. In these terms, foreign financing has no direct inflationary consequences and may allow monetary authorities to conduct monetary policy largely independent of the government's financing requirements.[13] A peculiar and attractive feature of foreign financing of the government liabilities then is that it is a possible method of financing with a reduced money-creation counterpart.

International interest rates can be prohibitive, however, for some developing countries if such rates include individual country risk premiums. Countries with already large public external debt loads face either market exclusion or a risk premium sufficiently large to make such foreign

---

[12]The attractiveness of non-Ricardian gains will be dependent on how constrained the aggregate supply side of the economy is. If shortages of supply are the constraining factor of development, any government spending with large current demand impacts but only future supply benefits, will have some inflationary costs. To this extent, the ability to import foreign capital goods, and thereby export current income gains, will be more attractive in the short run to a government wishing to maintain price stability.

[13]If the government is pegging the exchange rate, this is not necessarily true. Any foreign borrowing not paying for imported inputs (not matched by a corresponding outflow), will cause an appreciation of the exchange rate which will need to be offset by an increase in domestic currency to world markets. In this case, foreign borrowing may impinge on the ability to pursue an independent monetary policy and may have an inflationary impact on the economy.

borrowing prohibitive and unattractive.[14] For countries in this situation, concessionary loans and foreign aid may be the only foreign finance to which they have access. Concessionary loans from international agencies provide borrowers with more favourable repayment schedules and interest rates than do those available on international capital markets. Despite these advantages, countries may have limited enthusiasm for raising funds this way due to the costs associated with lending conditionality. In general, the recent conditionality accompanying loans from the IMF or World Bank has raised the implicit cost of the loans and makes such borrowing relatively unattractive. Developing countries, however, undertake such borrowing when their access to international credit markets is limited.

The government's residual demand for credit (that portion not financed abroad or from domestic non-bank sources) must be satisfied by recourse to the Central and commercial banks. In developing countries, such a residual is typically large and its financing will have a large impact on the dynamic behaviour of monetary aggregates.[15] The ability of commercial banks, and the necessity of the Central Bank, to satisfy this credit demand is, then, at the apex of the money-creation story. The ability and will of these two intermediaries to satisfy the credit demands of the economy will determine the size and speed of money creation in the economy.

CREDIT SUPPLY: THE CENTRAL BANK

The Central Bank in developing countries occupies the difficult position of being a net supplier of financial resources to the economy and the custodian of monetary policy. The lack of independence of the Central Bank from the government in these countries (de Haan and Zelhorst, 1990), suggests that the two functions are not easily reconciled. Governments, of varying

---

[14]In developing countries, there is a temptation for more shortsighted governments to believe that difficulties in raising revenue will decline over time. Governments with limited time horizons may then over-borrow in the present period and may push borrowing beyond socially optimal levels. The result of such excess borrowing is to make future revenue raising more difficult on the margin, thereby increasing reliance on domestic revenue sources.

[15]A large part of this residual will be satisfied by the government selling bonds to 'captive' buyers at yields below the market rate. Such a practice has been labelled the 'financial repression' tax, calculated as the difference between market rates of interest and the captive rate. Fry (1993a) calculates the average financial repression tax to be 1.9 per cent of GDP in developing countries.

degrees of prudence, look to the Central Bank to accomplish fiscal or other development policy goals.   Policy trade-offs, reflecting political pressures and general concerns about monetary stability which are often seemingly exclusive alternatives, present the Central Bank with a most difficult task. To arrive at some consensually agreed middle ground is not always possible and larger political forces often subjugate the Central Bank's monetary concerns to fiscal and development concerns.   The monetary authority does not need to function exclusively as a financial intermediary when it creates financial wealth, as it does not need to rely on deposit taking to fulfil this function.[16]   Rather, it creates financial wealth by monetizing borrowing through the act of purchase - of debt liabilities of either the governments or the commercial banks.   The act of purchase of such debt liabilities creates credit money drawable by the sellers of these debt instruments.   The seller then uses its credit at the Central Bank to redeem its liabilities.   For the government this means paying for its purchases and, in the process, creating income.   The increment in income leads to a further addition to deposits and currency (monetary base).   As such monetary assets increase, the commercial banks use the deposits as the base from which to further increase total liquidity and credit in the economy (Modigliani, 1987).   The increase in total liquidity and income has the immediate effect of stimulating aggregate economic activity.

Depending on initial conditions in the economy, the increase in aggregate demand   may   have   inflationary   consequences.   With   inflation,   the government reaps a capital gain through seigniorage and the inflation tax.[17] The idea of an inflation tax is best visualized by taking the rate of inflation to be the tax rate and the stock of outside money to be the tax base.   Also, government's debt liabilities with fixed interest rates are reduced in real

---

[16]Required reserves represent a cheap source of finance to the government and in this respect the Central Bank is acting as an intermediary. The often high level of required reserves provides tax revenue for the government, which is generally held as an aspect of financial repression which must be removed (Fry, 1993b). Nevertheless, a large part of government borrowing from the Central Bank is accommodated through monetary creation, as the Central Bank tends to be a net supplier of financial resources in most developing countries' financial systems.

[17]Fry (1993b) calculates the inflation tax to be, on average, around 2 per cent of GDP for developing countries.

terms by the inflation.[18] Seigniorage is the benefit to the government of financing its budget by virtue of its ability to print fiat money.   More seigniorage is then 'collected' if the Central Bank can succeed in giving the economy an inflationary surprise.   If the Central Bank issues currency beyond expectations, prices and the real money holdings of individuals will not adjust instantaneously to new equilibrium levels (Osband and Villanueva, 1993).   In this short-term adjustment period, the government can collect additional real tax revenues.   Benefits of seigniorage are limited by the ability of an authority to 'surprise' the economy as, in the face of persistent inflation, individuals will adjust their expectations and will decrease their holdings of cash balances (de Haan and Zelhorst, 1990).   When agents are economizing on holding money balances, the receipt from the inflation tax will be correspondingly small.   To secure a given amount of revenue, the Central Bank must then generate a high and increasing inflation rate.   High inflation rates tend to aggravate the nominal deficit by increasing the size of necessary outlays.   To the extent variable inflation depresses real activity by eroding domestic competitiveness, distorting relative prices and encouraging capital flight, income and revenue will also decline (Modigliani, 1987). Inflationary financing is, then, to be discouraged as profligate use of the inflation tax will increase the uncertainty in the economy.   Greater inflation leads to greater entrepreneurial pessimism, which serves to further undermine production.   Volatile inflation will also lead labour to demand indexing, which will bring further inflationary pressure to bear in the economy.   Once indexation takes hold, the inertial inflationary impulses will become very difficult to halt (Dornbusch and Reynoso, 1989).   Despite the pernicious effects of inflation, the government may rely on the Central Bank to monetize a portion of their debt if constraints on the other financing options are severe.

Fiscal/Development Policy Dominance

Given the financial constraints imposed by weak revenue-generating capacity, the Central Bank is often under political pressure to accommodate

---

[18]Furthermore, borrowers benefit in relation to savers, who face a reduction in their net purchasing power. Thus inflation serves to create a net transfer of resources from consumers to investors, provided that the borrowing is used for investment rather than consumption. Inflation can then be seen as a redistributive tax, the incidence of the tax falling on the consumer and the thrifty.

the financing needs of fiscal policy.[19] Even more extensive, however, is the use of the Central Bank and financial system in service of development policy. For the Central Bank, this entails accommodating the credit needs of private enterprise in priority sectors at the request of the government, often through the channel of the commercial banks. This is done by opening up access to the discount window in which the Central Bank issues advances to the commercial banks, supplying them with the necessary reserves to match their lending. In developing countries, priority lending under development policy is often made statutorily eligible for discount. In this situation, the Central Bank must pursue a policy of accommodation and monetize the debt liabilities of the government and/or the commercial banks. Fiscal and development policy become the ascendant policies in the economy and the duty of supplying financial resources dominates the monetary control function of the Central Bank. A regime of fiscal/development dominance, then, occurs when the monetary authority cannot influence the real government deficit net of interest payments, nor the amount of liquidity being created for certain sectors of the economy. That is, once financial markets have been saturated with government and private debt, fiscal/development dominance occurs if the monetary authority is forced to finance the residual credit needs created by policy. The monetary authority is, then, acting as a source of financial resources and credit. The first implication of such policy dominance is that under such a regime the supply of money becomes endogenous, responding to the credit needs of income generating government expenditure and development policy. The second implication is that any changes to discount (loan) policy can perturb the economy by directly altering the quantity of bank lending available (Gertler and Gilchrist, 1993).

A regime of fiscal/development policy dominance has implications for the entire financial system. The reason is that the Central Bank will need to reconcile its statutory accommodating stance with the need to fulfil a semblance of its now subjugated monetary policy goals. The task becomes exceedingly complicated when the monetary authorities must also administer interest-rate ceilings as another facet of government policy (Villanueva, 1988). The monetary authority must, then, try to manage the stock of money in the face of both accommodating policy and the artificially low interest rates which are encouraging excess credit demand. To accomplish the feat, the Central Bank must resort to highly restrictive quantity controls

---

[19]In the literature, a situation whereby fiscal policy dominates monetary concerns is known as a regime of 'fiscal dominance' (Sargent and Wallace, 1981).

on commercial bank lending activities to non-priority non-government sectors. The quantitative restrictions on credit range from direct lending ceilings on commercial bank loan portfolios, to restrictively high reserve requirements on deposits which binds the ability of the commercial banks to create credit money. The Central Bank must then use credit availability, and by extension credit rationing, as the primary tool of monetary policy under financial repression. The resulting monetary policy structure, aimed at limiting the liquidity in the financial system in the face of large sectoral accommodation, becomes the myriad of controls associated with a financially repressed economy (Cole and Patrick, 1986).[20] Financial repression is, thus, a response to the endogenous nature of money balances in these economies responding through the subjugation of monetary policy to development policy goals.

CREDIT SUPPLY: COMMERCIAL BANKS

The commercial banks dominate the regulated financial sector in most developing countries.[21] The commercial banks face demand for credit money from both the private sector and the government and are expected in turn to grant loans and issue demand deposits. The process of creating loans to finance income-creating activity, by monetizing primary securities, increases financial assets and liabilities in the system and thereby leads to an increase in the supply of money. The behaviour of the commercial banks under repression will, thus, have an important impact on the money supply story in developing countries.

In general, the quantity of loans and credit money created by the banking system is a function of both the willingness and ability of the banks to undertake debt creation. In this regard, the commercial banks profit maximize under dual informational and regulatory constraints. The informational constraint affects the willingness of the banks to create credit money, whereas the regulatory constraint affects both the ability of banks to create money and the final allocation of credit.

---

[20]For example, Hong (1986) argues concerning Korea that credit rationing has served as one of the most important policy tools to carry out its export promotion strategy.

[21]For example, see de Haan and Zelhorst (1990) and Fischer, B. (1989). Fischer reports that for most Asian countries, commercial banks mobilize between 75 per cent and 90 per cent of total savings in the organized financial system.

Commercial Banks: Willingness to Supply Credit

To begin, consider an economy with loan interest-rate ceilings. At any given time the banks will have before them a set of investment opportunities with widely differing expected returns. Given the low interest-rate structure and the limited size of the stock of reserves, the banks will face a greater demand for credit than they can effectively supply. In determining which investment projects will be financed, the financial intermediaries will need to assess the creditworthiness of the potential borrower. Banks are constrained from doing this due to the large information costs of distinguishing between the risk characteristics of different customers (Cho, 1986; Germidis, 1990).

The broad problem is that while individual borrowers are aware of the risk-return characteristics of their particular projects, the banks are constrained in knowing only the expected return and risk of the average project in the economy for that type of firm. Given this deficiency in information, the banks will find it difficult to sort out borrowers who have a high risk of defaulting on their loan from those that do not. A primary task of the banks in extending credit is, then, the classification of borrowers into categories that distinguish amongst risk characteristics. Of central importance to such subjective estimations of risk for banks is the 'financial information' which the banks may have acquired about the firm in the course of a customer relationship. In a non-repressed financial system, an efficient classification system would entail riskier borrowers being charged higher interest rates to account for the likelihood of default. However, in a repressed financial system, legal limits on interest rates, and sector-specific interest rates charged reflecting policy priority rather than risk, preclude the existence of such a response.

As riskier projects bring lower returns to the banks, banks have a vested interest to minimize the amount of risk that their loan portfolios bear (Cho, 1986). The task of the bank is, then, to maximize its expected revenue through the provision of the maximum amount of loan contracts with characteristics that minimize the amount of risk they bear. Banks do the latter by either influencing the borrowers' actions, short of direct monitoring, or by sharing the risk with another actor in the system. In the financial systems of developing countries, such risk-avoidance techniques lead to a tripartite classification of borrowers.

Group one borrowers: policy favour
The first group of borrowers are those to whom lending carries the minimum risk. In order to minimize the risk they bear, the banks rely on

implicit or explicit loan guarantees that substantially increase the probability of repayment.   For the banks, lending which carries significant guarantees are either loans to the government or loans to firms favoured under directed credit policy programs (both referred to hereafter as Group 1 firms). Directed credit programs are a direct appropriation of the allocative function of banks by the government, which sets active lending targets with interest-rate ceilings in favour of those firms in industries with a priority in development policy. Banks are administratively required (coerced) to funnel credit to these priority projects and industries, in order to provide the relevant financial support for the successful fruition of the government's development goals.   In undertaking the allocative role of financial intermediaries and forcing them to allocate credit on criteria other than risk, government intervention worsens the repayment prospects of commercial bank loan portfolios (Fry, 1993b). To compensate, governments entered into a risk-sharing relationship with the banks. In an effort which saw governments assume the majority of financial risk, loan guarantee agencies were created which explicitly guaranteed the repayments of loans extended under government hegemony.[22] In the absence of such explicit guarantees, it was widely assumed that policy lending was implicitly guaranteed by the government, as it had a moral obligation never to renege on its debt, nor allow widespread bank insolvency to result from its policy requirements (McKinnon, 1989; Virmani, 1989).

The dynamic response of banks to the government's willingness to act as a risk partner was to make the criteria of 'policy favour' a determining characteristic of the availability of credit to firms. In choosing to lend to priority firms, the expected repayments of banks grew correspondingly, regardless of the risk characteristics of the projects undertaken.   The inherent weakness in the provision of implicit/explicit loan guarantees which *de facto* absolved the banks from carrying the credit risk, is that it provided the bank with no incentive to alter the risk-taking behaviour of those firms. Group 1 firms, if banks have no reason to mitigate the extent of the credit risk, will lack an incentive not to undertake riskier projects in order to maximize expected returns in good outcomes. High risk projects are undertaken and this leaves the banks exposed to projects highly susceptible to failure. Once they no longer bore the negative consequences of their own lending, banks felt free to engage in lending which carried a

---

[22]Often, it was enough for government policy to be active in an industry for firms to qualify under the umbrella of an implicit guarantee, as such policy interest implied subsidization and profitability (McKinnon, 1989).

higher risk profile.

Contributing additionally to the banks' ambivalent position on risk are the over-extensive schemes of deposit insurance. Such blanket deposit insurance increased risk levels as banks could choose riskier lending strategies in order to benefit from large profits in good times, whilst any large losses were absorbed by the deposit insurance agency in bad times (McKinnon, 1989). Deposit insurance and explicit/implicit loan guarantees then combined to increase the fragility of financial systems by increasing the risk concentration in banks' portfolios.

Firms typically favoured by the directed credit programs are, or became by virtue of credit access, the large private and government-owned firms on which policy success and aggregate investment rest. This group of firms is fully served by the official credit markets and occupies a disproportionate importance in economic growth and the provision of aggregate investment in developing countries. For such firms, the banks have additional informational incentives as past lending to them creates a customer relationship which helps mitigate the problems of asymmetric information and reinforces the existing allocation of credit. The directed credit flows then generate a perpetuating flow of credit in which firms admitted to the official market, due to regulatory favour, build up an informational relationship with the bank over time. The financial information imparted to the banks further strengthens the position of these firms in appropriating the limited credit resources. As policy priorities change over time, firms no longer favoured by official policy but who now have a reputation in the financial market, are still granted access to credit. However, banks may then monitor the financial positions of these firms more closely by, for example, requiring the borrower to hold compensating balances.[23]

Group two firms: partially rationed firms

For the second group of firms, non-priority firms to which lending does not carry government guarantees, banks have an incentive to provide loan contracts which increase the cost to a borrower of defaulting. Banks do this by including in loan contracts non-price constraints on the borrower in terms of collateralized financial and tangible capital assets pledged to guarantee at least partial loan repayment. If a borrower defaults on the loan, the

---

[23]Compensating balance requirements are contractual arrangements whereby a borrower or holder of a line of credit is required to maintain a specified level of deposits with the banks. Banks can use these arrangements to monitor a firm's financial condition by observing the patterns and trends in deposit balances (Jaffee and Stiglitz, 1990).

collateral supplements the proceeds available to the lender. In the extreme case of a fully collateralized loan, the value of the pledged collateral will be sufficient to cover any shortfall in loan repayment. The presence of large collateral requirements encourages firms to undertake less risky projects, in order to increase the probability that their investment will be a success.[24]

Such firms carry an intermediate risk for the banks, but will only be offered a loan contract if the firm has some degree of reputation with the bank. This group of borrowers, typically medium-sized enterprises, will often demonstrate credit rationing in that some individuals (those with collateral and reputation) will be able to obtain loans while apparently identical individuals willing to borrow on the same price terms will not. Which individual firms in this group obtain finance from the official markets is dependent on the financial evolution of the firm, its reputation as a borrower and the level of credit rationing in the economy. As changes in the latter are the primary monetary tool under repression, the bulk of adjustment in response to policy will occur through this group.[25]

Group three firms: full credit rationing
The final group of potential borrowers suffers from the absence of active consumer relationships with the banks. For these predominantly small, urban-informal and rural borrowers, the severe informational asymmetries discourage banks from considering such groups as eligible for credit. Such groups tend to have a large variance of returns amongst their projects and since the lack of information precludes the banks distinguishing amongst individual borrowers, lending to any member of the group is viewed as inherently unprofitable on any terms.[26] The heavy collateral requirement

---

[24]Virmani (1989) reports that as a mechanism to level out the diverse risk-return characteristics of borrowers, commercial banks may adjust the collateral requirements of each sub-group of borrowers to make the expected return from lending to each group broadly similar. The potential failure of this levelling mechanism is that if any particular sub-group lacks the required amount of collateral, the sub-group will remain rationed from the official markets.

[25]Gertler and Gilchrist (1993) report that for developed countries, changes in monetary policy is felt most fully by the medium- and small-sized firms which rely on credit. The greater impact on small firms of changes in monetary policy is known as the Excess Sensitivity Hypothesis.

[26]Often, loan size is seen to be too small to warrant the administrative cost to the bank of extending the loan, and thus the bank will not offer the potential borrower a loan contract on any term. Bank discouragement of small deposits also means that such small enterprises will

they would be asked to secure is prohibitive and these groups are effectively excluded from the official market. Such borrowers are 'red-lined' in that, given their risk classification, no lender will grant them credit as they believe they cannot obtain their required return at any interest rate (Jaffee and Stiglitz, 1990). Such firms must satisfy their full credit demand from the unorganized money markets.

The Commercial Banks: Ability to Supply Credit

The ability of banks to satisfy the credit demands of those groups they would not willingly ration, and to do so independently of savings, depends on the characteristics of the banking system, its level of evolution, the regulatory constraints and, to some degree, the available stock of financial capital. The more rudimentary the existing financial institutions, the more binding the stock of financial capital is to the ability of financial intermediaries to create credit money (Chick and Dow, 1988).

In general, the banking institutions in developing countries have evolved sufficiently such that their liabilities are used as a means of payment. The implications are twofold. First, agents' holdings of banks' liabilities (deposits) represent money used to support consumption as well as representing savings. Second, the redeposit ratio from bank lending will be high and reserves will become the dominant constraint on bank lending rather than savings (Chick and Dow, 1988). To illustrate, consider a bank receiving an additional inflow of reserves - either a new primary deposit, a capital inflow, or due to an open market operation. The bank will desire to lend out a proportion of these funds and in doing so creates a secondary deposit used to finance an income-creating expenditure (e.g. investment). The increment in income will generate the additional savings the bank will be required to hold in reserve. An individual banking institution will be willing to lend beyond its reserves in hand to the extent it expects these lent funds will be redeposited with itself. The larger and more centrally placed the banking institution, the larger will be the redeposit ratio. The willingness and ability of the banks to create credit independently of their reserves will also depend on the existence of alternative sources of reserves

not be able to form the customer relationship with the bank which is a necessary prerequisite to obtain loans.

banks can rely on to make up any shortfall.[27]

In this regard, the most significant aspect mitigating the reserve constraint is the willingness of the Central Bank to act as a source of reserves - a lender of first and last resort. For bankers in developing countries, acquiring the necessary reserves from the Central Bank through the rediscount mechanism and acquiring them through savings mobilization are viewed primarily as substitutable activities (Patalinghug, 1987; Husnan and Theobald, 1991).[28] The rediscount mechanism functions through the commercial banks submitting summaries of their loan portfolios to the Central Bank. On the basis of these documents, the Central Bank issues advances to the commercial banks by crediting their accounts with the Central Bank. The interest rates charged on these advances are below market deposit rates for priority lending and thus commercial banks are not discouraged from using the discount window, or overtly encouraged to pursue savings mobilization (Patalinhug, 1987).

The extent to which the Central Bank opens the discount window is again determined by the development policy goals of the government. In practice, the Central Bank is obligated to monetize those loans which have been extended under a policy scheme, including loans to the government. As such policy schemes include interest rate ceilings and/or captive placement of government paper at low, often negative, interest rates (Cole and Patrick, 1986), the monetary authorities carry an obligation to discount these loans, otherwise it would be exceedingly difficult for banks to maintain some

[27] In most developing countries, a potential source of auxiliary reserves are the inter-bank markets which have been established with varying and limited degrees of success (World Bank Development Report, 1989). The significance of the inter-bank market is that it allows individual banks greater freedom in finding the necessary reserves to back the lending they have already decided to undertake. While the volume of credit creation is still dependent on the stock of reserves available to the system as a whole, the extent of bank lending is more likely to reach the limit of the deposit multiplier and the multiplier is more rapid (Chick and Dow, 1988). As inter-bank markets are still underdeveloped, it is not unusual for banks to use government securities markets instead as the necessary reserve cushion.

[28] The results for the economy are not identical, however, under savings mobilization and rediscounting. Savings mobilization has other benefits to the economy such as appropriate incentives and discipline for lending, income redistribution towards savers, forgone consumption and the provision of financial information. See Patalinghug (1987) and Husnan and Theobald (1991) for a discussion.

degree of profitability.[29]

The comprehensiveness of eligibility for discount of bills extended under the auspices of government development plans was an additional incentive to ensure the ability of the financial system to meet the goals set out by policy. Given the low deposit rates, governments were generally concerned that such developmental policy goals would be effectively thwarted by a savings bottleneck. To surmount the resource bottleneck, the authorities provided general access to the discount window at low interest rates for lending under the policy programs. Access to the discount window was seen as adequate compensation for undertaking policy lending which otherwise would have left the banks at a competitive disadvantage. Effectively, in providing blanket access to the window for categories of loans, the monetary authorities were providing the commercial banks with a potentially elastic supply of reserves. Banks can then undertake rudimentary liability management, funding their priority lending from the discount window and diverting deposits to fund non-priority Group 2 firms. In this way, banks can maximize the amount of credit money they create to groups which have, in their eyes, eligible credit demands.[30]

The elasticity of the supply of Central Bank reserves to commercial banks is, then, dependent on the extent to which the government borrows from the commercial banks to finance its deficit, and the extent to which the government opens the discount window (accommodates) in pursuit of its development goals. The more elastic the supply of reserves from the Central Bank becomes - the smaller the penal rate and the more constant the price of reserves from the discount window - the more endogenous become the reserves to the banking system and the more fully demand determined becomes the supply of deposits (Chick and Dow, 1988). As a consequence, the more elastic the supply of reserves, the more difficult it becomes to

[29]Commercial banks are often required to hold secondary reserves and/or a certain proportion of their portfolios of liquid assets in the form of government securities. Hutchison (1986) reports that virtually all Pacific-Basin countries employed captive private, or government affiliated, institutions to some extent in financing budget deficits domestically. Commercial banks are likely to be placed at a competitive disadvantage if they are forced to absorb a large amount of government debt at below market rates.

[30]In the absence of enough creditworthy Group 2 borrowers, the banks would hold excess reserves. The presence of substantial excess reserves makes it very difficult for the monetary authorities to alter liquidity conditions in the system. The commercial banks can use these excess reserves as a cushion to absorb any changes in monetary policy. The Central Bank may resort to penalizing commercial banks for the holding of excess reserves in developing countries.

control the amount of liquidity in the system and to maintain price control. The result is that the Central Bank must restrict liquidity creation by the commercial banks in relation to the banks' lending operations to non-priority sectors, in an attempt to maintain some degree of monetary control (Horrigan, 1988).[31]   Given their statutory accommodation, the task is exceedingly difficult and the macroeconomic environment becomes correspondingly unstable.   However, tight monetary conditions achieved through the manipulation of reserve requirements would serve to reduce non-priority sector loans.   The size of priority sector loans would remain largely unchanged and the bulk of adjustment to the new monetary conditions would be achieved in non-priority sectors.

To summarize briefly, the banks are trying to maximize their expected returns in the face of severe informational asymmetries. Additionally, the banks are trying to maximize the amount of credit they can extend, and in doing so maximize the total reserves in the system.   Lending under government auspices increases the expected return of bank lending by lowering the probability of loan non-recovery. Such lending also maximizes the supply of reserves available to the commercial banks by providing them with an all but elastic supply.   That is, access to the discount window increases the primary reserves from which the commercial banks could undertake lending to priority sectors (Group 1 firms). Credit rationing to the remainder of the economy, through the use of reserve requirements, discount window or monetary stabilization bonds, is then used to limit the inflationary consequences of that accommodation. In almost all developing countries, the allocation of commercial bank credit has been strongly influenced by government development plans (Okuda, 1990).[32]

---

[31]A reserve ratio requirement of 100 per cent would allow for perfect control of the money supply. The problem for Central Banks is to find the reserve ratio requirement that allows for maximum feasible monetary control in the face of existing policy goals. Here, the rationale for high required reserves is as a response to the endogenous nature of the money supply, rather than primarily as a source of revenue for the government. Horrigan (1988) develops a model of monetary control centred around required reserves but comes to the conclusion that other policy tools - adjusting the interest elasticity of the supply of reserves - are more suited to maintaining macro stability. The main problem with high reserve requirements is the detrimental impacts they have on the ability of commercial banks to engage competitively in financial intermediation.

[32] Hong (1986) argues that the government is able to institute a monopsonistic credit market for entrepreneurs by letting the entrepreneurs as a group maximize profits in setting real interest rates. In return, the government enjoys the power of credit rationing among entrepreneurs and of determining the sectoral flow of investment. Hong provides a similar argument on how the

FINANCIAL REPRESSION: CREDIT ALLOCATION

The potentially elastic supply of reserves for priority lending, combined with the use of credit rationing as the key tool of monetary policy, leads to skewed patterns in the distribution of credit which have a significant impact on how real expenditures respond to monetary policy.

Banks were most willing to lend to Group 1 firms as these loans enabled banks to maximize their expected returns, as well as maximizing the amount of credit they could extend. As a result, the portfolios of banks became highly exposed to this particular subset of the industrial population, making their solvency susceptible to any economy-wide adverse shock which universally threatens the success of all these firms. For their part, Group 1 firms with access to official credit were aware of their position and were able to respond to the institutional incentives to acquire bank finance (Hong, 1986). Borrowing under interest-rate ceilings was often acquired at low or negative real rates of interest (Mathieson, 1989). The low real rates did not encourage firms to economize on holdings of bank debt as they were benefiting from an effective subsidy paid for by depositors (Virmani, 1989).[33] In maximizing the amount of debt they can hold, priority firms maximize the amount of resource transfer from which they benefit. Additionally, due to their reliance on debt finance and the anticipated possibility of future credit rationing, firms view access to future credit as a potential supply-side bottleneck. Medium and large firms with access to official credit may have in the past, or expect to in the future, had investment plans thwarted by a lack of supply of credit. In order to overcome future potential bottlenecks, the firms will react by providing a buffer stock against these future contingencies. In order to build such a buffer, firms will acquire finance beyond their present investment needs and acquire speculative holdings of resources (Moore, 1988).

As banks are able to acquire an elastic reserve supply for this lending, many firms are able to succeed in increasing their own span of control by appropriating a larger share of bank credit. The result of firms holding large speculative balances is that the remainder of the economic system has

government and the entrepreneurial class are both satisfied in a financial system with credit rationing.

[33]Fry (1993b) argues that such subsidies also provided a strong incentive to delay loan repayment by creating an expectation that the whole loan could be viewed as a grant. Such delayed repayments contributed to the deterioration of banks' loan portfolios.

fewer resources than before, which causes greater supply-side difficulties for marginal firms (Group 2). The more efficient and resourceful firms with access to credit will tend to expand the market of inter-firm trade credits. Group 1 firms take on the role of financial intermediaries by supplying credit to those firms which are rationed (Cole and Patrick, 1986). Loans between firms are, then, used to finance the purchase of goods, and goods in progress. Here, official financial intermediaries begin functioning as wholesalers to the unofficial retail market which develops to serve the fringe of unsatisfied borrowers.[34] Where large interest-rate gaps between official and market rates exist, strong incentives arise for making illicit payments to those controlling the allocation of such funds, which supports the emergence of a UMM (Cole and Patrick, 1986). When firms begin acting as financial intermediaries, the level of reserves begins to respond passively to the need for credit in the economy and the amount of money balances in the economy becomes endogenously determined. The success of trade credit in allocating credit is due to the informational advantage that firms have, dealing directly with other firms, concerning the repayment ability of the firm in question.

The consequence of the over reliance of Group 1 firms on debt finance, for both speculative and working-capital balances, is that these firms end up highly leveraged with very high debt to equity ratios. Whilst it is true that existing debt-equity ratios are a function of what the corporate and banking sectors view as permissible and possible, the whole financial climate in developing countries conspires to produce firms with dangerously high debt-equity ratios (Sundararajan, 1985). The level of these debt ratios is of great importance due to the importance of these firms in the macroeconomy and their contribution to aggregate investment. Such debt-equity ratios become an over riding constraint when the authority attempts to shift the method of monetary control away from credit availability towards more indirect price measures.

THE MONETARY TRANSMISSION MECHANISM: FINANCIAL REPRESSION

As Group 1 firms are least likely to be credit rationed under these systems,

[34]The existence of such an urban UMM can increase the flexibility of the domestic financial system. Fry (1993c) argues that these UMM contracts are crucial in accounting for the success of Korea's and Taiwan's economic development programs.

the true effects of credit rationing are most strongly felt in the marginal Group 2 firms. As a rule, the more elastic credit is to Group 1 firms and the government, the greater the rationing of Group 2 firms will need to be if price stability is to be maintained. Beginning with an inflationary period, if the authority wishes to engineer a monetary contraction whilst being required to keep its loan policy in place, it will need to try and limit access to the discount window, raise reserve requirements or sell monetary stabilization bonds. Any of the above is aimed at decreasing the amount of primary reserves (liquidity) of the commercial banks, making it more difficult for them to satisfy existing credit demand. The banks will not need to deny Group 1 firms access, as without a change in loan policy the primary reserves to satisfy the credit needs of this group will still be available.   If Group 1 credit demand is large and requires large accommodation, the attempt at monetary contraction will fail to eliminate the primary source of the inflationary pressure.[35]   As such, the attempt at contraction will be ineffective and will not be able to engineer the desired reduction in inflation. The difficulty in maintaining price stability is the usual failing of this type of monetary regime. However, it is possible that the size of Group 1 credit demand will be compatible with some degree of price stability.   In general, this would require a fiscally 'responsible' government borrowing requirement. In this case, the banks would still be able to satisfy Group 1 credit demands, but would find their overall liquidity position tightened.

Banks respond by making more Group 2 firms marginal, denying them access to credit. As credit rationing limits their access to external finance, the new determinant of how much of their credit demand will be realized will be the internal liquidity of the firms and how much they can raise on the unorganized money market (UMM).[36]   Since the UMM loan rates are higher, rationed Group 2 firms would face a rising price for credit, altering

---

[35]Group 1 firms have been defined to include the government as a 'firm'. Large PSBRs requiring large monetary accommodation will be more inflationary, in general, than lending backed by deposits which requires forgone consumption by savers. In not requiring a prior reduction in aggregate demand, the ultimate impact on demand of such lending is greater. To the extent such lending creates income in the current period, but only brings supply benefits in the future, it will have an inflationary impact. The larger the PSBR, the larger the potential current inflation.

[36]The importance of firm liquidity in the face of rationing implies that spending behaviour may respond with a lag to changes in credit availability depending on the level of liquidity and on their willingness to use this liquidity.

their demands for external finance, despite no change in the official interest rate ceiling. Firms with contractually necessary outlays will borrow from the UMM in the present, but will reduce future desired investment and actual consumption in order to be able to meet their higher repayment obligations. If the firms did not expect to be able to meet payments obligations on liabilities with the UMM, they would decrease their demand for any portions of external finance which are variable. Firms would reduce actual current investment and seek to limit their current working-capital requirements. Reductions in investment levels and the reductions in working-capital outlays (on wage bills and raw materials) serve to reduce the level of income in the economy. As firm expenditure falls, robbing individuals of income, the consequential reductions in demand begin eliminating the inflationary pressure in the economy. The contraction begins working by requiring an alteration in the expenditure and financing decisions of Group 2 (and 3) firms.

The impact of the credit rationing will be most severe for the smallest of the marginal firms, which have yet to build a substantial reputation with the banks. Such firms may be fully credit-rationed from official markets following a credit contraction, and not offered the smaller loans that may be offered to firms in Group 2 with established reputations for repayment. Under a severe and prolonged period of repression, Group 2 firms will join Group 3 firms in needing to satisfy all of their financial requirements from the UMM. Obviously, the full effects of a monetary contraction in a repressed financial system will be dependent on the characteristics of the UMM.

RESIDUAL CREDIT SUPPLY: THE UNREGULATED MONEY MARKET

The contribution of these smaller, fully credit-rationed firms to measured aggregate investment in developing countries is, in fact, quite limited. Thus, although the impact of credit rationing is likely to impart a significant impact on the investment spending of smaller firms, these firms are likely to account for only a small part of the fluctuations in aggregate investment (Jaffee and Stiglitz, 1990). By extension, the UMM in developing countries is not of overriding importance in financing aggregate investment. Rather, it is important in mitigating the effects of credit rationing for broad sectors in the economy - the rural and urban-informal sectors - and thereby altering the spending decisions of these groups.[37]

The UMM develops in response to this large amount of unsatisfied credit demand which exists in a repressed system. The UMM is able to develop and survive as it can overcome the asymmetric informational problems by acquiring local information through close personal ties (see Llanto, 1990 and Fischer, 1989). The UMM is, then, essentially an endogenous response to the rationed demand for credit of firms. All borrowing on the UMM is demand determined and by its very nature independent from any direct manipulation of the monetary authorities. The extent to which a given UMM will be successful in supplying the remaining credit needs of the economy will be largely due to the country-specific features of its informal institutions. It must be emphasized that the UMM is heterogeneous between, and within, countries. It is also correct to distinguish between a 'traditional' sector and the 'urban-informal' sector (Cole and Patrick, 1986). The 'traditional' institutions are those which flourished before the establishment of commercial banks and which continue to be important, such as money lenders and pawnshops. The 'urban-informal' institutions are for those participants who do not have access to the regulated institutions or who cannot meet all their needs from the regulated sector, and for those participants in a position to arbitrage between the two markets. However, it is possible to make some broadly applicable generalizations on the activity of the UMM.

In general, the UMM has a competitive advantage in providing high return but highly illiquid assets. Deposits with the unregulated intermediaries are seen as a relatively safe instrument for savings - lending carried out on a close, informal basis with supra-legal means of recovery often available to the lender. The level of returns on deposits held in the UMM differs amongst intermediaries, but the rewards of saving with the UMM are seen to be quite high, regardless of whether they are of an explicit interest-bearing type or not.[38] Fernando (1988) discusses factors affecting interest-

---

[37]Part of the credit demand that is likely to be satisfied on the UMM will be those who may be engaged in black-market/underground economy activities and as such will necessarily not orientate their demand to official markets (Fernando, 1988).

[38]A large proportion of informal lending is free of interest and such lending is often made to friends and relatives. The incentives for extending such loans are due either to value placed on continuing existing social relationships, or to establish reciprocal obligations on which participants can draw in time of need. The latter type of loan constitutes part of a complex social mechanism for spreading risk and such lending carries with it this implicit return (Fernando, 1988). Burkett (1989) analyses how rotating organized savings and credit

rate determination in the UMM, and concludes that the general presumption of a large monopoly profit element in UMM lending is not borne out by actual experience. Rather, he points to a large risk premium and demand-push pressure as factors pushing up the interest rate on UMM lending. The reason demand pressure exerts such a large influence on UMM rates is because the quantity of deposits available for lending is limited. The characteristic of these deposits on the UMM is that they generally do not act as a means of payment (Bhaduri, 1989). UMM institutions act purely as an intermediary between primary savers and actual investors. As the UMM does not benefit from having funds redeposited, their ability to create liquidity is constrained. The amount of credit money the UMM is able to create is then limited directly by the amount of the initial deposits which implies that investment is perfectly limited by the initial quantity of savings.[39] In other words, the theoretical credit multiplier of the UMM is unitary and reflects the amount of resources allocated from portfolios to UMM liabilities.

Whereas other aspects of the UMM tend to reduce its general efficiency (for example, its segmentation, lack of a mechanism for pooling of funds and risks, inability to achieve economies of scale in lending - for good discussions see Owen and Solis-Fallas, 1989; Germidis, 1990; Fischer, B.L. 1989; and Cole and Patrick, 1986), the inability of UMM institutions to have their liabilities used as a means of payment is most telling in its lack of ability to extend credit on a scale comparable to that of commercial banks.

The Monetary Transmission Mechanism Revisited

Any increase in system-wide credit rationing due to a decrease in the availability of official credit, will lead to greater competition for the existing quantity of funds present in the UMM (Shahin, 1990; Lin and Chu, 1989).

---

associations (ROSCA) work in Malaysia. ROSCAs are effectively a type of group lending whereby there is an organized framework for creating reciprocal obligations to gain access to credit in future and no explicit interest rate is paid to the depositors.

[39]Bhaduri (1989) finds that many UMM intermediaries are not deposit takers, and hence their lending is limited to the intermediaries' private surplus wealth. Also, without a legally stipulated cash reserve ratio or an institutional lender of last resort, private money lenders must rely entirely on their personal creditworthiness. Both of these factors limit the effectiveness of the UMM in creating liquidity and supplying the credit demands it faces. Llanto (1990) argues that the UMM is unable to sustain the credit needs of a growing rural economy.

The excess demand for funds in the market should elicit a positive response of interest rates. As UMM interest rates rise, the market attracts a larger source of loanable funds and a portion of credit demand is discouraged (adverse selection). As the cost of UMM credit rises with the increase in rationing, firms will attempt to reduce current expenditure and investment, and will need to reduce future desired investment to meet their higher required payment obligations. As firms reduce their income-generating behaviour, the reduction in personal incomes feeds through to spending decisions. These reduced consumption decisions multiply the reduction in income and serve to choke off any inflationary impulses in the economy.

If the UMM is large and has a fairly elastic supply of funds, as would be the case with inter-firm credit supplied by Group 1 firms, the rise in the UMM interest rates may not be particularly high. If rates do not rise significantly, firms will not be discouraged from borrowing for their financing needs and their spending/investment decisions will not be altered. The converse of this is that an economy with a small UMM, or one predominantly used to finance consumption, will be unable to meet residual credit demands. Thus, rationed firms will face severe credit bottlenecks, resulting in the need to curtail spending and investment decisions.

However, the more elastic the credit supply from the UMM, the more difficult will it be for the monetary authorities to accomplish their monetary goals. A very robust UMM is thus undesirable from the monetary authority's point of view, as it makes it more difficult to alter the general liquidity available in the economy and thereby affect spending decisions of firms. The ability to maintain price stability, which relies on the monetary authorities' ability to change the behaviour of firms, is thus undermined as firms' response to changes in policy becomes more lagged and variable.

To sum up, all credit created on the UMM is an endogenous response to demand for finance by agents engaged in economic activity but rationed out of official credit markets. However, the UMM lacks the coherence and development necessary to create credit independently of savings. In this sense, the extent to which the UMM is able to act as a sufficient source for firms seeking finance is completely dependent on the quantity of savings allocated to UMM liabilities. The greater the amount of deposits in the UMM - the lower the official market real deposit rate, the larger the interest rate gap between the two markets - the greater becomes the endogeneity of the supply of credit money in the economy, and the more difficult it becomes for the monetary authority to manipulate the general liquidity position in the economy.[40]

OPEN-ECONOMY EXTENSION

The above analysis of monetary policy is applicable to the array of developing countries which have maintained pervasive capital controls on international financial flows. However, not all countries have maintained such financial autarky. Economies with more liberal capital regimes will have had the movements of their monetary aggregates influenced to a greater extent by international capital flows. In allowing the free international flow of capital, a conduit is created through which foreign influence can alter the supply of money in the domestic economy. Such an 'outside' source of monetary change is typically held to introduce a new source of endogeneity into the money supply. That is, the presence of international financial flows which can alter the supply of liquidity in the economy, and do so regardless of the desire of the monetary authority, endogenizes the money supply. However, there is a much more fundamental source of endogeneity present in the form of credit demand, as international financial flows will move in response to the financial needs of the economy.

The Behaviour of International Capital Flows

The behaviour of international capital is usually analysed in a standard portfolio balance approach, whereby investors weigh up the relative returns on competing assets and make allocation decisions based on these considerations. These movements of international capital are responsive, in general, to interest rate differentials adjusted for the expected movement of domestic currency, and the expected rate of domestic inflation.

In the first instance, capital movements are sensitive to the differential between the domestic and foreign rates of interest. A domestic economy with a policy of interest-rate ceilings, which keeps domestic interest rates below world rates, will expect to discourage the inflow of capital whilst

---

[40]The UMM's influence and ties to the official market are generally analysed in a competing assets portfolio model (Shahin, 1990; Owen and Solis-Fallas, 1989). The more repressed the official market and the lower the rate of interest in it, the greater is portfolio substitution and loans in the UMM. Thus, it is arguable that the more repressed the official markets, the more endogenous becomes total liquidity in the system due to the larger UMM component.

encouraging outflows (Snowden, 1987). Any negative interest-rate differentials which encourage capital outflows, will serve to erode both the domestic and foreign deposit base of domestic commercial banks. As the deposit base is eroded, the reliance of the commercial banks on the Central Bank for the supply of primary reserves is increased. Capital flight, therefore, increases the importance of the function of the Central Bank as a net supplier of financial resources to the economy.

As international financial flows involve the use of more than one currency, interest-rate differentials must be adjusted for expectations concerning the movements of the relevant currencies in determining the ultimate direction of capital flows. The possibility of a depreciation of the domestic currency, which would entail a capital loss for any prospective investor, serves to discourage the inflow of any purely financial capital. To the extent that a depreciating exchange rate is desirable for reasons of trade, the loss of financial capital will be accepted. The expected rate of currency depreciation will be sensitive to the performance of the current account and the type of exchange-rate regime. However, even with a fixed exchange-rate regime, investors may form expectations of a devaluation, particularly if the exchange rate becomes over-valued and the monetary authority lacks monetary credibility.[41]

Capital flows will also respond to expectations of domestic inflation. In economies with high and variable inflation, foreign currency and foreign currency denominated assets will serve to provide an inflation hedge. As domestic investors see in these assets a more stable store of value, flow of capital out of the county will be expected.

The above standard portfolio analysis is applicable to capital flows which enter an economy to purchase domestic equity and bonds. However, in developing countries the large proportion of financial capital entering the country does so as debt - direct borrowing from a foreign financial institution - or as foreign direct investment. The flow of such capital does not respond to portfolio-based decisions, which seem more applicable in explaining capital flight than capital inflows. Rather, the size of debt-based inflows will be based on the desired foreign borrowing of domestic decision makers and the perceived creditworthiness of these domestic (public and private) borrowers. The size of capital flows in the form of direct

---

[41]Such expectations have a penchant for becoming self-fulfilling prophecies. If investors fear a devaluation and move large quantities of financial capital outside the country, the loss of foreign reserves further increases the likelihood of an actual depreciation by eroding the Central Bank's ability to maintain its exchange rate target.

investment will be based on the desire of foreign investors to benefit from some particular resource of the country - particularly low labour costs.

Levels of foreign borrowing

The size of desired foreign-debt borrowing will be based on the economy's need for foreign exchange. The extent to which the country lacks foreign exchange will be due to the presence of persistent current account deficits, the financing of which may be made more difficult still by capital controls. If such is the case, the required quantity of foreign currency needed to pay the import bill may be substantial. The government, or domestic firms, will need to enter into a foreign-currency denominated debt contract to acquire the financial resources (currency) to meet these international payment obligations. The quantity of desired debt will be endogenous, responding to the excess of domestic investment and consumption decisions requiring imported goods over their export capacity. The propensity to import from domestic spending decisions and the movement of external prices will specifically determine desired foreign borrowing. As domestic agents make decisions regarding the creation of future higher-valued goods and these decisions require the import of productive inputs, the desire to enter into a foreign-currency denominated contract will arise. As business confidence increases stimulating investment, or the price of foreign goods increases, so will the country's desired foreign borrowing. Once a domestic actor enters into a foreign-currency denominated debt contract, the need to make interest and amortization payments in the future occurs. The domestic borrower will, thus, borrow on the expectation of future (export) revenue gained, which will be balanced against future expected repayment obligations. An unexpected change in either of these, the external interest rate or external demand for domestic export goods, will succeed in changing the foreign credit (currency) needs of the economy. Thus, unexpected costs or revenue shocks, would require increments in foreign borrowing.

The perceptions of the international financial community of a country's creditworthiness will be based on the expected repayment ability of the borrower. As most foreign borrowing is by the public sector or with explicit government guarantees, a primary element in such perception, is the size of existing (sovereign) debt particularly in relation to the economy's perceived export potential. The export potential is important as it provides the source from which future debt and amortization repayments will be made. The larger the existing debt or the smaller the export capability, the more difficult it will be for the country to service existing and future debt obligations. As the international financial markets make judgements on the creditworthiness of a particular country, they will levy a risk premium which reflects these considerations. As risk premiums rise, foreign financing will become a relatively expensive method of financing, requiring a reduction in the demand for foreign debt by domestic agents. The reduction in the demand for foreign-currency denominated debt by domestic agents will be accomplished by the curtailment of current-period consumption and investment decisions. Thus, the extent of foreign borrowing will be determined by the past and present investment and consumption decisions of domestic borrowers - past decisions reflecting current repayment ability.

If either credit demand or credit supply decreases, the scale of foreign borrowing will decrease. If a large risk premium exists, then, the country's foreign credit demand must be reduced and the country will be suffering from international credit rationing. The current amount of credit rationing will then be a function of the size of previous capital flows, and the perceived repayment ability of the country. As foreign borrowing will be almost exclusively used for the purchase of imported capital and primary goods, an increase in the international credit rationing of the economy will require a decrease in both actual investment and consumption levels.[42]

Levels of foreign direct investment

Capital which is in the form of direct foreign investment will enter an economy for a perceived cost advantage. A foreign investor will move capital in the joint expectation of receiving a future income benefit and of being able to produce at cost-minimizing levels. Thus, capital will enter for purely productive reasons, seeking out benefits provided by the recipient economy. As such, expectations of domestic exchange rate movements and domestic inflation rates will be important. Changes in either variable will be able to significantly alter domestic cost advantages and, ultimately, profitability. For instance, the reduction in the value of domestic currency following a depreciation may help offset any increase in the domestic price level which was eroding domestic cost competitiveness. The expectation of depreciation would, then, encourage the inward flow of direct investment. However, if a foreign investor was wishing to repatriate income rather than re-export goods, the depreciation would reduce the foreign-currency value

---

[42]The presence of international credit rationing of a country's credit demands provides a rationale for the liberalization of capital controls. To the extent a liberalization of capital controls provides an additional source of foreign exchange (through capital inflow), it reduces the level of foreign borrowing needed to satisfy any given level of foreign exchange. Thus, a liberalization of capital controls can be seen as reducing the scale of a country's international credit rationing (also called a foreign exchange bottleneck).

of that income. Therefore, expectations of a depreciation could discourage the inflow of capital. Nevertheless, capital in the form of foreign direct investment will enter for a myriad of reasons, based on the current and future characteristics of the recipient domestic economy. Capital will enter purely for reasons of production, once an investment decision has been made by a foreign investor.

International Financial Flows and the Money Supply

The inflow of foreign capital can alter the domestic money supply in one of two ways. First, foreign financial capital which purchases a domestic debt liability monetizes that liability. In this case, the Central Bank acquires foreign exchange reserves, and the firm (or issuer of the liability) receives the value of their liability in domestic currency. The firm (or government) can then use the finance acquired to undertake desired investment or working-capital expenditure. The expenditure creates income, and a multiplied effect on income and money is stimulated as this income is spent and finds its way into the domestic banking system. Thus, foreign finance is desired by domestic actors in order to fund investment and consumption decisions already undertaken.

The second way is if foreign capital enters directly into the banking system. The Central Bank still receives an increase in foreign exchange reserves but the banking system can then use this foreign capital as the primary reserves from which to undertake lending to domestic customers. As the commercial banks can create a multiplied increase in credit from these primary deposits, the increase in the liquidity of the system is greater than that just accruing to the size of the capital inflow. The ability of foreign capital to enter the system as a primary reserve enhances the ability of the domestic banking system to create credit independently of the monetary authority's discount window. The larger the inflow of capital, the greater the deposit base of commercial banks from which to undertake credit expansion.[43]

A fixed exchange-rate regime
The key to the initial burst of domestic monetary creation is in the Central Bank acquiring foreign exchange reserves in exchange for domestic

---

[43]In general, the Central Bank would attempt to control this type of lending in the same way as lending from domestic deposits - through the use of required reserve ratios and monetary stabilization bonds.

currency, to allow foreign finance to monetize domestic debt liabilities. The extent to which this will happen will depend on both the type of exchange rate regime and the amount of direct restrictions on capital transactions. In many developing countries, the size and quantity of foreign exchange dealings are limited by the government. In this case, the government will be the dominant supplier of domestic currency to the foreign exchange market. A fixed exchange-rate regime will require the government to supply any deficiency, or absorb any surplus, of currency required by the markets to maintain an exchange-rate target. Thus, the government is constrained with a fixed exchange rate to supply all the domestic currency the foreign exchange market requires, given its balance of payments position. This subjugation of domestic monetary policy to the needs of an exchange-rate target is the commonly cited source of endogeneity in the money supply.

However, it is not necessarily the case that all inflows of capital will lead to a corresponding increase in domestic money supply. If the Central Bank sets a ceiling on the expansion of reserve money, it will be required to sterilize the impact of any capital inflows above that ceiling. The Central Bank sterilizes capital inflows by offsetting the international flow with a corresponding reduction in the domestic credit extended by the Central Bank. The sustainability of such a policy of sterilization depends on the cost of reducing Central Bank domestic credit and on the scope and persistence of these flows (Mathieson, 1988).[44] If capital inflows are sterilized, no additional domestic monetary creation will occur.

Additionally, it is important to realize that a large part of the international financial transactions of domestic agents will have no impact on the domestic money supply. A large element of measured capital inflow into a developing country is in the form of debt - a government or a firm acquiring a foreign-currency denominated loan or floating foreign-currency denominated (sovereign) bonds in a foreign financial market. A feature of this debt is that it will have no immediate domestic monetary consequences. The 'neutral' character of foreign borrowing *vis-a-vis* domestic money arises because such borrowing is done in a foreign currency *for* spending decisions carried out in a foreign currency. Thus, foreign reserves are not acquired

---

[44]Fry (1988) has estimated a set of 'offset' coefficients capturing the extent to which these countries have sterilized their capital inflows. Fry reports that for a selection of Pacific-Basin developing countries these ratios are similar to those estimated for most OECD countries, sterilizing about two-thirds of their capital inflows.

and no domestic monetary creation counterpart is entailed.[45] Hence, the innate neutrality of foreign borrowing in terms of domestic money creation has allowed most developing countries to pursue monetary goals independently of world monetary conditions.[46]

Whereas debt can be domestic money neutral, foreign direct investment will exert the greatest source of expansionary pressure on the money supply. The source of domestic monetary expansion will in this case be the need to finance working-capital budgets denominated in domestic currency. Once the decision has been made to proceed with a project, the actual act of investment and production will create domestic currency working costs as domestic inputs and variable factors of production are hired. The hiring of local factors then creates domestic incomes. In order to finance this increase in domestic incomes, the foreign investor will need to acquire domestic currency, and does this by supplying foreign exchange (reserves) to the Central Bank. Domestic money is then created in response, allowing the investor to finance the domestic income creation accompanying the foreign capital. The larger the flow of investment into a country, the greater will be the monetary stimulus occurring due to the ensuing increase in domestic incomes. As domestic incomes grow, a portion of this will find its way to the commercial banking system. The increase in their primary reserves will thereby improve their ability to create credit. A secondary increase in the money supply then occurs. The key in the first round, however, is that increments in the money supply, due to foreign capital, will be *caused* by the accompanying creation of income in the domestic economy.

A floating exchange-rate regime

If the exchange-rate regime is floating, the monetary authority will not need to supply additional currency to the markets with an inflow of capital.

---

[45]To the extent that such foreign currency spending is on imported capital goods, a second-round monetary effect may occur. The increase in capital (or production) will increase the marginal productivity of labour, increasing the real (and by extension nominal) wage rate. The increases in wages and incomes will then call forth increments in the money supply.

[46]The money supply's independence from world monetary conditions implies that the typical international source of endogeneity is not that relevant for developing countries. Rather, developing countries' demand for foreign currency is endogenous, responding to the investment and consumption decisions of domestic actors, foreign prices, foreign demand and world interest rates. Foreign aid, particularly if it is tied, is a good example of such domestic monetary-neutral capital flows (Hutchison, 1986).

Rather, the increased demand for domestic currency will, *ceteris paribus*, lead to an appreciation of the exchange rate. As the monetary authority does not acquire additional foreign reserves, there is no additional domestic monetary creation component. However, if the government has a managed float and aims to engineer a persistent depreciation of the domestic currency, say for trade reasons, inflows of capital would require the creation of domestic money. In general, such exchange rate arrangements are characterized by a foreign exchange market intervention rule which will specify the scale of the authority's purchases or sales of foreign exchange. Foreign exchange will then be bought or sold for domestic base money, in reaction to the departures of the exchange rate from a desired level. Monetary authorities may then be 'leaning against the wind', and in so doing will create or destroy money in response to balance of payments surpluses or deficits. The larger the capital inflow, *ceteris paribus*, the greater the corresponding increment of domestic money supply.

The Monetary Transmission Mechanism with the Open Economy

In looking at the monetary transmission mechanism in an open economy, the type of international financial flows which will be of interest are those which cause a corresponding change in domestic money supply. As a practical note, it would seem that the level of equity and bond investment in developing countries is quite limited. This is due to the absence of secondary markets for bonds and the presence of highly speculative equity markets. Also, the financing of current account deficits by foreign-currency denominated debt would have no first round implications for the conduct of monetary policy. That said, it is instructive to understand theoretically how movements of financial capital influence the monetary control process.

Capital flight and monetary control

The effects of a financially repressed monetary regime on the conduct of open-economy monetary policy will be coloured by the existing loan policy of the Central Bank and the direction of capital movements. In the case of capital flight, although the scale of capital outflow can be potentially large, it is not expected to impact much on domestic money supply, the reason being that most capital flight is in response to large inflationary pressure. As such rampant inflation is invariably caused by an excess of money in the system, the reduction in domestic money supply engendered by capital outflows will be very little in comparison. Capital flight is a response to monetary disequilibrium but although undesirable, it is not a hindrance to monetary control (expansion).

The undesirable effects of capital flight will be concentrated in the foreign exchange market. If the authority is pursuing a fixed exchange-rate target, there will be continuous pressure from capital flight to supply foreign exchange reserves to the market. The sustainability of this is going to be limited, especially if the economy also suffers from chronic current-account imbalance. Capital flight will, then, erode the foreign exchange resources of the country and increase the likelihood of a devaluation of the domestic currency. The erosion of foreign reserves may create a foreign exchange bottleneck, requiring a reduction in the actual import of input and capital goods by domestic entrepreneurs. This reduction in capital spending will reduce domestic production and incomes, with associated contractionary effects throughout the economy.

A floating exchange rate regime with large capital outflows will require the continuous depreciation of the exchange rate. A large depreciation will serve to increase the cost of imported inputs. Without foreign exchange controls, a loan policy consistent with a repressed financial system would imply that the main importers of intermediate and capital goods, Group 1 firms, will retain enough access to credit to pay for the increase in cost of imported inputs. Domestic monetary accommodation of the credit demands of these groups, to pay for the increased costs, would then lead to increments in the supply of domestic money and the broad accommodation of inflationary pressure. Such monetary accommodation to pay for imported inputs would put further pressure on the domestic currency to depreciate, encouraging greater capital flight and stimulating more domestic inflation. A vicious circle would then result, entrenching inflation (particularly with wage-indexation) and making monetary contraction very difficult.

Capital inflow and monetary control

In general, the presence of capital inflows will lead to increases in income and provide the domestic banking sector with a new source of primary reserves from which to undertake credit creation. Given a repressed regime, the authority will want to direct this credit into priority sectors. However, with the standard required accommodation of these regimes, basic liability management by banks would imply that the quantity of credit which the banking institutions would be able to create would increase. Thus, the presence of international financial flows creating primary deposits increases over all liquidity in the banking system, and thereby may serve to decrease the actual credit rationing of Group 2 firms. However, if the Central Bank then wanted to engineer a monetary contraction, it would need to attempt a greater reduction in the capacity of banks to create credit. That is, it would have to sell a greater quantity of monetary stabilization bonds, or raise reserve requirements to a higher level.

With a fixed/managed exchange rate, the initial increase in domestic money supply from the Central Bank acquiring foreign reserves would, then, require a greater amount of domestic credit rationing. That is, the required sterilization of the capital inflows would require the monetary authority to engineer a greater reduction in domestic credit than would otherwise be the case with financial autarky. The monetary authority would then need to increase its attempts at reducing the credit-creating ability of commercial banks, through a more extensive control of the domestic financial system. Once commercial banks have their credit-creating ability squeezed, they will need to increase the amount of credit rationing in the economy.

As credit rationing falls most squarely on Group 2 firms, the increase in domestic credit rationing would entail greater exclusion from official markets for these types of firms. This exclusion would put greater pressure on the UMM and cause a similar adjustment pattern as displayed under a closed economy. The net effect, then, of international financial flows which carry a positive monetary stimulus, particularly direct foreign investment, is that they require the subsequent increase in credit rationing of those domestic firms most sensitive to changes in credit availability.

SUMMARY

The present chapter has analysed, using a broad institutional framework, the monetary transmission mechanism under a regime of financial repression. The essence of the argument is that the regulatory framework of financial repression serves to create a financial climate in which the commercial banks rely on the Central Bank for their credit-creating capability. The Central Bank is hindered from directly regulating the size of credit by the legislative requirements for accommodation. These requirements exist so that they ensure the satisfaction of the government's development policy. The required accommodation by the Central Bank, and the subsequent reliance on the window by the commercial banks, endogenizes the money supply and compounds the Central Bank's difficulties in maintaining price control. To reduce liquidity in the system, then, requires the broad credit rationing of those firms not involved in policy priority activities. Thus, the transmission mechanism of monetary policy in the economy works through altering credit conditions to non-priority firms. The cost of adjustment to monetary contraction is then borne mainly by those sectors of the economy suffering credit rationing. To the extent that the UMM can alleviate this credit rationing, the UMM mitigates the adjustment costs of these firms to changes in policy. In doing so, the UMM makes it more difficult for the monetary authority to control liquidity conditions in the economy. The UMM is, then, an endogenous response to the credit needs of sectors suffering from policy-induced rationing.

In the open-economy framework, the presence of large capital inflows, particularly direct foreign investment, requires a greater rationing of domestic firms to maintain a given level of price stability. Again, the costs of adjustment will be borne primarily by Group 2 firms. For a situation of capital flight, the broad accommodation in a repressed economy will lead to a vicious circle of depreciation and inflation.

The crux of the argument is that although the commercial banks rely on the Central Bank for primary reserves, the required accommodation means that the amount of credit in the system will be endogenously determined by the needs of development policy. However, this selfsame reliance on the Central Bank by the financial system implies that a possibility exists for the Central Bank to severely disrupt credit flows. For this to happen, there must be a change in regulatory conditions which will allow the Central Bank greater scope for altering access to its discount window. If there is a change in regulatory apparatus - a financial liberalization - the significant alteration of credit conditions (both price and quantity) will have large adjustment consequences. These adjustment costs to large changes in regulation (financial liberalization) serve as the focus for the next chapter.

6. Short-Run Macroeconomics: Adjustment to Financial Liberalization

INTRODUCTION

In analysing the short-run effects of a program of financial liberalization, the institutional structures or starting points of the economy will have a large impact on the actual adjustment path the economy follows. As a result, it is imperative that such institutional realities are built into the theoretical models of how financial liberalization works. In chapter 5 it was argued that firms' high debt-equity ratios, the concentration of credit amongst a group of dominant firms, the over-exposure of banking groups' portfolios to these firms, and the role of the Central Bank as a net supplier of financial resources will have important roles to play in the transmission mechanism of a change in monetary policy. The present chapter will seek to incorporate these effects into an adjustment story capturing the effects of financial liberalization on a developing economy. The chapter will be divided into two main parts. The first part will consist of a purely heuristic explanation of the likely response of the economy to a financial liberalization. This intuitive approach will distinguish between unannounced and announced policy shifts, as well as including an open-economy extension. The second part will be the presentation of a formal model which will be broadly post-Keynesian and which will formally assess the adjustment path of the economy to a liberalization. The chapter will conclude with a discussion of policy implications from the formal model.

A Heuristic Exploration of Short-run Adjustment to a Financial Liberalization

In analysing the economy's short-run adjustment path, it is assumed that the immediate results of financial liberalization will be a dramatic increase in both nominal and real interest rates. Additionally, elements of financial dualism will be assumed such that there are two types of firms in the economy. The first type of firms, Group 1 firms, are the large industrial concerns which manage to appropriate the lion's share of credit under repression. Group 1 firms do not suffer from tight or binding credit constraints but rather are highly leveraged and benefit from a highly elastic credit supply. As these firms are highly dependent on bank credit, a change in the price of that credit will have a large bearing on their behaviour.

The second type of firms are the group 2, medium- and small-sized firms which are either partially or fully rationed from the official credit markets. Such firms must rely on alternative forms of finance to satisfy their financial requirements. Typical alternative sources of finance include the unofficial money market (UMM or curb market) and retained earnings. The firms are not reliant on bank credit, and access rather than price is their primary financial concern.

AN UNANNOUNCED LIBERALIZATION PROGRAM

Behavioural Response of Group 1 Firms

The initial effect on Group 1 firms dominating the official credit market is that the carrying cost of existing debt obligations, contracted under a previous set of expectations, has risen. To the firms carrying large debt loads, the change comes as an exogenous cost-push shock which interacts with their current cash flow, the revenue of these firms being determined by the aggregate demand-side behaviour of the economy. With a fixed current return on capital (firm income), the increased payment obligations are equivalent to an adverse income shock. The firm must curtail its present consumption activity, and will revise its expectations of future profitability in line with the new interest-rate expectations (Buffie, 1991).

In the immediate aftermath, however, the firm is faced with rising fixed costs and cannot fully offset those costs by creating higher-valued goods.[1] Due to their large quantity of outstanding debt, the additional costs of debt servicing become a binding constraint to production as firms must meet

---

[1] An implicit assumption is being drawn that the increase in costs will be reflected initially in increases in prices. However, as credit is used to finance increments in debt costs rather than labour costs, it is assumed that real wages will fall. The reduction in aggregate demand then implies that firms cannot pass the whole increase in costs to customers. Thus, real payment commitments will continue to exceed expected revenue.

these higher costs from current budgets. As the size of its required debt payments has risen sharply, the consumption of the firm will be reduced to its minimum possible level, and the firm will seek additional supplementary credit in order to meet its commitments. The additional financing requirements pushes the firm into a Ponzi-game whereby it is caught in a double-bind of increasing costs (Minsky, 1986). On the one hand, the firm faces increasing costs associated with the increases in the short-term rate of interest. On the other hand, it faces increasing costs due to the forced increase in the size of the debt overtime. The double increase in costs has a cumulative effect whereby the total amount of outstanding debt to the firm continuously increases and reaches levels in which its expected future receipts will not be able to cover. Firms, then, are not borrowing to finance increments in production or capital accumulation, based on expectations of future profitability, but rather are borrowing just to maintain solvency. In doing so, the firms are acquiring liabilities that they cannot expect to repay given their own current expectations. The financial position of these productive firms deteriorates steadily, and their survival is called into doubt.

Behavioural Response of Commercial Banks

For the commercial banks, the effect of an unannounced change in interest-rate policy is that the banks immediately face a greater demand for credit. The increased credit demand is due to the higher financing requirements of Group 1 firms being reflected in higher credit demand. The banks, in turn, are drawn into a severe moral hazard in which they are forced to lend. The banks lend in order to ensure that the firms to which they are highly exposed do not suffer insolvency and bankruptcy. The failure of any of these firms would threaten the banks' own solvency. Thus, it is in the banks' perverse short-term self-interest to continue lending to these firms, even though the assets they are acquiring are rapidly becoming non-performing.[2] As a result, the banks' overly exposed position in loans to Group 1 firms ensures that the largest proportion of new loans will go to these firms. In the immediate post-liberalization atmosphere, then, it is in the banks' own interests to ensure that most new credit is used primarily to meet existing payment commitments, rather than funding new investment.

---

[2]The solution is perversely optimal as if these firms fail the banks themselves will fail. Thus, in propping up the firms with finance, although causing a worsening of an already bad situation, it staves off the ultimate demise of the firms and thus ultimately of the banks themselves (Dooley and Mathieson, 1987).

However, as this game continues, bank portfolios continue to deteriorate, as the growth in debt has helped create an accumulation of non-performing loans. Additionally, the commercial banks are constrained from diversifying these deteriorating portfolios by asymmetric information problems. The inability to clearly assess the creditworthiness of new customers reduces the ability of the bankers to diversify their present risk. Previously rationed firms may remain largely excluded from official credit markets in the initial aftermath of liberalization. The internal dynamics of the Ponzi-game, thus create an atmosphere of rapidly deteriorating financial assets and the continual worsening of the financial positions of firms and banks.

Accommodation Policy: the Central Bank

The extent to which the Ponzi-game will be played will be based on the ability of the commercial banks to fund the game. The ability of the banks to fund the game will be a factor of the accompanying policy stance of the monetary authorities.[3] In the direct aftermath of liberalization, the Central Bank may accommodate the credit needs of the Ponzi-boom in an effort to ensure the solvency of the financial system. The dilemma facing the Central Bank is that the firms caught up in the Ponzi-game are precisely the ones which dominate aggregate macroeconomic activity. Additionally, these firms are those which were favoured by, and encouraged to devour debt by, government directed credit. As the solvency of the commercial banks, and ultimately the financial system, depends on the continued viability of these firms, the authorities have a certain moral obligation not to allow the banks, or the firms, to fail. The Central Bank could then be drawn into a moral hazard position due to the need to maintain the solvency of the financial system. The moral hazard arises from the endemic tiering of risks in the

---

[3]Whereas the banks face a credit demand surge from firms on which the banks already hold financial claims, the ability of the banks to meet the demands has increased due to an influx of primary deposits to the official market. The process at work here is that the increase in official interest rates causes a portfolio substitution amongst savers who take the additional resources either out of loans in the UMM, inflation hedges, or other financial assets. Regardless of where the portfolio substitution comes from, the net effect is the banks have an increase in primary reserves which can then be on-lent. The amount of credit extended, independent of the Central Bank discounting, then increases following the policy shift, yet it is unlikely to be enough to satisfy the needs of the Ponzi-boom. It is more reasonable to expect that firms' debt requirements will be increasing faster than increments in deposits. The extent to which the Ponzi-boom will be fuelled will therefore be dependent on the Central Bank's policy position.

system, whereby the monetary authorities assume the credit risks of the associated lending of commercial banks. The commercial banks must lend to indebted firms to maintain their solvency, and the Central Bank must supply the required reserves to the financial system to maintain its stability. As a result, the direct aftermath of reform may see the Central Bank allow the supply of reserves to the banking system to become perfectly elastic. As the supply of money begins responding endogenously to meet the need to finance outstanding debt obligations, the elasticity of the money supply grows.[4] In taking this stance, the Central Bank is able to maintain general solvency of the financial system.

Reform-Induced Instability: Changing Policy Options

In anything but the immediate aftermath, a policy stance of full Central Bank accommodation is untenable. The Ponzi-induced borrowing leads to a rapid build-up of non-performing assets, congruent with the deterioration of the financial positions of firms and banks. The net overall debt structure in the economy is not in a position to be honoured, as aggregate payment conditions far surpass aggregate expected cash flows. The possibility looms of a general debt deflation and the accompanying loss of productive resources. Also, as the financing requirements of a Ponzi-boom infinitely expand, the accommodative and excessive rate of credit creation will lead to a rapid inflationary period as firms attempt to reduce the real size of their outstanding debt. This growing macroeconomic instability and build-up of non-performing debt cannot be sustained. A bounded but rational monetary authority must realize that it is on the proverbial road to hell. The unsustainability of this adjustment path will, therefore, force the monetary authority to alter its existing policy stance.

The first of the two policy options available to the monetary authority is that it can pursue a policy of non-accommodation of the Ponzi-boom. For the monetary authority, this option would be most consistent with its liberalization policy, as it would entail closing access to the discount window.[5] Such non-accommodation will also allow for the achievement of stabilization goals, as it presupposes a large reduction in the rate of money

---

[4]Snowden (1987) argues that for this reason, liberalization may conflict with the conduct of disinflationary monetary policy.

[5]In general, financial liberalization programs contain an element of reduction in the discount window. The scale of accommodation is usually reduced and access to the window is rationalized.

creation. Once a general non-accommodative stance is undertaken, a general debt deflation will occur with firms being unable to meet their debt obligations, resulting in a divestiture of capital or bankruptcy. The widespread failure of large-scale producing concerns represents a process in which the economy suffers from a large loss of industrial capacity. This loss of productive resources to the economy is a destruction of its income-generating capacity, in both the short and medium terms. The real loss in national income following on from the loss in income generating processes has multiplied negative income effects throughout the economy. The multiplied loss of income and employment exerts further contractionary pressure on the economy, allowing the general stabilization of the price level.

The level of non-performing loans will continue to rise with the increase in firm failure. As loans become non-performing, bank asset values collapse, placing many financial institutions in a position facing insolvency and failure. The failure of any dominant financial institution will carry the risk of systematic contagion, which if realized further hinders the official market's ability to create credit.[6] The large-scale reduction of liquidity creation in the system will bring additional deflationary pressure to bear on the economy, further limiting any price instability suffered at the beginning of the reform. Thus, the non-accommodating stance will be successful in halting the Ponzi-boom and restoring price stability, but will do so only at a high cost in terms of output, employment and human welfare. The result of the unannounced change in loan policy is then unambiguously negative in the short run, in terms of its effect on both productive capacity and capital accumulation. The liberalization, however, will have a positive price stabilization effect, once the initial inflationary surge is eliminated.

The Alternative Policy: Reintroducing Control

The second option available to policy makers is to reverse the liberalization process and attempt to institute a period salvaging the financially distressed firms. Foremost, the monetary authority will need to reimpose interest-rate ceilings and provide a package of subsidized emergency credit, in order to eliminate the source of the Ponzi-boom. The most financially distressed firms will need to be put through painful restructuring at often sizeable

---

[6]Contagion refers to a situation in which the failure of one financial institution damages confidence in the system, causing liquidity and solvency difficulties for other financial institutions.

resource costs. In order to minimize the size of these costs to the real sector, it is usually more feasible for the government to use the banks as a main channel of adjustment. That is, the government will require the banks, rather than industry, to absorb significant losses through a *de facto* write-off of sizeable chunks of the non-performing debt. In compensation for the large adjustment costs borne disproportionately by the financial sector, the government will be required to provide an additional degree of financial and administrative support to the banks. The usual form such help takes is that the Central Bank agrees to be the lender of first and last resort for the banks. Also, the banks are often given substantial inflows of new capital resources. The bulk of non-performing debts are then subsumed by a fund operated by the monetary authority.

The net effect is, then, to increase the level of government intervention in the financial system - financial repression. Although the credibility of the monetary authority for undertaking and staying with reforms in the future would be damaged, the authority would be successful in reducing the short-run welfare losses associated with a pure non-accommodating stance.

Unannounced Liberalization: Behavioural Response of Group 2 Firms

A program of financial liberalization will also have adjustment implications for firms using, and agents supplying, credit to the UMM.   A portion of the primary reserves entering the banking system in response to higher official interest rates, will be from savers' portfolio assets.   Portfolio substitution to bank deposits will include funds lent on the UMM and, as a result, the amount of credit extended by the UMM will decrease. The nature of the UMM is such that the lending ability of the market is constrained directly by the quantity of funds the intermediary is able to acquire.   Any loss of resources from the UMM must result in a decrease of the lending ability of the market. To the extent that funds are siphoned from the UMM, agents supplying this market will either have to be satisfied with a lower quantity of transactions, or will need to compete for funds by offering higher interest rates on their liabilities. As UMM deposit (loan) rates rise and the cost of credit rises, firms reliant on this market for their working-capital financing requirements will suffer cost-push effects. Unlike the official markets, a Ponzi-boom will not occur as intermediaries lack the resources and the elastic supply of reserves to be able to rapidly create such credit. Additionally, firms rationed out of the official market are unlikely to be highly leveraged, as the typical credit available on the UMM will have very short maturity structures, and will not be for large amounts (Owen and Solis-Fallas, 1989). Instead, the effect of higher UMM interest rate effects would be to make access to credit a greater supply-side constraint, increasing the amount of credit rationing and leading to greater adverse selection problems. The only firms willing to borrow at the higher rates will be those firms engaged in projects with the highest expected future profits - those which also carry the riskiest profile. The bulk of Group 2 firms will be forced to reduce, in the immediate aftermath, their demand for working-capital finance. In order to reduce their required borrowing, these firms will need to rely more on retained profits, reduced variable costs of production, and delayed capital purchases. That is, for risk-averse small entrepreneurial agents, higher real loan rates are equivalent to an adverse income shock which will depress investment spending and lower the rate of capital accumulation. For those firms too small to pursue these options, the alternative may be to cease production entirely.

Again, the primary path of adjustment will come through the supply side, with a smaller amount of available credit acting as an additional supply-side bottleneck. The loss of income and capital stock will not be as large as for Group 1 firms, but will still add contractionary effects to the economy.

Longer-Term Behaviour: Implications for Group 2 Firms

The immediate response of Group 2 firms is coloured by the fact that the firms remain rationed from the official credit markets. As time passes, the enlarging of the official credit market may increase the access of these firms to official credit. As the firms enter the market, their financing constraints are loosened and the firms find that they can act with greater financial freedom. The extent of the new access of the firms to official markets will be ultimately determined by the Central Bank's accommodative policy, and the ability of each firm to overcome informational problems with the banks. The informational problems will only be surmounted with time, as the firm builds up a customer relationship with commercial banks. As the firms' market access increases, it will substitute official market credit for UMM credit and will also increase its net indebtedness. If credit conditions in the longer run are made too easy following the liberalization, this may encourage excessive risk on the part of both banks and entrepreneurs. The result may be that these firms become heavily indebted and financially vulnerable.

AN ANNOUNCED LIBERALIZATION PROGRAM

In analysing the effects on the economy of a prior announcement for a loan policy change, a distinction must be made between credible and non-credible announcements. The credibility of any given announcement will be determined by the reputation of the monetary authority and individual agents' expectations regarding future policy.

The Behavioural Response: a Non-credible Announcement

If the announcement of a future policy change lacks credibility in the eyes of economic agents, the information will not enter into future expectations, nor will it alter current behaviour. With current behaviour unchanged, the dynamics of the system will be as above since the actual policy change will enter as a shock. The rationale for agents fully discounting the announcement could be due to a past history of policy announcements which have been reneged on, or not completely implemented, by the authority. The result of an announced change for a non-credible authority is, then, that the liberalization is unsustainable with large costs in terms of capital accumulation in the short run.

The Behavioural Response: a Credible Announcement

When a credible monetary authority makes a prior policy announcement, the behaviour of economic agents will change with this new information. Responding to the announcement, Group 1 firms build into their expectations a future negative income shock. The negative income shock will be due to the increased cost of debt and the elimination of any implicit subsidies gained from the interest-rate ceilings. In order to minimize the size of this future loss in real income, firms will attempt to reduce their current debt obligations, thereby lowering their leveraging. In order to reduce their future loan and interest payment commitments, the firms will seek alternative sources of finance with which to substitute away bank credit. Given the shallowness of existing equity markets in developing countries, firms will be limited in their financial options to placing a greater emphasis on retained earnings. Additionally, firms may seek to offset some of the future reduction in income by accumulating a larger amount of capital prior to the policy change. The firms will increase their current-period capital accumulation, in order to have more goods in progress with which to fund future higher debt payment obligations. The extent to which capital accumulation will jump upwards will be dependent on the firms' expectations of future profits *vis-a-vis* future payment obligations. If the future increase in interest rates, and therefore future expected payment commitments, is seen to be greater than the future return on capital, the firm will not borrow to increase its capital stock. Rather, new capital accumulation will be limited to what can be financed through retained earnings. The greater the time lag between the announcement and the actual policy change, the greater will be the ability of firms to lower their leveraging and increase their capital accumulation.[7] The greater the credibility of the announcement, the larger will be the response of firm behaviour and expectations. As firms reduce their leveraging and accumulate capital, the susceptibility of the productive sector to financial collapse is reduced, and the magnitude of the adverse consequences of the shift in the loan rate is lowered. Capital accumulation is able to offset some of the policy's negative income consequences, and the loss of productive capacity by the system is reduced. However, the reliance on bank credit by these firms for meeting their financial requirements casts some doubt on the actual ability to diversify their credit sources. Thus, the effectiveness of a credible policy announcement in mitigating adjustment costs may be limited.

The Commercial Banks and a Credible Announcement

The commercial banks will respond to a credible announcement of a policy shift by altering their expectations and lending behaviour. If commercial banks fully expect higher real loan rates and a substantial non-accommodating policy, the banks will seek to lower their risk and, therefore, their exposure to highly leveraged firms. The banks may accomplish this by refusing to roll over additional credits and/or by calling in existing loans. The banks may also attempt to acquire new customers in the hope of diversifying their existing portfolios and minimizing the amount of credit risk they face. Hindering the attempts of banks at restructuring their loan books is the pressure from highly indebted firms which rely on credit in order to survive. The banks are placed in a dilemma in which

---

[7]An implicit assumption in the analysis is that the bulk of borrowing is done through variable interest-rate contracts. If fixed interest-rate contracts are widely available, the firm will be encouraged to increase its borrowing once an announcement has been made. Thus, it is possible that an initial increase in outstanding debt (and capital accumulation) will occur once a credible announcement had been made. Once the actual policy is introduced, the level of borrowing and capital accumulation would be expected to drop back to its new equilibrium level.

continued lending to troubled firms increases the banks' exposure, but to stop lending would be to suffer large losses immediately. The banks might then extend credit in the hope that the firm will be able to turn around its financial fortunes and begin to honour its liabilities. However, a fully credible policy announcement will cause bank expectations to become more pessimistic by increasing the probability of a future failure of these loans. Thus, with the announcement, bank lending to these firms will reduce. Such firms may slip immediately into bankruptcy if they cannot diversify their financing, and the commercial banks will bear the corresponding losses before the actual change in policy. The immediate losses the banks will suffer will be less than if the same firms became insolvent due to a Ponzi-boom following the actual policy shift, as the debt overhang is not as large. Thus, an initial deterioration of banks' portfolios may occur before the actual policy shift, although the corresponding financial instability will be reduced.

To the extent that the commercial banks can restructure their lending and reduce their exposure, the financial instability following the policy announcement will be mitigated. Some firm bankruptcies and bank losses may occur following the policy announcement. Mitigating the beneficial effects of the announcement, however, is the problem of asymmetric information which casts serious doubts on the banks' ability to diversify their portfolio quickly. Also, the greater the credibility of the announcement in the eyes of the bankers, the greater will be the subsequent response. Thus, the longer the gap between announcement and implementation, the greater the ability of the banks to reduce their exposure to troubled firms and diversify their portfolios.

The Behavioural Response: the UMM

The effect of a prior policy announcement on the UMM stems from its effects on individual agents' portfolios. Once an announcement has been made, firms with access to official markets will substitute away from bank credit towards retained earnings. As a portion of funds available on the UMM comes from firms with official credit market access, these firms will reduce the amount of credit they are willing to create in order to restructure their leveraging. The policy announcement will, thus be followed by an initial contraction of transactions exchanged on the UMM prior to policy implementation. The contraction will not be as severe as following the unannounced policy, as this initial contraction will be followed later by a further contraction following the actual change - caused by the portfolio response of savers to the change in relative interest rates. The effect of an announced policy change on the UMM is, then, a staggered reduction in credit extended, and a staggered reduction in capital accumulation for the firms reliant on UMM credit.

OPEN-ECONOMY EXTENSION: A CAPITAL-ACCOUNT LIBERALIZATION

Up to this point, the analysis has dealt solely with a closed economy. The closed economy case is equivalent to a liberalization undertaken with a closed capital account, and one which does not attempt to liberalize its international financial transactions. However, if a financial liberalization was undertaken with an open capital account, or undertaken concurrent with a capital-account liberalization, the presence of international financial flows would alter the adjustment path.

The impact that the open economy exerts on the transmission mechanism comes from financial flows responding to the interest-rate differential between domestic and foreign assets, and the expectations of relative currency movements. In an open economy, the net effects of a financial liberalization will be determined by the initial portfolio response of domestic and foreign savers to the new domestic interest rate. In general, the new higher (positive) interest rate will cause, *ceteris paribus*, a portfolio substitution away from UMM and foreign deposits in favour of domestic deposits, including the repatriation of capital from abroad. The inward flow of deposits will swell the domestic deposit base and help commercial banks create credit more independently of the Central Bank. If the economy functioned previously with an open capital account, the inflow of capital would include repatriated capital that had gone abroad (capital flight), as well as the influx of new capital. If the capital account was previously closed, the amount of capital inflow would be less, as it would primarily include new foreign investors only. Thus, the initial effect of the higher interest rate occurring due to financial liberalization is a capital inflow into the domestic financial system. The effects of this financial inflow will be dependent on the exchange-rate regime pursued by the monetary authority.

Financial Liberalization in the Open Economy: Flexible Exchange Rates

Assume that the monetary authorities undertake an unannounced financial liberalization, and have done so with an open capital account and a flexible exchange rate.[8]

The immediate impact on Group 1 firms in the domestic economy, in terms of suffering from negative cost and income shocks, remains the same. As capital flows into the economy, the consequential increased demand for domestic currency also puts upward pressure on the country's exchange rate. With a flexible exchange rate, the enforced appreciation reduces the demand for the country's exports. To the extent that the heavily indebted firms are engaged in the tradables sector, the loss of international competitiveness by the firm reduces both current income and reduces the expectation of future income streams.[9]   The rise in interest costs, combined with the additional loss of revenue, leads to a greater reduction in the firm's total welfare in this period than in the autarkic case. Thus, the size of the negative income shock to the firms has increased with the more open economy. Given this situation, the possible demise of firms through a situation of financial insolvency will be more rapid with an open economy. As expectations of future income fall, the expectation of being able to cover debt obligations in the future also decreases, increasing the likelihood of ultimate firm bankruptcy.[10]   The genesis of a Ponzi-boom has arisen and firms begin their futile, but necessary, search for greater quantities of debt.

The banks, however, find an immediate swelling of their deposit base as capital flows inwards in response to the increased interest rate.   The repatriation of capital and new inward financial flows increase the ability of the commercial banks to create credit independently of the Central Bank. The commercial banks in the immediate aftermath, as they get pulled into a moral hazard, can then supplement their discounted credit in feeding the Ponzi-boom. As the monetary authority realizes the growing instability in the domestic financial system, it will seek to stop the Ponzi-boom by changing its accommodation stance. The tools available to the monetary authority to decrease the rate of credit creation are altering access to the

---

[8]The analysis is limited to financial flows entering due solely to an increase in the domestic rate of interest. Debt and foreign direct investment are not expected to be directly influenced by a financial liberalization.

[9]An implicit assumption is made that the export demand for developing countries' goods is elastic. If export demand is inelastic, a revenue increase would occur, offsetting the negative aspects of a liberalization.

[10]The appreciation of the exchange rate is also likely to work against their policy goals, such as trade liberalization. The deleterious effects of capital flows are why sequencing of liberalization is seen as desirable, with liberalization of the capital account coming last.

discount window and increasing lending ceilings and/or reserve requirements. However, the latter two policies are associated as part and parcel of the financial repression that the financial liberalization seeks to replace. The monetary authority will, then, seek to stop the Ponzi-boom by a reassessment of its discount policy. As the discount policy becomes increasingly non-accommodating, the commercial banks find that their ability to lend, using Central Bank funds as a source, has decreased. The banks, however, may still be able to fund the Ponzi-game to a limited extent, based on their newly enlarged deposit base. Thus, the international and domestic portfolio behaviour has allowed the banks greater autonomy from the monetary authorities in creating credit.

As the autonomous ability of commercial banks to create credit grows, the ability of the monetary authority to achieve its monetary policy objectives in the short run becomes increasingly impaired. The initial swelling of liquidity from international financial flows, independent from the Central Bank, may therefore contribute to post-reform instability in terms of allowing a more prolonged financing of the Ponzi-game. The inability of the monetary authority to limit the size of this new credit creation, due to the liberalization, will increase the post-reform instability. The size of the debt overhang in the economy will grow, and the future debt deflation will impose higher losses. The ultimate reduction in capital, employment and output therefore will be greater with an open economy.

Alternatively, the monetary authority may retreat from liberalization and reimpose direct controls on the creation of credit by commercial banks. This step would help to limit directly the additional monetary instability from reform, but would be a reversal of liberalization and a reduction in the authority's credibility.

Financial Liberalization in the Open Economy: Fixed Exchange Rates

With a fixed exchange rate, the initial problems of a reduction in competitiveness do not arise. Thus, the negative income shock to firms will be of a similar magnitude to that in the closed economy. However, the need to maintain the fixed exchange rate in the face of large capital inflows will require the Central Bank to increase the supply of domestic currency.[11]

---

[11]The monetary authority may choose to sterilize the impact of capital inflows by ensuring that the amount of currency created to maintain the exchange rate is matched by a reduction in currency from an alternative sector in the economy. To the extent international capital flows are sterilized, the additional inflationary impact will be blunted.

As the monetary authority must become accommodative to maintain its targeted exchange rate, it loses control over part of its domestic money supply. The commercial banks are able to use these reserves then to fund the Ponzi-boom. It is likely that by effectively choking off domestic money creation, the monetary authority can still bring about a general debt deflation. However, the two policies are theoretically at odds and the larger the capital inflows, the more difficult it will be for the monetary authority to restore monetary stability. Ultimately, the monetary authority may need to choose between its exchange-rate target, and the maintenance of the domestic financial system's stability. A one-off appreciation of the exchange rate would, then, be consistent with the financial liberalization. However, the enfeebling of domestic competitiveness is usually at odds with the export orientation of most developing countries.

The effect, then, of the capital account being open, concurrent or part of a financial liberalization, is that it introduces greater instability into the post-reform atmosphere. As the ability of the banks to create credit independently from the Central Bank increases, the efforts of the monetary authority to choke off the Ponzi-boom becomes increasingly futile. If the monetary authorities lose control over domestic monetary creation, particularly with a fixed exchange-rate regime, the instability from the reform may be prolonged and deepened. If the authority loses the ability to choke off the distress borrowing, the net deterioration in both firms' and banks' financial standing is increased. As loans turn non-performing and firms fall into bankruptcy, the stability of the domestic financial and industrial system is endangered. The only option for the monetary authorities may be a forced retreat from financial liberalization and a reimposition of a semblance of the direct controls which will allow them to maintain some monetary stability. The adjustment costs to a financial liberalization are then likely to be even greater in an open economy than those in the relatively autarkic case.

SUMMARY OF SHORT-RUN ADJUSTMENT TO FINANCIAL LIBERALIZATION

The short-run effects of a financial liberalization in an econmy with previous substantial financial repression are likely to be as follows. For an unannounced policy shift, commercial banks will expand the rate of credit creation in order to satisfy distress borrowing which has been entered into by firms whose costs have risen on their existing debt loads. The banks, in a position of severe moral hazard, draw on an elastic supply of reserves and succeed in financing the game whilst worsening both their own, and the firms', solvency positions. As payment commitments begin to exceed aggregate cash flows, a general debt deflation occurs causing bankruptcies, capital divestment, and bank insolvency. The productive and income-generating capacity of the economy is duly eroded. Additionally, substitution out of UMM deposits in to commercial bank deposits restricts the UMM in its ability to create credit, and causes firms reliant on UMM finance to reduce their optimal amount of capital accumulation. Firms active in this market face higher interest-rate charges and view this as a permanent adverse income shock. The fall in income in both sectors, as the monetary authorities become increasingly non-accommodating, serves to constrain aggregate demand and rein in any existing inflationary pressure. As distressed productive concerns go bankrupt, the destruction of income-generating capacity and reduced liquidity are able to stabilize prices. The stability of prices is therefore achieved, but only at the cost of reducing employment, investment and real output. Accompanying this is financial instability, large bankruptcies, bank failures, income inequality and a widening gap between actual and potential output. In the direct aftermath of liberalization, then, money may turn completely endogenous, responding to the credit needs of a Ponzi-boom. The more non-accommodating the authorities become subsequently, the greater will be the ensuing contraction and difficulty for both the productive and financial sectors. The only way for the monetary authorities to stop the Ponzi-boom once it has started, is to bear the large adjustment costs or to reverse the liberalization policy.

A credible prior announcement is able to mitigate some of these effects by allowing firms time to build the new information into their expectations. With the announcement, then, there would be a one-off reduction in credit demands as firms would seek to reduce the size of their indebtedness and begin substituting away from official market finance. The commercial banks would also stop extending new loans to highly indebted firms, as future expected repayment ability of these firms would have decreased. The reduction in the quantity of credit supplied, caused by the announcement, reduces the adjustment costs associated with the actual policy change. However, some financial instability may arise at the time of the announcement if the heavily indebted firms cannot diversify their credit sources.

The opening up of the economy at, or prior to, a liberalization is likely to increase the costs associated with adjustment. The international financial flows responding to the liberalization will initially put upward pressure on the exchange rate. The loss of international competitiveness the firms, then, reduces both current income streams and the expectations of future income. The reduction in incomes is accompanied by a swelling of domestic liquidity due to the international financial flows. The monetary authorities may still be able to engineer a debt deflation by non-accommodating domestic monetary creation, but the banks will remain more highly liquid.[12] The greater the financial capital inflow, the greater the potential prolonging of the instability.

A FORMAL THEORETICAL MODEL OF ADJUSTMENT TO FINANCIAL LIBERALIZATION

The model sets out the adjustment paths to a financial liberalization in order to analyse the issue of whether a liberalization is sustainable. The issue of sustainability revolves around whether a program of liberalization can actually be maintained in a developing economy. The issue is of importance as many problems of reform have been subject to broad amounts of policy 'slippage' or retraction (Greenaway and Morrissey, 1992). Few countries have managed to fully maintain policies of financial liberalization and monetary authorities have often resorted to reintroducing a large degree of intervention in financial markets.

The model is set up as a simple policy game. The dynamic behaviour of the system is driven by a group of infinitely lived firms responding to policy shocks.[13] To facilitate exposition and simplify the dynamics, the game has been split up into a series of discrete time periods beginning with an initial steady-state period. The rules of the game are as follows: (i) the government (monetary authority) can only enter the game at the end of a time period, and (ii) a time period ends when the monetary authority observes a change in its switching function.

These two rules are supplemented by a number of specific qualifications. First, it is assumed that the government has a reaction or switching function which encapsulates its desired values for particular macroeconomic

---

[12]The banks in being more liquid may, then, have another source of liquidity with which to survive the non-accommodation of the monetary authority.

[13]The usual justification for assuming infinitely lived firms (entrepreneurs) is that succeeding generations will be linked by a set of operative bequests (Buffie, 1990). The firms, thus optimize without a view to any final terminal state. An infinite horizons framework allows unanticipated shocks to be dealt with satisfactorily. An infinite planning horizon also rules out any short-term behaviour which would cause a Ponzi-game prior to the policy change.

aggregates. The Central Bank attempts to maximize this objective function by using its policy tools. Once a policy choice is made, the government must wait to see the effects of its choice before further adjusting its behaviour. In the game framework, the length of the time period is then determined by the behaviour of the government, but the government is not free to continuously enter the game and alter policy. Rather, the government is assumed to be faced with a discrete switching function. Once the value of that switching function is *observed* to alter (deteriorate), a policy switch is triggered. That is, the government will have certain target levels of macroeconomic variables from which deviations are measured. As deviations from target levels are observed to grow, the government then enters the game by using one of its policy tools. The rationale for this is that in the real economy, there is always an inherent time lag between the authority implementing a policy and observing the response of the system. The response of the system is determined by the behaviour of firms in the economy. Thus, the government does not continually make policy changes. Additionally, it is assumed that the government does not have perfect foresight regarding the effects of its own policy actions. Hence, policy can improve or reduce the size of deviations from the government's target levels. A further assumption is that all policy changes are treated by the firm as policy shocks. No prior announcement regarding policy changes is introduced and the firms do not build them into their expectations. Firms are undertaking maximizing behaviour continuously, and the policy shocks succeed in changing where that maximization behaviour leads.[14]

The game further assumes that the government has two policy tools which it uses in response to the value taken by its switching function. In order to assess financial liberalization, the policy tools are the rate of interest on lending, r, and the monetary authority's position on accommodation, ϕ $(0 \leq \phi \leq 1)$.[15] If $\phi = 1$, through use of discount and reserve policy, the

---

[14]In terms of game theoretic terminology, the firm could be said to be the leader whilst the monetary authority takes the role of the follower. Government actions are thus predicated on the ultimate behaviour of firms.

[15]The two policy tools are assumed to be independent. In general, monetary theory would hold that there should be an interdependence between the two tools, as the monetary authority would only be able to control either the price or the quantity of credit (but not both). However, under financial repression, the monetary authority controls both price and quantity in the *official* credit market. Financial liberalization is then a movement to a regime where the government only attempts to control quantity or price. Thus, the two policies may be treated as independent for a developing country.

authority is fully accommodating towards the credit demand of those firms which have access to official monetary institutions. If $\phi=0$, then the monetary authority is being perfectly non-accommodating to firms' credit demand.[16]   The policy tools are used in an attempt to minimize the values of the following policy switching function:

$$\Pi = \frac{1}{2} \left[\left(\frac{L}{K}\right) - \left(\frac{L}{K}\right)^* \right]^2 + \psi \qquad (6.1)$$

where L is the level of outstanding debt in the economy and K is the level of capital stock.   The L/K ratio is a 'real' version of the debt/equity ratios in the economy and * denotes a social target level the authority wishes to realize.   It will be assumed that the monetary authority has correctly identified the socially optimal (L/K) ratio and uses this socially efficient level as its target.[17]

ψ is a parameter which captures the perceived loss to the government from a loss of credibility in their monetary policy. The authority has a *perception* as to the value of its credibility to the economy.[18]   Any loss of credibility, due to the reneging of a policy commitment, will be seen as carrying negative welfare effects, and these will be modelled as a one-off increase in ψ. If the perceived value of $\psi > 1/2[(L/K)-(L/K)]^2$, then the authority will not renege on its current policy commitment. If perceived $\psi < 1/2[(L/K)-$

---

[16]The model completely abstracts from concerns over the demand for money. The reason for this is that the model seeks to demonstrate that the demand for credit determines the adjustment path to a financial liberalization. As such, money demand concerns are subsumed implicitly under the government's accommodation stance.

[17]The derivation of this socially optimal (L/K) level is part of a much bigger problem beyond the scope of this chapter. In general, the monetary authority will, at the very least, have some broad idea of what represents socially prudent debt-equity ratios.

[18]Credibility is, in general, a non-cardinal concept. Credibility concerns policy makers in developing countries for two main reasons. First, credible monetary announcements quickly enter expectations, and thereby rapidly alter the behaviour of agents in the economy. If a monetary reform is undertaken with credibility, the actual goals of the reform will be easier to achieve as agents expect the reform to be permanent. Second, credibility is likely to be important for relationships with international lenders and donors. Many reforms are undertaken as conditionality for the receipt of e.g. IMF loans and funds. Credibility in reform may be seen as a guarantee for future access to such funds. The magnitude of the increase in ψ, thus, will be determined by the importance the authority places on these issues.

$(L/K)]^2$, then reducing the loss accruing due to the debt-capital ratios will override any concerns for credibility.

If the target level $(L/K)^* = (L/K)$, the actual level, then the economy is efficiently allocating and using credit and by assumption does not suffer from financial repression. However, two other possibilities may exist which would be consistent with a situation of financial repression:

1. $(L/K) > (L/K)^*$ where the actual debt-capital ratio is greater than the socially optimal debt-capital ratio. What this may imply is that credit is being used inefficiently by firms, and thus a motivation for the policy game (liberalization) is to improve the efficiency of credit in the economy.
2. $(L/K) < (L/K)^*$ where the actual debt-capital ratio is less than the socially optimal debt-capital ratio. This may imply that firms are being credit rationed and must rely on other financing sources, primarily retained earnings, to finance the acquisition of capital. The rationale for the policy game is to increase the quantity of credit intermediated in the economy.

Time Period One: Firm Behaviour in the Steady State

To begin the game, it will be instructive to start with an economy in a non-socially-optimal steady state from which policy analysis can proceed. At this point in time, the firms' position has been determined by past maximizing behaviour in the face of constraints. The firms have maximized their objective function:[19]

$$\max_{C} \int U(C)e^{-pt} \, dt \qquad (6.2)$$

where C is consumption, p is a constant rate of time preference, and U is total utility, subject to the following constraints:

$$C = R(K) + B - rL - \delta K - \dot{K} \qquad (6.3)$$

$$\dot{K} = I - \delta K \qquad (6.4)$$

---

[19]The model of firm behaviour is a substantially modified version of Buffie (1990). The model has been modified to make it much more Post-Keynesian than that presented in Buffie.

$$\dot{L} = B \qquad (6.5)$$

(6.3) defines firm consumption as the return on capital stock, $R(K)$, and bank borrowing, B, less debt servicing, rL, depreciation on capital, δK, and changes to the capital stock, K (with a dot denoting a time derivative). The rate of change of the capital stock (6.4) is investment, I, less depreciation. As the economy is a non-growth steady-state, the growth in the capital stock will be zero. The stock of outstanding debt simply grows by the amount of new borrowing (6.5), which will be at a constant non-zero level in the steady state. For simplicity, it will be assumed that new increments of debt are offset by repayments on existing debt so that net outstanding debt is not increasing. Substituting steady-state values of (6.4) and (6.5) into (6.3) then gives a fixed consumption level in the steady state:

$$C = R(\bar{K}) - r\bar{L} - \delta\bar{K} \qquad (6.3a)$$

The firms' current amount of borrowing, B, will in general be determined by the financial sector and the firms' own desired level of borrowing. Strict financial dualism will be assumed here as the firm will either have access to the official markets (Group 1 firm) or will be excluded from the market (Group 2 firm).

Group 1 firms
Group 1 firms have access to official markets and under repression will have their credit demands fully satisfied. For such firms, they will face a set of financing constraints characterized as:

$$B^* = B \qquad (6.6)$$

$$B < Z \qquad (6.7)$$

$$Z = h + \phi B^*, \quad h > 0 \qquad (6.8)$$

(6.6) simply sets out that the firms are able to satisfy their target or desired borrowing completely from the credit market. (6.7) states that firms' demand for credit is less than the amount of credit the banking system can provide, Z. Z captures the ability of the banks to provide credit, which is dependent on the open market stimulus of the authorities (modelled as a one-off increase in h), and some proportion of firms' credit demand which is determined by the authority's monetary policy stance, ϕ. As these firms are given favoured access to official markets, it is assumed they are not subject to credit constraints and have all their credit demands accommodated, $\phi=1$.

If $(L/K) > (L/K)^*$, then Group 1 firms dominate the macroeconomic topography of the economy.[20]

Group 2 firms

Group 2 firms are those which are excluded from the official markets and face a high degree of credit rationing. For them, their financial constraints are binding:

$$B^* > B + B_u \tag{6.9}$$

$$B = Z \tag{6.10}$$

$$Z = h + \phi B^* \tag{6.11}$$

$$B_u = Z_u \tag{6.10a}$$

$$Z_u = \lambda (1 + r_u - r) D \tag{6.11a}$$

Here, (6.9) states that the firms' desired borrowing is greater than their actual borrowing (credit rationing) from the official, B, and unofficial or curb, B_u, markets. The financing constraints from the official and unofficial sector are biting (6.10) and (6.10a). As the firms are subject to credit rationing, only a fraction of their credit demand is satisfied on the official market so that $0 \leq \phi < 1$. The firms can also satisfy some of their credit demand from the unofficial sector. The ability of the unofficial markets to extend credit, Z_u, is dependent on the amount of deposits in that market. A subscript u denotes variables pertaining to the unofficial money market. λ

---

[20]It is a necessary condition for $(L/K) > (L/K)^*$, that the firm be Group 1 (not rationed). Thus, if $(L/K) > (L/K)^*$ the correct adjustment behaviour is that of Group 1 firms.

is an elasticity determining the portfolio behaviour of deposit holders, such that some proportion λ of total deposits, D, will be held on the UMM. The parameter value will be influenced by the interest-rate differential which will increase the amount of deposits held on the UMM as the size of the differential increases.

If $(L/K) < (L/K)^*$, then Type 2 firms dominate the macroeconomic topography.

The Policy Game: Financial Liberalization

Given the rules of the game, the monetary authority sees the steady state $(L/K) \neq (L/K)^*$ and is advised to undertake a financial liberalization in order to eliminate the loss accruing in its objective function. Following orthodox policy advice, the monetary authority adopts a liberalization of its policy tool, r. The liberalization is modelled as a one-off significant increase in r.[21]

Case One: Group 1 Firms' Dominance

Time period two: financial liberalization with accommodation

The present period will analyse a situation where the response of Group 1 firms will dominate the macroeconomic adjustment. For expository reasons the capital stock will remain a fixed variable, but the firms will have full access to borrowing in this period.[22] The only control variable for the firms in this period will then be B. The firms still maximize:

$$\max_{c} \int U(C)e^{-\rho t}\ dt$$

But now subject to:

$$C = R(\bar{K}) + B - rL - \delta\bar{K} \tag{6.12}$$

---

[21] An implicit assumption is made that the majority of past borrowing has been done with a variable interest rate debt contract.

[22] Intuitively, the firm will not initially use its capital stock to offset the increase in costs, because it can borrow to meet these new costs. The firm will see the selling-off of capital as a non-optimal course due to the utility increasing quality of $R(K)$. As long as it does not have to sell off capital to meet the higher debt payments, it will refrain from doing so.

$$\dot{L} = B \tag{6.13}$$

Also, the firms are still subject to the financial constraints that are embodied in equations (6.6)-(6.8) which are non-binding in this case.

The time path of the firms' control variable is determined by the current-value Hamiltonian:

$$\max_{B} H = U(R(\bar{K}) + B - rL - \delta\bar{K}) + m_L(B) \tag{6.14}$$

and the first-order conditions (6.13) and:

$$\frac{\partial H}{\partial B} = U_c + m_L = 0 \tag{6.15}$$

$$\dot{m}_L = -\frac{\partial H}{\partial L} = U_c r + \rho m_L \tag{6.16}$$

where m_L is the shadow-price of outstanding debt.[23] Solving through yields the time path for L:

$$L(t) = \beta e^{rt} - \frac{C(0)}{\rho} e^{(r-\rho)t} + \frac{(R-\delta)\bar{K}}{r} \tag{6.17}$$

where β is a constant of integration.[24] Given the presence of the first term, a positive exponential, and the third term, a positive constant, the time path can be inferred to be positive explosive and is thus unstable.

The economic interpretation for the exponentially increasing path is that for the firm, the initial impact is from the immediate costs of debt servicing exceeding its fixed expected income receipts ($R(K)$). However, as long as (6.6) and (6.7) hold, the firms can borrow to finance all the necessary increases in debt servicing. In increasing their borrowing, however, they

---

[23]The specific form of utility function employed in solving the system is $U = \log(C)$, with $U_c > 0$, and $U_{cc} < 0$.

[24]See Appendix 6 for full derivation of this solution.

begin a Ponzi-game whereby the increases in present B, serve to increase the rL term, thereby increasing future debt service obligations and required borrowing. The firms, thus, begin to borrow to alleviate a temporary liquidity crisis, but in doing so start to create their own solvency crisis.

The firms can play the game as long as (6.7) holds, which is dependent on (6.8). For the duration of this period of the game, $\phi=1$, and the amount of credit created by the banking system will be responding to the dictates of the Ponzi-game.[25] The ever increasing L, given a fixed capital stock, continuously and rapidly increases the size of the value in the government's switching function. Once the authority observes this, it prepares a policy change to move the economy off the explosive unsustainable path and brings the second time period to an end.

In order to stem the increasing value in the government's switching function, another discrete policy shift is undertaken by the monetary authority. The monetary authority can readjust r and suffer from losing credibility for reform, or it could change its accommodation policy and maintain its thrust towards liberalization. Given the presence of ψ in its switching function, it is assumed that the authority chooses the latter and, for sake of simplicity, the new policy stance is a movement from $\phi=1$ to $\phi=0$. Credit policy turns non-accommodative and the credit constraint for the firms bite.

Time period three: post-liberalization with non-accommodation
The effect of the policy shift on firms is that they can no longer borrow in their maximising behaviour. Thus, outstanding debt will have reached its zenith and the firms will now be completely credit rationed. The firms will still be maximising their objective function, but will be subject to:

$$C = R(K) - r\bar{L} - I \qquad (6.18)$$

$$\dot{K} = I - \delta K \qquad (6.19)$$

$$\dot{L} = B = 0 \qquad (6.20)$$

---

[25] As the firms' costs from ever increasing outstanding debt begin rising, the firms will attempt to pass these costs on to consumers. Thus, a certain degree of inflationary pressure will result from financial liberalization in the immediate aftermath. Infinite planning horizons rule out a Ponzi-game prior to the change in policy.

(6.20) embodies the financial constraints of (6.9),(6.10) and (6.11) with $\phi=0$ (and $h=0$) substituted into those constraints. With complete credit rationing, the dynamic control variable for the firms becomes their capital stock. The time path of its capital stock is determined by the new current-value Hamiltonian:

$$\max_{I} H = U \left(R(K) - rL - I\right) + m_K \left(I - \delta K\right) \qquad (6.21)$$

with the first order conditions as (6.19), (6.22) and (6.23).

$$\frac{\partial H}{\partial I} = -U_c + m_K = 0 \qquad (6.22)$$

$$\dot{m}_K = -\frac{\partial H}{\partial K} = -m_K R(K) + \delta m_K + \rho m_K \qquad (6.23)$$

where m_k is the shadow price of capital. Solving through with constant returns to scale yields:

$$K(t) = \beta e^{(R-\delta)t} + \frac{C(O)}{\rho} e^{(R-\delta-\rho)t} + \frac{r\bar{L}}{(\delta-R)} \qquad (6.24)$$

with β as a constant of integration. The path the capital stock will take will then be dependent on the particular values of each parameter (R, δ, ρ). To solve analytically, some assumptions will be made regarding the nature of the relationships. The assumptions made are that (i) $R>\delta$, but (ii) $R<\delta+\rho$.[26] Given this, the first term on the right-hand side will be an unstable, exponentially increasing function. The middle term will be an exponentially decreasing function, and the final term will be a substantial negative constant value. Inferring from the summation of the terms suggests that there would be a potentially protracted reduction in the value of the

---

[26]With regard to assumption (i), it would be *intuitively implausible* for $R<\delta$, as this would imply the impossibility of growth in the capital stock. Additions to capital stock would always be less then depreciations. Regarding assumption (ii), in the middle of a Ponzi-boom, business expectations would be very pessimistic, leading to a much higher time preference for the current period. Thus, it is *intuitively most likely* that $R<\delta+\rho$.

capital stock. The greater the outstanding debt payments, rL, the lower the capital stock will fall, and the longer the time period of decrease before the capital stock eventually begins its upturn. Again, the economy is on an unsustainable path as a result of the policy shift.

The economic rationale for such a time path is that in being completely credit rationed, the firms must find a new source of funding to offset the much higher rL term dominating their objective function. As the firms are required to repay their outstanding debt, they must reduce their current period consumption (to its minimum) and they must undertake negative investment. The forced repayment thus causes the firm to choose a course of capital divestment in the current period. The reduction in capital stock resulting from the sale of capital to meet payment obligations will, however, reduce the future repayment ability of the firms.[27] Thus, in disposing of their assets to meet payment obligations, the firms are in a position whereby it becomes increasingly difficult to maintain their solvency and repay any future obligations. Only once the large debt overhang is eliminated from the economy, will there start to be a recovery in capital stock. The selling off of physical assets, or firm bankruptcy, by driving down K, increases the already exaggerated (L/K) ratio in the economy.

The size of the switching function has again increased, triggering a policy change by policy makers that will put the economy back on a stable path. In doing so, the authorities bring the third time period to a close.

Time period four: a policy jump - reintroducing repression

By this period, the main goal of the authorities will be to place the economy back on a stable time path. As long as costs accruing to the authority dependent upon $[(L/K)-(L/K)^*]$ (i.e. the costs of a domestic financial collapse) are greater than costs associated with lost credibility, ψ, the authority will renege on its commitment to financial liberalization. The authority will, thus, undertake the necessary policy steps to restabilize the economy. Specifically the authorities will undertake discrete reductions in r and L, combined with an increase in accommodative stance, so that $0<\phi<1$. The discrete reductions in r and L will jump the economy back to a new stable adjustment path by eliminating the source of the instability (the Ponzi-boom). This new path will be associated with a higher level of L per unit of capital stock, however, as each firm remains more highly indebted than it was in the pre-reform period.

---

[27]In developing countries, the often large collateral requirements accompanying loans mean capital divestiture is likely to be a very prevalent result of such interest-cost shocks.

The reduction in L, not previously a policy tool, will only be accomplished by increasing the level of government participation in the financial markets. A debt write-off rescheduling whereby current repayment obligations of the firms are reduced to manageable levels, given current income expectations, will be required. The total amount of non-performing debt in the economy will have increased as a result of the failed liberalization. In support of the reduction in L, interest-rate controls will be reapplied and r will be managed downwards. The reduction in r is obvious policy 'slippage', in direct contravention of what is generally held to be financial liberalization.

The increase in ϕ gives back to the firm some access to official credit markets. As the firm moves along its new stable path, it will be able to recover some, but not all, of the capital it lost in the previous period. It cannot reacquire all of the capital because it is subject to some financing constraints, as long as $\phi \neq 1$. The model economy will finally come to rest at a new steady-state path associated with less capital stock and more outstanding debt.

Figure 6.1 traces the adjustment path of the whole game. The economy begins at steady-state point (a) in time period one characterized by curves $L=0$ and $K=0$. At this point, the policy makers decide to undertake a financial liberalization in response to the perceived costs of financial repression. The policy they choose is a discrete increase in nominal and real interest rates which affects the firm as a policy shock. The initial policy shock, corresponding to time period two, leads to a Ponzi-type increase in L with a fixed K. Thus, the economy is pushed into an unsustainable adjustment with an explosion in L (line 2). The unsustainable path increases the deviations from target levels and triggers a change in policy to monetary non-accommodation, which chokes off the growth in L. With the fixed level of L, the adjustment to the new policy comes through a reduction in K as fixed capital assets are lost through firm shut-down and bankruptcy. The economy moves along adjustment path 3. As this path is also unsustainable and increases deviations from the target levels, the policy switch is again triggered. In order to put the economy back on to a stable adjustment path, there must be a discrete reduction in r and L. This done, the economy jumps down to a new saddle path associated with a higher steady-state level of outstanding debt in the economy, $L'=0$. With an increase in ϕ, the firm borrows again and the economy moves along this stable path to reach a new equilibrium point at (b). (b) is associated with a lower capital stock and a higher level of outstanding debt. The failure of the liberalization has then made the economy worse off than it was prior to the attempted reform experience. Thus, if the economy's macroeconomic response will be dominated by firms characterized by $(L/K) > (L/K)^*$, it is highly likely that the financial liberalization will be unsustainable, and that the economy will be worse off than if it had not attempted reform.   The economy will then behave in a manner as suggested by the stylized model.

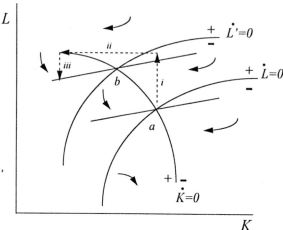

*Figure 6.1: Group 1 firms'
response to financial
liberalization*

Case Two: Group 2 Firms' Dominance

Time period two: financial liberalization with financial constraints

In a world where Group 2 firms dominate the macroeconomic response, a financial liberalization would be expected to generate a different adjustment path.   For simplicity, set $\phi=0$ (and $h=0$) so that all Group 2 firms are completely credit rationed from the official markets ($Z=0$).   The firms will then be subject only to financial constraints (6.9), (6.10a) and (6.11a), expressible as:

$$B^* > \lambda\ (1 + r_u - r)\ D = B_u \qquad\qquad (6.25)$$

In maximizing their objective function, the firms will be subject to:

$$C = R(\bar{K})\ +\ B_u\ -\ r_u L_u\ -\ \delta\bar{K} \qquad\qquad (6.26)$$

and the equations of motion for K and L_u.   Again assuming period two to be consistent with a fixed K, the sole control variable for the firms will be L_u.   If r_u represents the 'free market' rate of interest, r will rise to equal r_u

in the post-reform period.[28]   This one-time increase in r will be felt initially in the financial constraint of (6.25). As $r=r_u$, the constraint in (6.25) now reduces to:

$$B^* > B_u = \lambda D \qquad\qquad (6.25a)$$

λD is by its nature a fixed, non-zero amount.[29]   By causing a portfolio adjustment away from the unofficial market, the liberalization has reduced the ability of that market to create credit to λD. Thus, the new equation of motion for L_u will be:

$$\dot{L}_u = \bar{B}_u = \lambda D \qquad\qquad (6.27)$$

Substituting (6.25a) and (6.27) into (6.26) gives:

$$C = R(\bar{K}) + \bar{B}_u - r_u L_u - \delta \bar{K} \qquad\qquad (6.26a)$$

which has a fairly trivial solution as the firms' only control variable is bounded upwards, short of what is desired by the firms. From (6.27), the solution for L is:

$$L_u(t) = \lambda D t + G \qquad\qquad (6.28)$$

where G is a constant of integration. The firms will thus borrow all they can, and that amount will be determined by the portfolio preferences of savers.

The reduction in Z_u, reduces B_u, and drives a further wedge between the firms actual and desired level of credit. The reduction in B_u leads to an

---

[28]The assumption that $r=r_u$ in the post-reform market contains a rather stringent condition that no curb market premium will exist after the reform. The assumption is subsequently relaxed.

[29]The level of B is thus completely dependent on the ability of the unofficial market to create credit. As long as λ does not equal zero, this will be a fixed non-zero amount. The model implicitly assumes that the total level of deposits in the system does not alter after a liberalization of interest rates. All that happens is a portfolio switch from unofficial markets to bank deposits. This is not to ignore the possibly substantial savings held in real assets in these countries. The result does not change, however, as during this period the firm is constrained by access to the informal market only, which would not *a priori* be a recipient of substantial new deposits post-liberalization.

immediate reduction in the welfare of the firms. With all other elements constant, the reduction in B_u will require an immediate reduction in firms' consumption.

As the drop in B_u to its new lower level pushes down L_u, the economy moves to a position with a lower total value of debt for the existing level of capital stock. The reduction in total L increases the loss in the switching function, triggering a policy switch which will seek to increase L to achieve its policy goals, thereby bringing the period to a close.

Time period three: post-liberalization with increased accommodation

The authorities, ever concerned with credibility, will resort to the alternative policy tool, ϕ, to achieve their policy goal. The monetary authority becomes more accommodating to these firms' credit demands so that $0 < \phi < 1$. Group 2 firms are then given access to the official credit markets to meet some of their credit demands, and are now subject to the financial constraints of (6.9), (6.10) and (6.11).[30] The financial constraint can thus be expressed as:

$$B < \frac{Z - h}{\phi} \tag{6.29}$$

The firms are able to utilize both control variables, I and B, in their maximization strategy. The firms will maximize their current-value Hamiltonian:

$$\max_{I,B} \ H = U(R(K) + B - rL - I) \tag{6.30}$$
$$+ \ m_L(B) \ + \ m_K(I - \delta K) \ + \ \eta(\frac{Z - h}{\phi} - B)$$

with respect to B and I. The first-order conditions are:

$$\frac{\partial H}{\partial B} = U_c + m_L - n = 0 \tag{6.31}$$

---

[30] The amount of borrowing on the unofficial market has already adjusted to the new fixed lower quantity. The constraints can therefore be assumed away without the loss of any important information. That is, the new constraints associated with the official credit market will determine any new behaviour of the firm.

$$\frac{\partial H}{\partial I} = -U_c + m_K = 0 \qquad (6.32)$$

$$\dot{m}_L = -\frac{\partial H}{\partial L} = U_c r + \rho m_L \qquad (6.33)$$

$$\dot{m}_K = -\frac{\partial H}{\partial K} = -U_c R + \delta m_K + \rho m_K \qquad (6.34)$$

$$\frac{\partial H}{\partial n} = \frac{Z-h}{\phi} - B \geq 0 \qquad n \geq 0 \qquad n\frac{\partial H}{\partial n} = 0 \qquad (6.35)$$

Solving for L and K yields:

$$L(t) = \frac{Z-h}{\phi}t + G \qquad (6.36)$$

where G is a constant of integration and:

$$K(t) = \beta e^{(R-\delta)t} + \left(\frac{Z-h}{\phi}\frac{1}{\delta-R}\right)\left(1 + \frac{rt^2}{2}\right) \qquad (6.37)$$
$$+ \left(\frac{C(o)}{\rho}\right)e^{(R-\delta-\rho)t}$$

where $\beta = Ae^{-k} + G$ which is a constant of integration.[31]

As the firms now have access to official markets to supplement their borrowing on unofficial markets, total outstanding debt increases. Although some of the new borrowing will be used to acquire new capital stock, some will go on compensating for the loss in consumption in the first period. The path for the capital stock can be inferred using the same assumptions regarding relative parameter values. With a positive (first term) and a negative (third term) exponential term, the path for capital will be at some point increasing. The presence of the positive increasing middle term,

---

[31]See Appendix 6 for full derivations.

however, suggests that there will be an initial increase in capital stock (or only a short initial period of reduction), with the rate of capital accumulation increasing over time. As a result, the (L/K) ratio will increase and there will be a reduction in loss, or an increase in benefit, to the economy. The economy is better off with a higher level of debt and a higher level of capital, at the new steady-state level. The liberalization is, thus, sustainable and is primarily beneficial to the economy. Alternatively, as the economy did not enter a Ponzi-boom, the liberalization may have led to investment optimism as firms now have la · access to credit markets. Thus, the rate of time preference may not be as high as under the previous adjustment period. If the rate is not suffici· ly high for $R > \delta + \rho$, then the capital stock will increase exponentially The implication this holds is that the absence of macroeconomic instability following the reform is a crucial component in ensuring its success.

Case Three: Alternative Response with Group 2 Firms

The preceding adjustment path assumed that interest rates in the formal market had no impact on the informal market interest rate. Changing the assumption to allow for a change in r_u, resulting from a prior change in r, alters the adjustment path. Assuming that r_u moves upwards to maintain a fixed spread with r, the initial effect of the financial liberalization is to increase the repayment obligations of the firms. The increase in current repayment obligations has increased the firms' desired borrowing. However, with a fixed level of D and a constant spread, the ability of the informal markets to create credit has not increased. Thus, the wedge between actual and desired borrowing increases. The firms actual borrowing is given by the constraint:

$$\dot{L}_u = \bar{B}_u = \lambda \ (1 + r_u - r) \ D \qquad (6.38)$$

Substituting into (6.26) gives:

$$C = R(\bar{K}) + \lambda(1 + r_u - r)D - r_u L_u - \delta\bar{K} \qquad (6.26b)$$

Therefore, with a fixed K and an inability to borrow more, firms must decrease their consumption in the face of higher borrowing requirements.[32] In the immediate aftermath, the liberalization causes a reduction in firm utility and welfare. The inherent limits on the unofficial financial markets ability to create credit have then served as a break on the playing of the Ponzi-game. The Ponzi-game cannot arise as the firms are limited in their borrowing, and instead must compensate for their higher debt obligations by decreasing their consumption. As no change in observable borrowing has occurred, the government has not succeeded in reducing the size of its loss function, and correspondingly must increase its accommodation to achieve its policy goals.

As the firms gain access to the official credit market, they become subject to the new set of official market financing constraints. The new borrowing they undertake, however, would largely be used to substitute for the much higher priced unofficial market credit. If the pre-reform Z_u was greater than the new Z, the total amount of borrowing is unlikely to have increased as a result of the reform. If $Z_u=Z$, then the total amount of borrowing in the system should remain unchanged. However, if $Z_u<Z$ after the reform, the total amount of borrowing in the system should increase, and a portion of the new borrowing will go to supplement the firms' investment and consumption.[33] In this last case, the observable (L/K) ratio would increase and the government would find that it had been successful in reducing the size of the loss in its switching function.[34] Total amount of debt and capital in the system would have increased and the liberalization would be successful in achieving its policy goals. However, the liberalization is not as successful as in the previous case which had no interest rate effects in the

[32]The solution for L is then:

$$L(t) = (\lambda(1 + r_u - r)D)t + G$$

over which the firm has no direct control.

[33]The disagreement between new-structuralist (e.g. van Wijnbergen) and neo-classical economists such as McKinnon and Shaw can be seen in these terms. The new-structuralist argument is that $Z_u>Z$, whereas the neo-classical argument is that $Z_u<Z$ in the post-reform environment.

[34]As borrowing on the unofficial markets is largely unobservable to the government, debt substitution whereby official market debt is used as a substitute for unofficial market debt, would be sufficient to raise the observable (L/K) ratio and lower the value of the government's loss function. Thus, the reduction in size of the unofficial market can be seen as a policy goal in its own right.

UMM.

LONG-RUN IMPLICATIONS OF FINANCIAL LIBERALIZATION

The model, as presented thus far, has not dealt with the long-run implications of a liberalization program. The model is not set up to deal specifically with the long run and this is likely to be satisfactorily only dealt with in a much more general modelling framework. However, some points of reference regarding the long run may be inferred from the story.

In the first case, with initial conditions such that Group 1 firms dominate the economy, the long-run implications of liberalization follow from its inherent instability. The result of the failed liberalization is that the economy moves to an inferior position, with more outstanding debt and less capital stock. Arguments of cumulative causation, as found in endogenous growth theory, would suggest that the negative effects of this reduction in capital would persist in the economy (hysteresis). Endogenous growth theory argues that capital accumulation triggers a learning process, which is a public good, and manages to raise economy-wide efficiency (Fry, 1993b). The reduction in capital stock following a liberalization reduces this learning, hindering the long-term growth prospects of the economy. Furthermore, the large policy slippage from the reform means the economy will be left with more or less the same financial policy baggage as before the reform. Any future attempts at reform will be made more difficult by the loss of credibility from the current policy failure.

In the alternative case, with Group 2 firms dominating macroeconomic response, long-run implications arise as the liberalization is maintained beyond the short and medium terms. The financial liberalization, in this case, represents a loosening of the financial constraints to which the firms are subjugated. As the financial constraints are loosened, both total debt and total capital stock are likely to rise. The greater the loosening of ϕ, the accommodation stance, the larger the corresponding increases in B and L. If the credit constraint grows sufficiently so that the firm is no longer constrained, the financial conditions of (6.6) to (6.8) apply. The solution path for L becomes:

$$L(t) = \frac{h}{1-\phi}t \qquad (6.39)$$

As ϕ approaches 1, the L term grows infinitely large (as $\phi \to 1$, $L \to \infty$).[35] The continuous and steady upward growth of L in the newly liberalized and highly accommodative atmosphere, then pushes the (L/K) level in the economy above the social optimum. The increase in outstanding debt increases the potential instability in the economy. As the L term dominates the firm's objective function, the firm becomes financially susceptible to any large changes in revenue or the price at which credit is created. If an exogenous shock or contractionary monetary policy follows which pushes the price of credit upwards, a Ponzi-style situation and general debt deflation will loom. A prolonged increase in the interest rate will exacerbate any instability, causing a reduction in capital stock and employment as firms become bankrupt. The potential for financial instability following a successful liberalization is, thus, greater the more accommodative the monetary authority is post-reform. If the liberalization creates conditions allowing licentious credit creation by commercial banks, greater instability in the economy will be the inevitable result of the financial liberalization.

POLICY IMPLICATIONS

The short-run time paths throw up some very interesting implications for policy implementation, particularly with regard to the observation of initial conditions, the degree of liberalization and the prudent level of accommodation.

Group 1 Firm's Dominance

As shown, the starting points or initial institutional structures are very important for the ultimate short-term sustainability of a liberalization program. The institutional structures created by financial repression will thus be a determining factor in the response of the system to any large policy shocks. In general, two alternative starting points are possible: a situation whereby firms are characterized by $(L/K) > (L/K)^*$, so that financial repression has created a large group of heavily indebted firms that dominate

---

[35]The corresponding path for K would then be:

$$K(t) = \beta e^{(R-\delta)t} + \frac{h}{(1-\phi)(\delta-r)}\left(1-\frac{rt^2}{2}\right) + \frac{C(0)}{\rho}e^{(R-\delta-\rho)t}$$

the macroeconomy, or, alternatively, $(L/K) < (L/K)^*$ in which the dominant firms all suffer from credit rationing and must rely on retained earnings or other financial sources to finance their capital accumulation.

If policy makers observe the former case as applicable, the likelihood of a full-scale financial liberalization achieving its goals is unlikely. The poor prospects are due to the large L term dominating the firms' objective function, and the large increase in r which is the *sine qua non* of liberalization. The two factors unite in the firms' rL term to drive the Ponzi-game and create the financial instability in the economy. As a result, the costs associated with the liberalization are prohibitively high, rendering the program ultimately unsustainable. In this case, financial liberalization leads financial instability, as a horse would lead a carriage. With regard to financial policy, the goal of the policy maker must then be to limit the size of the rL term. In accomplishing this, the elements of policy are twofold.

First, the policy maker should seek initially to reduce the debt overhang in the economy. In general, this can be accomplished in a gradual manner, by weaning firms off the easy credit conditions to which they have been accustomed. Financial policy should be on one level, therefore, geared at encouraging firms to find alternative sources of financial capital. In order to accomplish this, there must be a discrete and gradual reduction of access to the discount window so that firms will be encouraged to use a smaller quantity of borrowing more efficiently. By gradually reducing the supply of loans to heavily indebted firms, such firms will have time to adjust their borrowing behaviour and account for the new borrowing conditions in their expectations. As their expectations alter, firms can minimize their credit requirements and actively compete for funds in other markets. As the fund-raising activities of firms spread to other financial markets, this will provide a stimulus to growth in the capital and secondary markets which will help broaden the scope for indirect methods of monetary control. With the growth and deepening of these additional financial markets, the ability of the monetary authority to control credit and monetary creation in the post-liberalization atmosphere is enhanced. Thus, potential post-reform instability will be minimized by a committed prior policy which seeks to gradually reduce the size of the debt overhang in the economy. The closer L approaches L^*, the lower will be the initial costs to firms from any subsequent liberalization.

The second element of policy, complementary to the first, is the gradual reduction of the interest rate subsidy. All past maximizing behaviour of firms included the implicit subsidy received, and the expectation of the maintenance of this subsidy, which was granted by the application of interest-rate ceilings. As such, firms were encouraged to over-indulge in credit, and the quantity of debt amassed ended up far surpassing that quantity of debt which was congruent with financial stability in the face of adversity. If this subsidy element were to be eliminated immediately, firms would then find that they faced a reduction in an income source as well as the increase in costs from higher interest rates and a higher quantity of outstanding debt. An unexpected change in the price of credit, then, becomes an adverse price and income shock which is capable of sowing the seeds of a Ponzi-boom and setting off a financial crisis. However, a gradual change in the price of credit, especially if pre-announced, will give firms time to build this information into their decision-making expectations. The behaviour of the firm will, thus, alter with the expectation of higher future interest payments, causing a reduction in current borrowing and ultimately a reduction in outstanding debt. With less current borrowing available at slightly increased prices, firms can begin to substitute debt for lower-priced finance and will begin to minimize their total credit demand. Thus, a gradual and flexible adjustment upwards of interest rates, with adjustment time allotted for firms, is preferable to a one-off elimination of interest-rate ceilings. In this framework, the monetary authority can limit the rise in r to a level which does not endanger the stability of the system.

The reduction in L, which the rapid increase in r of the 'big bang' could not deliver, is thus more aptly achieved by the joint gradual reduction in access to the discount window and a gradual increase in the price of credit. Thus, the two keys to creating the basis for a sustainable liberalization are the need to ensure that the initial level of L is not too big, and that the increase in r is not too rapid and too severe. The gradual approach also increases the probability that any policy action will be sustained, allowing the monetary authority to gain credibility for their reform efforts. As the efforts become increasingly credible, the response of firms' expectations will be congruently greater, further altering favourably the financial characteristics of the firms.

Alternatively, the monetary authority could institute a liberalization in which outstanding debt contracts are to be held at fixed (repressed) rates.[36] New debt contracts, however, would be charged at the new, higher, liberalized rates of interest. A prior policy announcement in such a scheme would be undesirable as it would stimulate a large increase in outstanding debt prior to the actual implementation of the policy. A surprise reform of this nature would be successful in reducing excessive levels of credit

[36]I am grateful to Maxwell Fry for this policy suggestion.

demand without causing a large Ponzi-boom. However, existing expectations would be incompatible with the new financial climate. Thus, the increase in the cost of new debt, and reduction in the implicit subsidy, would still come as a price-revenue shock to firms. As a result, there would be perhaps an inevitable scaling down of existing investment and consumption decisions. A contractionary period would then follow, but the costs of adjustment would be greatly reduced. The levels of firm bankruptcy and bank insolvency would be correspondingly reduced.

Group 2 Firms' Dominance

If the policy makers observe an institutional structure which is characterized by $(L/K) < (L/K)^*$, then the aim of reform will be to ease existing credit constraints of the firms. The rapid liberalization with accommodation is likely to be sustainable in the short run at least. As the logic of the reform is the easing of credit conditions, the greater the accompanying accommodation the greater will be the success of the liberalization. However, a prolonged period of easy credit may allow firms to acquire greater levels of debt than are prudent. Commercial banks may also connive in this to bolster short-term profitability and undertake large quantities of lending to particular sectors. The possibility of increased risk due to the concentration of debt and large debt overhangs, implies unconstrained liberalization can increase the potential instability in the economy. The possible destabilizing long-term effects of the liberalization, therefore, must be carefully watched by the regulatory authorities. Thus, a financial liberalization must be undertaken with a substantial increase in the amount and quality of prudential regulation and supervision. If the authority lacks the regulatory framework whereby this supervision is made possible, the wisdom of undertaking a liberalization must be called into question.

At first glance, the two goals of liberalization and regulation/supervision, seem to be at least contradictory in spirit. On the one hand, the authority is aiming at freeing the market from pervasive interference from the monetary authority. On the other, it is being suggested that the monetary authority should impose greater regulatory control over the market. Strictly speaking, this perception of contradiction is justified as the two elements are pulling in opposite directions. However, the nuts and bolts of the situation is that the two forces together represent a recognition that unfettered liberalization is inherently likely to increase the instability present in the financial system. As a result, liberalization must have limits set upon it which decreases the likelihood of excessive risk taking by financial agents.

These limits are to be provided for by the presence of a prudential regulator which can ensure that the level of risk in the financial system is not concentrated, and that debt levels do not grow to levels which represent a potential threat to the stability of the financial system.

The regulatory goals of financial stability ar additionally served by limiting the extent of the increment in accommodation following the liberalization. Although a greater increase in accommodation will allow the goals of the liberalization to be achieved more rapidly, such a rapid increase in credit creation is unlikely to be in the best interests of the long-term stability of the system. If L grows too large, too fast, the financial position of firms will be precarious, in danger from a rapid change in credit conditions brought on by a non-anticipated exogenous event. By limiting the increase in ϕ, though, the ultimate increase in L is limited (see (6.39)) and the potential for acquiring a debt overhang, with the associated destabilizing properties, is consequently reduced. Thus, in not allowing a credit boom to arise, the financial system will remain more robust in the face of any future adversity. The seeds of a Ponzi-boom and a general debt deflation are not sown.

APPENDIX 6: MATHEMATICAL SOLUTIONS

Solution for Group 1 Firms: Time Period Two

$$\max_{B} H = U(R(\bar{K}) + B - rL - \delta\bar{K}) + m_L(B) \qquad (6A.1)$$

$$\frac{\partial H}{\partial B} = U_c + m_L = 0 \qquad (6A.2)$$

$$\dot{L} = B \qquad (6A.3)$$

$$\dot{m}_L = -\frac{\partial H}{\partial L} = U_c r + \rho m_L \qquad (6A.4)$$

From (6a.1) and (6a.4),

$$\dot{m}_L - (\rho - r)m_L = 0 \qquad (6A.5)$$

so that:

$$m_L(t) = m_L(0) \, e^{(\rho - r)t} \qquad (6A.6)$$

and:

$$U_c = -m_L(0) \, e^{(\rho - r)t} \qquad (6A.7)$$

$$U = \log (C) \quad \text{so that} \quad C = \frac{1}{\partial U / \partial C} \qquad (6A.8)$$

From (6A.7) and (6A.8):

$$C = -\frac{1}{m_L(0)e^{(\rho - r)t}} \qquad (6A.9)$$

so that:

$$C(t) = C(0) e^{(r-\rho)t} \tag{6A.10}$$

$$C(t) = R(\bar{K}) + B - rL - \delta\bar{K} \tag{6A.11}$$

Substituting (6A.10) and (6A.3) into (6A.11) gives:

$$\dot{L} - rL = C(0)e^{(r-\rho)t} + (\delta-R)\bar{K} \tag{6A.12}$$

Solving through for $L(t)$ gives:

$$L(t) = \beta e^{rt} - \frac{C(0)}{\rho}e^{(r-\rho)t} + \frac{(R-\delta)\bar{K}}{r} \tag{6A.13}$$

where $\beta = Ae^k + G$ which are constants of integration.

Solution for Group 1 Firms: Time Period Three

$$\max_{I} H = U(RK - r\bar{L} - I) + m_K (I - \delta K) \tag{6A.14}$$

$$\frac{\partial H}{\partial I} = -U_c + m_K = 0 \tag{6A.15}$$

$$\dot{K} = I - \delta K \tag{6A.16}$$

$$\dot{m}_K = -\frac{\partial H}{\partial K} = -U_c R + \delta m_K + \rho m_K \tag{6A.17}$$

From (6A.15) and (6A.17),

$$\dot{m}_K - (\delta + \rho - R)m_K = 0 \tag{6A.18}$$

Solving gives:

$$m_K(t) = m_K(0) \; e^{(\delta + \rho - R)t} \tag{6A.19}$$

From (6A.19), (6A.15) and (6A.8):

$$C(t) = C(0)e^{(R-\delta-\rho)t} \tag{6A.20}$$

$$C(t) = RK - r\bar{L} - \delta K - \dot{K} \tag{6A.21}$$

From (6A.20) and (6A.21):

$$\dot{K} + (\delta - R)K = -C(0)e^{(R-\delta-\rho)t} - r\bar{L} \tag{6A.22}$$

Solving for K(t) yields:

$$K(t) = \beta e^{(R-\delta)t} + \frac{C(0)}{\rho} e^{(R-\delta-\rho)t} + \frac{r\bar{L}}{\delta - R} \tag{6A.23}$$

where $\beta = Ae^k + G$ which are constants of integration.

Solution for Group 2 Firms: Time Period Three

$$\max_{I,B} H = U(RK + B - rL - I) + m_L(B) + \tag{6A.24}$$
$$m_K(I - \delta K) + n\left(\frac{Z-h}{\phi} - B\right)$$

With first order conditions:

$$\dot{L} = B \tag{6A.25}$$

$$\dot{K} = I - \delta K \tag{6A.26}$$

$$\frac{\partial H}{\partial B} = U_c + m_L - n = 0 \tag{6A.27}$$

$$\frac{\partial H}{\partial I} = -U_c + m_K = 0 \tag{6A.28}$$

$$\dot{m}_L = -\frac{\partial H}{\partial L} = -U_c r + \rho m_L \tag{6A.29}$$

$$\dot{m}_K = -\frac{\partial H}{\partial K} = -U_c R + \delta m_K + \rho m_K \tag{6A.30}$$

$$\frac{\partial H}{\partial n} = \frac{Z - h}{\phi} - B \geq 0 \;\; ; \;\; n \geq 0 \;\; ; \tag{6A.31}$$

$$n\frac{\partial H}{\partial n} = 0$$

From (6A.28) and (6A.30):

$$\dot{m}_K - (\delta + \rho - R)m_K = 0 \tag{6A.32}$$

Solving yields:

$$m_K(t) = m_K(0)e^{(\delta + \rho - R)t} \tag{6A.33}$$

From (6A.28) and (6A.29):

$$\dot{m}_L - \rho m_L = r m_K \tag{6A.34}$$

Substituting (6A.33) into (6A.34) and solving yields:

$$m_L(t) = \beta e^{\rho t} + \frac{r m_K(0)}{\delta - R}e^{(\delta + \rho - R)t} \tag{6A.35}$$

where β is a constant of integration.

From (6A.25) and (6A.31):

$$\dot{L} = B = \frac{Z-h}{\phi} \qquad (6A.36)$$

Solving for $L(t)$ yields:

$$L(t) = \frac{Z-h}{\phi}t + G \qquad (6A.37)$$

where G is a constant of integration.

From (6A.22), (6A.33), and (6A.8):

$$U_c = \frac{1}{C} = m_K = m_K(0) \ e^{(\delta+\rho-R)t} \qquad (6A.38)$$

or

$$C(t) = C(0)e^{(R-\delta-\rho)t} \qquad (6A.39)$$

From:

$$C = RK + B - rL - I \qquad (6A.40)$$

and substituting in (6A.26), (6A.36), (6A.37), and (6A.39) into (6A.40) yields

$$\dot{K} + (\delta-R)K = \frac{Z-h}{\phi} + r(\frac{Z-h}{\phi}t) \qquad (6A.41)$$
$$- C(0)e^{(R-\delta-\rho)t}$$

Solving for $K(t)$ then gives:

$$K(t) = \beta e^{(R-\delta)t} + (\frac{Z-h}{\phi}\frac{1}{\delta-R})(1 + \frac{rt^2}{2}) \qquad (6A.42)$$
$$+ \frac{C(0)}{\rho}e^{(R-\delta-\rho)t}$$

where $\beta = Ae^k + G$ which are constants of integration.

7. Experiences of Financial Liberalization in the Pacific Basin

INTRODUCTION

As discussed, most developing countries, including those in the Pacific Basin, have had their policy regimes influenced by the developments in financial liberalization theory. The periods of active reform began in the early 1980s and have persisted, on and off, until the present. The incentive for early attempts at financial liberalization was, in general, a combination of adverse external and internal conditions. Externally, developing countries were faced with a period of deteriorating terms of trade - as commodity prices dropped, interest rates rose and the world entered recession. The growing problems in financing energy and interest costs, combined with subsiding world demand, created financial difficulties for the private and public sectors in most developing countries.

The external shocks served to aggravate stresses which had begun to appear in domestic financial markets. The 'financial repression' of subsidized interest rates, directed credit and direct monetary control measures had been leading to the usual problems. Deficiencies in resource mobilization, inefficiencies in credit use, and difficulties in maintaining price stability were evident. As a result, most developing countries embarked on either IMF-supported or independently declared programs of financial liberalization which varied across countries in terms of duration, ambition and success.

The present chapter seeks to outline the experiences of Indonesia, Korea, Malaysia and the Philippines, with regard to financial policy and liberalization. The purpose of the chapter is to recount the experiences of these countries with financial liberalization in order to be able to present an analysis of these events consistent with the post-Keynesian viewpoint outlined in the previous chapters. That is, the chapter seeks to use the case studies as illustrative evidence of the ideas embodied in the theory developed

211

throughout the book. The countries have been selected for their position as emerging developing countries which have all achieved different levels of success. Also, the relatively successful attempts at development in this region (South-East Asia) make the experiences particularly illuminating for economists interested in development. The case studies will trace the experiences of these countries with financial policy through the last two decades. The most ambitious attempts at reform were found in those countries with the most pervasive macroeconomic problems - Indonesia and the Philippines. In general, all of the countries felt the need for some change in their financial systems and hoped the reforms would bring this about. The countries also shared different experiences with regard to the openness of the capital account, exchange rate policies and development goals. Despite this heterogeneity of characteristics amongst the cases, dominant themes of experience emerge which serve to underlie the conclusion that distinct limits exist to the amount of financial liberalization that is possible and desirable.

INDONESIA

The 1970s: Financial Policy and the Macroeconomy prior to Reform

Developments in the financial sector in Indonesia have been influenced largely by developments occurring in the petrochemical sector. The Indonesian economy as a whole benefited from its position during the 1970s as a net oil exporter, and recorded growth rates of real GDP averaging around 12 per cent p.a. for the period 1973-83. Also, reflecting the favourable impact that burgeoning oil revenues had on the economy were domestic investment rates of 27.6 per cent of GDP and a gross domestic savings ratio of 14.8 per cent of GDP for the same period. The effect of oil revenues was felt most strongly on the fiscal system as the government began to rely increasingly on oil revenue as its chief source of revenue.[1] Paradoxically, the surge in oil revenue during 1973-83 did not result in decreased government borrowing abroad, but rather served to supplement

---

[1]The reliance on oil revenue for financing government expenditure increased from 26 per cent in 1969 to 71 per cent in 1981. Such reliance led to a skewed and underdeveloped tax system that was to cause problems after the reduction in oil revenues from 1982. As a result of the balanced budget, the government had no need to float bonds in the domestic market.

it by encouraging the government to increase its spending (Figure 7.1).[2] The Soeharto government pursued a 'balanced-budget' rule from 1968 which removed recourse to monetary creation as a means of financing a deficit. Instead, financial shortfalls were bridged by foreign loans which the government classified as foreign revenue (Figure 7.2). Fiscal policy was not dominant in terms of the Central Bank directly accommodating the government's financing requirements with domestic money creation. However, the conversion of oil revenue and large foreign borrowing into rupiah at a fixed dollar exchange rate to finance the government's domestic spending, increased the money supply and added to inflationary pressure (Woo and Nasution, 1989).

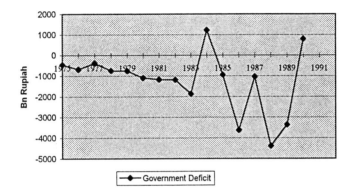

Figure 7.1: Indonesia - government deficit

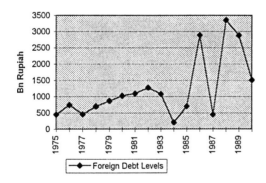

Figure 7.2: Indonesia - government foreign net borrowing

[2] The data source for all figures in this chapter is the *IMF International Financial Statistics*.

During the 1970s, the Bank of Indonesia (BI) used the extension of liquidity credits to the banking system, state enterprises and private companies as a main instrument of monetary control. The liquidity credits, extended at subsidized rates and fixed maturities, were an important element in the government's pursuit of policy objectives. In conjunction, the BI set up a complicated rediscount financing system for loans to state banks, in order to influence the direction and quantity of credit. For example, in the government rice intensification program (BIMAS) the government provided state banks with 100 per cent of the funds they loaned out. The percentage of automatic rediscount available for other sectors was determined on the basis of priority and ranged from 20 per cent to 80 per cent of the value of the loans. Access to the window was limited primarily to the state banks which became the dominant players in the banking sector. Funds available under the ambitious rediscount program were charged at low discriminatory rates ranging from a quarter to a half of their loan rates. The combination of high rediscount percentages and low rediscount rates ensured that the direction of credit from the state banks was in harmony with the government's development objectives. Between 1977 and 1982 liquidity credits rose by an average of 40 per cent p.a. and had become the major source of funds on the margin for deposit money banks (Sundararajan and Molho, 1988). By the end of 1982, loans supported by liquidity credits accounted for nearly 80 per cent of total credit by all banks. At the same time, liquidity credits made up nearly a third of total liabilities of state banks. In order to ensure a subsidy element in the lending, the BI enforced ceiling controls on deposit and loan rates. As time passed, the gap in interest rates between state banks and private banks grew as controlled interest rates became misaligned; 6-12 per cent point gaps appeared, depending on the maturity of the deposit, by 1982.

The fixed maturity of the liquidity credits precluded the government from engineering reductions or increases in the money supply at will. In order to stem the inflationary pressure from cost-push pressures and foreign borrowing, the BI began using lending ceilings which were to persist until the early 1980s. The use of credit ceilings on individual banks, including private and foreign banks, was carried out in conjunction with the use of subsidized liquidity credits to meet policy objectives. Over time, the BI began to introduce more detailed credit ceilings, distinguishing between types of credit for each bank. Within the overall ceilings were still further sub-ceilings differentiated by category of loan. Such restrictions extended to credit ceilings for *Pribumis* (indigenous Indonesians) which the government had hoped would create credit access for them and thereby increase their participation in the economy (Woo and Nasution, 1989). The ceilings were of two varieties, one type of ceiling acting as a target or quota to be met and the other acting as a limit not to be surpassed. The efficacy of the ceilings in controlling the growth of the money supply was undermined by the constant increase in net foreign assets and the rapid expansion of BI's liquidity credits (Cho and Khatkhate, 1989). The control of monetary expansion necessitated more highly binding ceilings. The ceilings resulted in a large accumulation of surplus funds held in the banking system, especially by the state banks. The extent of the excess funds was largely determined by the effects of the discriminatory access to BI's liquidity credit by bank ownership. The position of the state banks as recipients of preferential funding treatment and the lack of competition for deposits due to interest-rate ceilings allowed the state banks to become the dominant financial intermediaries. The state banks during this period became responsible for approximately 90 per cent of commercial bank business (Sundararajan and Molho, 1988).

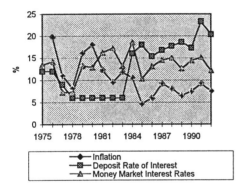

Figure 7.3: Indonesia - inflation and interest rates

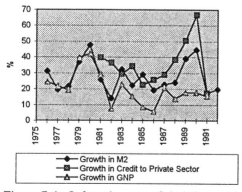

Figure 7.4: Indonesia - growth in M2, credit to the private sector, GNP

By granting state banks guaranteed access to the discount mechanism, loans were increasingly financed through liquidity credit facilities. With most loan financing secured through BI accommodation, state banks had little incentive to mobilize savings and could use excess reserves for more speculative purposes.   The majority of mobilized resources for state banks came from captive customers' deposits, such as state enterprises, who were required to bank with state-owned institutions. Given the breadth of credit ceilings, the excess funds were then either on-lent in the domestic inter-bank market in Jakarta or were held in the form of foreign assets.[3]   Hence, the pattern of monetary control resulted in the contradictory situation whereby below market interest rates coincided with excess liquidity in the highly regulated state-owned banks.

Woo and Nasution (1989) suggest that possible reasons why state banks held such large excess reserves were:

1.   Bad banking practices, encouraged by the state bank's monopolies on types of business, made them unable or reluctant to serve small and less profitable customers.
2.   Project selection was constrained by the need to find both economically and politically viable projects.
3.   Bank officers may have demanded too high side payments from prospective borrowers and in this way decreased the demand for loans from the private sector.

The result was that certain priority firms (usually state-owned enterprises) appropriated the lion's share of credit and the bulk of middle- and small-sized enterprises remained credit rationed.   The credit rationing of these non-priority firms required the firms to readjust downwards any investment plans which could not be self-financed. The lack of access to credit, thus reduced the ability of these firms to invest in modern technologies which helped reduce the dynamism inherent in the economy.

For domestic private companies operating in a priority sector, debt financing was less expensive relative to the costs of raising and servicing equity.   Credit from state banks carrying subsidized interest rates was plentiful, and could easily be rolled over. Priority sectors generally covered industrial enterprises and the inherently conservative state banks favoured

---

[3]The inter-bank market, due to these excess holdings, remains an important source of bonds for private banks and non-bank financial intermediaries (NBFIs) which lack access to the discount window. In terms of acquiring foreign assets, the share of BI in total international reserves held by the banking system fell from over 90 per cent in 1977 to less then 50 per cent in 1983 (Sundararajan and Molho, 1988). In response, BI sought to reassert its dominance and required state banks to hold special deposits with BI.

lending to enterprises which were large, established, and carried implicit government backing.   The subsidy implicit in the debt also led firms to increase their borrowing requirements, requiring greater credit rationing of other firms.   Favoured firms acquired large debt burdens and the risks present in the financial system became concentrated amongst a specific group of corporate firms.   Although data on financial corporation structure in Indonesia is quite scarce, the debt/equity ratio has been estimated to be around 900 per cent for this period (Cho and Khatkhate, 1989).   Often what passed as equity was also loosely disguised debt.   Thus, the financial structure which resulted after a prolonged period of repression began showing characteristic weaknesses.   The interaction between development policy goals, the needs of monetary policy and the lending practices of banks overly subordinate to policy resulted in high leveraging of the priority corporate sector.   Money was responding to the needs engendered by policy, but did so in a framework which encouraged distortions.   The result was a weak, overly dependent financial system and a banking system over-exposed to the dominant state-owned industries.   These circumstances were to be the starting points of reform.

Financial Liberalization: Elements of Reform

The weaknesses and flaws in the ability of the BI to control monetary expansion were again revealed by the second oil price rise in 1979.   The true impetus to monetary and financial reform, however, came with the series of negative external shocks of 1982.   The deepening world recession and weakening in world oil markets caused a reduction in Indonesian oil revenue from Rpa 7.8 billion in 1981-82 to Rpa 6.9 billion in 1982-83 (Woo and Nasution, 1989).[4]   The drop was felt as a real reduction in government non-debt budgetary expenditure, which impacted unfavourably on economic growth.   The effective end of the oil boom made financing the investment-savings and foreign exchange gaps much more difficult, and government debt levels began to rise.

In responding to the growing adverse macroeconomic environment, the government undertook a broad structural adjustment policy which included a reform of the financial system.   The goals of the reform were to increase domestic resource mobilization to help offset the loss of oil revenues, to

---

[4]The price of oil was to decrease from $35 per barrel in 1982 to $25 in 1985, and further to $12 per barrel in 1986. The price of oil has now hovered around $19 per barrel for the remainder of the decade.

increase the efficiency of financial intermediation, to provide attractive rupiah-denominated assets to prevent capital outflow, and to improve more indirect methods of monetary control. Financial reform began in earnest with a wide and sweeping package of measures introduced in June 1983 (Arndt, 1987).

As a cornerstone of the reforms, commercial banks were largely freed from direct BI control of their lending activities through credit ceilings. Although the credit ceilings continued to apply to the priority categories which acted as targets rather than constraints, these categories were to be greatly simplified. With this step the BI attempted to reduce the use of credit ceilings as a tool of allocative policy and monetary control.

In conjunction, the BI attempted the phased removal of particular (non-priority) loan categories from access to BI liquidity credits. The removal of a wide range of loan types from eligibility for liquidity credits was inclusive of categories estimated to account for 50 per cent of outstanding bank assets.[5] The BI was keen to stress the gradation of the process of reducing outstanding liquidity credits, and permitted some non-priority sectors to remain temporarily eligible to give the banking system time to adjust. Priority sectors remained eligible with some post-reform increases in the quantity of available liquidity credits, and some new categories were made eligible. As a result of the reform, the share of private credit financed by rediscount from BI's window gradually decreased from 56 per cent in March 1983 to 49 per cent a year later, only to recover again to about 59 per cent by September of 1984 (Balino and Sundararajan, 1986).

In an effort to increase the competitiveness of the monolithic state banks, interest rates on most categories of deposits and loans, excepting priority loans, were deregulated. As a result, the interest rates charged by state banks began to rise to a range of 14-17 per cent by September, up from 6-12 per cent in March, and remained close to the deposit rates of foreign and domestic private banks (Balino and Sundararajan, 1986). Higher bank funding costs were correspondingly reflected in higher loan rates. The most notable feature of these real interest rates was their high level and volatility (Cho and Khatkhate, 1989). Given the weak current account, real interest rates displayed downward rigidity as market participants continued to expect a devaluation of the rupiah. These expectations kept interest rates high

---

[5]The withdrawal of non-priority categories from liquidity credits was concentrated primarily in large investment loans. The development raises the question of where long-term lending levels should be maintained and where banks will get such resources once banks' recourse to liquidity runs dry (Balino and Sundararajan, 1986). The categories that remained eligible were chiefly BIMAS farmers, smallholders, small-scale enterprises and private estates.

(open-capital account) and fanned inflationary expectations. As a result, the nominal interest rates remained high despite a drop in actual inflationary pressure.

In the newly deregulated atmosphere, new methods and tools of indirect monetary control were needed. To help foster the task, the BI issued its own debt certificate, the Sertificat Bank Indonesia (SBI) early in 1984 using a conventional auction system.[6] The pertinent sale and purchase of SBIs was to allow the authorities the ability to absorb, or inject, bank reserves at their own initiative and thereby influence domestic money market conditions (Achan, 1986). The success of SBIs as a monetary control tool has been hindered by recurrent episodes of speculation against the rupiah which has given rise to large capital outflows. To increase the attractiveness of SBIs, the BI nominated the government-owned First Indonesian Finance and Investment Corporation (Ficorinvest) as a rediscounter of SBIs. Ficorinvest stood ready to discount SBIs at the original rate of interest, regardless of remaining maturity, and in turn was able to rediscount them with the BI. By providing a 'secondary' market where automatic repurchase was available, BI made SBIs as liquid and risk-free as liquid reserves (Sundararajan and Molho, 1988).

In conjunction with the new instrument, the BI introduced two new discount facilities to support attempts at monetary control. The first facility was designed to aid the day-to-day reserve management of financial institutions, by providing short-term liquidity support. The second facility was designed to encourage long-term lending by giving temporary relief to banks facing maturity risks from a shortening of deposit maturities following deregulation (Sundararajan and Molho, 1988). Access to each facility was limited and the basic rate was maintained at a penalty rate above most deposit and inter-bank rates. The facilities were primarily viewed as having a lender-of-last-resort function, and were therefore used only when banks lacked recourse to other funds.

The final new element introduced was the Serat Berharga Pasar Uang (SBPU) money market instrument, first subscribed in February 1985 (Achan, 1986). The new instrument was introduced to allow the BI to more consistently inject and remove liquidity at will. SBPUs included the use of promissory notes/trade bills issued by customers and inter-bank promissory notes drawn up according to pre-specified regulations and were envisaged to be traded amongst banks, NBFIs and the BI. Ficorinvest was made

---

[6] Although the SBIs were sold at weekly auctions, rates were usually determined beforehand by the BI (Cho and Khatkhate, 1989).

market maker, ready to buy and sell SBPUs, and was able to fund its holdings and activities by recourse to the money markets on a special 'liquidity line' arrangement with BI. The initial response of the market to SBPUs was quite positive with the volume of SBPUs rising sharply during 1985-86 and SBPUs succeeding in broadening participation and expanding the range of maturities of paper traded.

Impact of Financial Liberalization

The reform was followed by a sharp rise in interest rates which had an adverse impact on the financial positions of many of the large, indebted, Indonesian corporate bodies. The large increase in interest rates was incongruous with the levels of borrowing undertaken with a different set of expectations. As payments on existing loans began to surpass revenue flows, many firms found their ability to service existing debt obligations had ended (Cho and Khatkhate, 1989). With financial ruin imminent, the firms turned to bank finance to smooth the cost shock and finance the new higher level of payment obligations. The ability of the firms to find this finance was dependent on the ability of the state banks to access the reserve window.

As the reform included a broad reduction in the categories of loans eligible for rediscount, the state banks found that their ability to create credit was reduced. The large increase in credit requirements of the priority firms, combined with the reduction in the credit-creating capability of the state banks, rapidly led to financial problems. Without further credit, firms had no choice but to default on their outstanding debt liabilities. The state banks, already plagued by bureaucratization, became increasingly hindered by the serious problem of non-performing loans (Cho and Khatkhate, 1989). The loan portfolios collected under a policy structure providing inadequate incentives for project selection and implicit government credit guarantees, began showing frailty (Woo and Nasution, 1989). Indonesian banks began showing heavy arrearage in all sectors. State-owned banks developed loan exposure so large that their solvency was at risk as they could not have recovered the principal and interest, through asset transfer or sales, in the advent of foreclosure on borrowing firms. The persistence of exceedingly high interest rates resulting from reforms exaggerated the problems. Banks, trying to compensate for their heavy and mounting arrears, increased loan rates by as much as two percentage points. Such short-sighted action had the unintended effect of worsening the financial position of borrowing firms and accelerating the growth of non-performing loans (Cho and Khatkhate, 1989).

The impact on the profitability of banks was predictably adverse, declining after the reform for all categories of banks. Profit to total asset ratios for all banks declined from 2.7 per cent in 1982 to 1.8 per cent in 1985, mainly as a result of a sharp decline in loan portfolio performance and a rise in funding costs (Cho and Khatkhate, 1989). Interest-rate margins eventually declined as competition began to increase and non-performing loans took their toll. The volatility of interest rates after the reform also forced the banking industry to adjust its lending terms to minimize interest-rate risk. The primary result was a reduction in long-term bank credit with maturity over 12 months falling as a proportion of total bank credit.[7]

In the aftermath of this first attempt at reform, the state banks still dominated the financial system, holding up to 75 per cent of bank business by 1989. The BI intervened in the market to secure the solvency of these banks and partially reopened access to the discount window. State banks remained subject to regulatory control and continued to extend large amounts of credit under priority credit programs and to powerful clients able to exert political leverage. As a result, liquidity credits from the BI remained an important source of funding to the banking system, despite the changes wrought in the mechanism by the reform.

1985-1992: Recent Developments and Subsequent Measures of Reform

The first reform package had little success in achieving its goals and weakened the financial system by aggravating the problems with non-performing loans. The problems came to a head in 1987 when capital flight began in earnest, stimulated by a higher than expected current account deficit and prompting instinctive fears of a rupiah devaluation. The BI decided by June 1987 that the new open market tools were not functioning efficiently enough to raise interest rates quickly and stem the flow of capital. As a stopgap measure, the BI ordered state enterprises to withdraw Rpa 1.3 trillion from state banks to be placed in BI securities. The BI also sold Rpa 800 billion of bonds to the commercial banks during the month which sharply reduced the availability of rupiah financing (Woo and Nasution, 1989). Large domestic corporations felt the liquidity squeeze and repatriated foreign assets for use as working capital. With the immediate

---

[7]Cho and Khatkhate (1989) report that the proportion of long-term credit to total bank credit fell from 41.2 per cent in 1983 to 39.8 per cent in 1987, although they argue that such statistics must be treated circumspectly given the paucity of the data. Structural factors which may also account for the shortening of maturity levels include banks' poor credit appraisal capabilities and their faulty collateral practices.

crisis abated and the flow of capital reversed, the BI found it desirable to address the underlying weaknesses in the financial markets. A second 'big-bang' package of liberalization was introduced, beginning in 1988.

The reform package was announced in three stages, the *Pakto* (banking regulation) October 1988, the *Pakdes* in December 1988, and the *Pakjan* (credit deregulation) in January 1990 (Lowenstein, 1989). The reform was aimed at stimulating the mobilization of domestic savings and strengthening the efficiency of the financial markets by increasing the amount of competition. The keys to the reforms were the removal of the monopoly of state-owned banks over the deposits of state-owned enterprises, and the permission for existing financial institutions to engage in broader areas of activities.[8] Foreign banks and NBFIs were allowed to increase branch networks previously confined to Jakarta and new foreign banks were allowed to enter the market by establishing joint ventures.[9] By early 1990, the tiers of subsidized loans that the BI used to direct credit were dismantled. In their place, new banks were instructed to make 20 per cent of their loans to businesses with no more than Rpa 600m in assets and less than 50 staff. Lending limits of 20 per cent of banks' total capital to any one borrower and 50 per cent to any group of borrowers, were imposed in an effort to strengthen the resilience of the banking sector to external shocks.

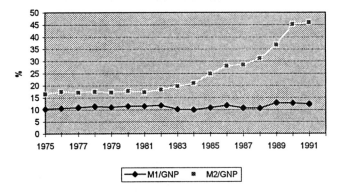

Figure 7.5: Indonesia - M1/GNP, M2/GNP ratios

---

[8] The change in relationship between state banks and the 225 state-owned enterprises stipulated that state companies could now put 50 per cent of their deposits with non-state banks (Lowenstein, 1989).

[9] By September 1990, the finance ministry had issued new operating licences to 29 private national banks, 132 secondary banks and 11 joint ventures (*The Banker*, Sept. 1990).

In response to the reforms, the banking sector doubled in size. By the end of 1989, time deposits had grown to Rpa 26 trillion, savings deposits doubled to Rpa 4.2 trillion, and more than 135 new commercial banks had set up business. The banks took on inexperienced staff to lend the growing volume of funds and competition for funds pushed interest rates up so that prime lending rates were well above 20 per cent. The high interest rates made bank finance an expensive source of capital and stimulated growth in Jakarta's stock market. The total funds generated on the market surged from US$110m in 1988 to over US$1.2 billion in 1989 (*The Banker*, May 1990). Banks also became involved in raising equity capital and lending it out became a licence to print money. A large amount of these funds were channelled into speculative activities and Jakarta's stock exchange boomed, becoming one of the best-performing in the world.

Amidst the rapid expansion of financial markets, accusations of foul play arose along with more general concerns about over-heating and whether companies would survive a recession. Too much money was seen as being diverted into speculation, and gains made in the property and stock markets were producing a speculative bubble which the authorities were keen to burst. To stop the tide of speculation, the BI entered the market and reopened its SBI lines. The BI offered up to 2 per cent points more than commercial banks were offering on time deposits, and completed this liquidity crunch by requiring all liquidity credits to be repaid to full maturity (*The Banker*, Sept. 1990).

Inter-bank rates shot up to 40 per cent overnight as the banks began competing in earnest for the shrinking pool of funds. The liquidity squeeze had its impact and by mid-1990, reports were circulating in Jakarta that eight banks were already in difficulties having failed to meet their clearing commitments (*The Banker*, Sept. 1990). By the end of the year, the fifth largest bank had to be rescued by the BI due largely to losses that banks suffered from wild speculation on foreign exchange. In February 1991, three private banks suffered liquidity crises and had to turn to the BI to cover their liabilities on daily clearing.

The underlying cause of the bankers' problems was the non-performance of loans, caused by an unrelenting increase in lending rates which had reached 30 per cent by March 1991 (*The Banker*, May 1991). The risk of bad debts from firms required to refinance their operations at record interest rates was particularly pronounced in agriculture and industry, which were the primary benefactors of the complicated system of subsidized loans now being almost completely dismantled. The new loan rates were not compatible with previous expectations of loan repayment levels. As these industries rolled over and refinanced their outstanding loans, state banks were no longer able to rely on rupiah credits to satisfy the demand. It was estimated that more than Rpa 2 trillion of liquidity credits was sucked out of the banking system following the dismantling of the subsidized credit program (*The Banker*, 1991). As the state banks felt the squeeze, they moved rapidly into the deposit markets and further pushed up interest rates, crowding out the smaller banks.

As the upward movement of interest rates continued increasing credit demand, the decrease in available credit created a spate of bad debts plaguing the financial institutions. Additionally, a large part of the new credit created in the liberalized atmosphere went into speculative pursuits. The imprudent concentration of risks in these areas left the financial system vulnerable to any adverse changes in confidence and the performance of these markets. The effect of the BI's contractionary policy was to eliminate the income gains to firms and this effectively ended the upward price spiral in the markets. As property prices dropped, outstanding debt values began to rise above the value of the physical assets on which such debt was secured. A large increase in non-performing loans then threatened the solvency of the financial system.[10]

The crisis reached its nadir with the collapse of Bank Summa late in 1992 (*The Banker*, May 1993). The problems of bad debt became so severe that the BI refused to bail out the bank and promptly called in the receivers. The collapse of the Bank Summa further triggered runs on three smaller private banks and public confidence in the system was sent reeling. The root of Bank Summa's problems was excessive lending to related companies which then subsequently failed to service their loans. The laxity of supervision and easy credit following the 1988 *Pakto* allowed the bank the freedom to engage in poor lending practices which saw it become victim to an over-exposed portfolio. Despite subsequent moves to re-regulate, the BI was criticized for failing to act quickly enough against the many banks which exceeded their legal lending limits.

By mid-1991, the fragile state of the financial system led to the consensus that Indonesia's three year long banking experiment was going too far and too fast (*The Banker*, May 1991). The BI reacted with a new host of financial rules introduced to curb the worst excesses of previous years. Apart from separating banking from underwriting and broking to prevent

---

[10]By mid-1993, it was estimated that state-owned commercial banks had non-performing loans of between 15 and 25 per cent of their total loans. Private banks were much better off but their bad debt exposure had increased to 5.9 per cent of total loans in 91/92 from 3.9 per cent the previous year (*The Banker*, May 1993).

any potential conflict of interest, the new 1991 *Pakto* expected commercial banks to meet BIS capital standards by the end of 1993.[11]   The BI also wanted better scrutiny of bank directors and set higher bad debt reserve levels for banks.   New rules aimed at reducing foreign exchange speculation and share trading by banks were introduced.   The new web of regulations represents a retreat from the over-exuberant and essentially imprudent process of liberalization of the late 1980s.   It is symptomatic of a growing awareness of the importance of prudential regulation and supervision of the financial system, especially with a financial industry that is undergoing teething problems.

As the competition for domestic deposits continues to soar and the BIS standards bite, Indonesian banks will be forced to look offshore for extra capital funds.   Already, financial institutions have raised more than US$5 billion offshore, which has increased private sector foreign-denominated debt.[12]   However, amidst all the change and switches in policy, Indonesia's banking sector is at least achieving real competition, better services and more sources of finance.   The private banks have increased their share of total credits from 25 per cent in 1989 to 37 per cent by the end of 1991 (*The Banker*, May 1993).   Only time will tell if the banking sector is at a stage whereby it can effectively meet the financing needs of an ever expanding Indonesian economy.   If the government can provide adequate regulation and supervision, the banks and the economy may be able to surmount the problem of bad debts which remains a current hindrance.

[11]The BIS standards of capital adequacy stand at 8 per cent for new loans. A chronic shortage of capital at the state banks will make it difficult for them to comply without a cash injection. The major private banks are expected to be able to reach the 8 per cent capital adequacy without assistance.

[12]The government has pursued a policy of managed depreciation of the rupiah to maintain export competitiveness. This has been hindered by a rise in debt interest payments, leading to a balance of payments deficit of $1.5 billion. Such problems have led to the continued reliance on foreign borrowing, much of it denominated in yen, which steadily appreciated in the late 1980s. Indonesia's debt service ratio peaked at 38 per cent in 1988, but had declined to 35 per cent by 1990.

KOREA

Financial Policy prior to Reform and Macroeconomic Background

Korea has had a long history of financial policy change. The Korean economy underwent a short period of financial deregulation in 1966 which was followed shortly by a more prolonged period of financial re-regulation. As the Korean economy entered the 1970s, the government, through the Bank of Korea (BOK), was directing credit to priority areas and controlling interest rates. At this time, an element of inertial inflation existed and this was subsequently exacerbated by a devaluation of the won in 1971 (Figure 7.6). The devaluation was seen as a necessary step for improving the competitiveness of the export sector which had become the new focus of development policy (Kim, W., 1988). The won had become 'overvalued' from the standpoint of trade considerations, due to a continuous large inflow of foreign capital (Cho, 1989). The ensuing devaluation increased costs for domestic enterprises by increasing payments due both on outstanding foreign debt and those necessary for imported inputs. Due to the cost-induced profit squeeze, Korean firms problems servicing their external debts and the country developed a financial crisis in 1972. In an effort to alleviate the position of firms, the BOK decreased the rate of interest by 4 per cent points and the loan rate by 3 per cent points in January 1973.

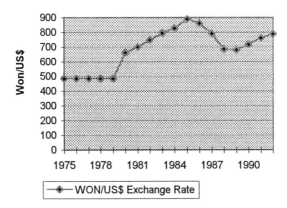

Figure 7.6: Korea - WON/$ exchange rate

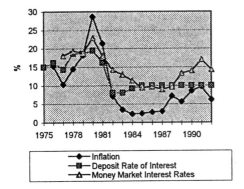

Figure 7.7: Korea - inflation and interest rates

As the real economy continued to deteriorate, a presidential decree was issued in August 1972. The primary purpose of the decree was twofold. In the first instance, the decree was intended to improve the financial structure of private loan-ridden corporations, and to institutionalize the loans being extended on the Unorganized Money Market (UMM). In a move to absorb informal intermediaries and bail out troubled firms, the BOK set up a group of non-bank financial intermediaries (NBFIs). NBFIs, such as finance companies, were created to provide instalment savings facilities and short-term business and household finance. The role of the NBFIs was enhanced by making them subject to less regulation than the banking sector, with greater freedom in the pricing of their liabilities. Owing to this greater autonomy and flexibility, the NBFIs were able to compete directly with the banks and grow rapidly. The new owners of the NBFIs tended to be the powerful families and *chaebols* (corporate bodies) which used them to further concentrate financial and economic resources in the hands of the preferred sectors (Cho, 1989).

The second element of the decree helped mark a shift in industrial policy which would dominate development policy for the remainder of the decade. Korea began pushing forward investment in heavy and chemical industries. In the previous years, Korea had adopted an outward orientation as the key to their development strategy. The new emphasis was complementary to the old strategy in the sense that it aimed to foster the production of currently imported inputs necessary for the newly established export industries. This went hand in hand with the development of new export opportunities in heavy industries such as ship building.

However, even the newly emerging *chaebols* were unwilling to invest in heavy and chemical industries at their own risk due to the large fixed capital investment required, the long gestation period, and the uncertainty of return associated with these projects (Cho, 1989). To create private sector interest, the government expanded the scope of low interest loans and opened up access to the discount window to encompass intermediate goods industries and machinery and construction. With this policy, the BOK supplied credit to the banking system either through the discounting of commercial bills or by extending general loans to the banks based on the collateral of certain assets. The BOK classified the eligibility of bankers bills for rediscount into prime borrowers, ordinary enterprises, those guaranteed by the credit guarantee fund, and bills for trade promotion and other sectors designed for preferential treatment.   Trade promotion bills were automatically rediscounted at full face value and their quantity was therefore outside the control of the BOK. Additionally, exporters were given access to short-term loans which were tied to the gross value of export sales and extended at subsidized and preferential rates. Such short-term export loans were also automatically extended without limit to those with valid letters of trade (invoices), irrespective of domestic value-added content of the exports, and for values of up to 80 per cent of domestic production costs. As part of the policy, credit was allocated on industry specific grounds, with the primary recipients being the emerging *chaebols* which began to dominate the heavy and chemical industries. For the remainder of the decade, the provision of credit subsidies was used to bolster efforts towards development and was of the magnitude of 10 per cent of GNP per year, on average (Hong and Park, 1986).

Accompanying subsidized credit were explicit and implicit loan guarantees.[13]   Both the banks and industry became aware that the government would not allow the larger emerging firms to become insolvent or bankrupt.   Essentially, the government was partaking in Korea's development program in the capacity of a risk taker, and it assumed the majority of risk through the use of a subservient financial sector.   By bearing the down-side risk, the government allowed firms to earn the entire excess of returns over the cost of loans, less the cost of credit, whilst at the same time expecting the banking sector to bear the cost of losses (Cho, 1989). Thus, firms had the dual incentives of available, subsidized credit on the one hand and a lack of negative down-side risk on the other, to be involved in those sectors which were favoured by government policy.

---

[13] An example of an explicit loan guarantee was the Korea Credit Guarantee Fund (KCGF) which guaranteed the value of various loans extended under the policy auspices of the government.

Over time, the government adopted an increasingly complex structure of interest rates which favoured certain categories of borrowers.   A combination of adjusted interest rates, credit ceilings and access to the discount window were used and reflected changes in the government's priority towards growth and development in specific industries.   The government control of credit allocation during this period was pervasive and by the late 1980s, it was estimated that the government was allocating 50-70 per cent of domestic credit (Layman, 1988). Government regulations were extensive and included direct influence of the management and organizational structures of most commercial banks.

The program to develop strategic sectors was implemented by relying on the expansion of monetary liabilities and a large inflow of foreign capital. As the government was providing an almost elastic supply of credit to the preferential sectors, it continued to rely on required reserve ratios to reduce the ability of commercial banks to lend to non-priority enterprises.   The frequent adjustment of the required reserve ratio, and their high levels, caused instability in the money multipliers and further complicated the management of bank balance sheets and the money supply. In theory, banks unable to meet their required reserves had to pay penal rates to the BOK. However, the BOK usually extended general loans to the banks to make up any deficiency, which decreased the effectiveness of the reserve instrument in monetary stabilization (Layman, 1988).   In order to supplement their waning control over the money supply, the BOK introduced monetary stabilization bonds in 1973 which were to be subscribable through private auction.   Subsequently, in 1977, the BOK began issuing government bills aimed at financing budgetary deficits from sources other than borrowing from the BOK (Figure 7.8).

Even these additional measures of monetary control were, however, undermined by the continued subservience of monetary objectives to the dictates of development policy.   The fungibility of credit funds allowed firms with access to elastic supplies of credit to inflate their real credit demands and divert the excess to rent-seeking activities. The real problem was the large subsidized component of the credit which did nothing to discourage rent seeking and inefficiencies. The subsidy element led firms to become reliant on bank credit, stunting the growth of the equity market and leading to increasingly high financial leveraging (Hong and Park, 1986).[14] The result of the large accommodation of the credit demands of

[14]Rent seeking in Korea was highly concentrated amongst a core of powerful groups (*chaebol*) while the bulk of government officials and bankers were relatively clean.

priority sector firms, combining with the BOK's attempts at direct monetary control, led to a growing dualism in the financial sector. While industrial firms could satisfy all credit needs from the banking sector, smaller non-priority firms and households were forced to rely on the UMM (curb market) to satisfy their credit needs. It was estimated that the size of these informal markets was around won 1.5 trillion or about 12 per cent of the average level of banking claims on the private sector by early 1980 (Layman, 1988). Access to credit had then become as, or more, important than the cost of credit, in Korea. Such restricted access to credit served to influence the direction of resource allocation and industrial growth in the Korean economy (Park, 1989).

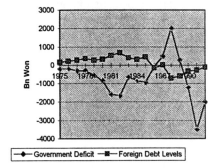

Figure 7.8: Korea - government deficit and foreign borrowing

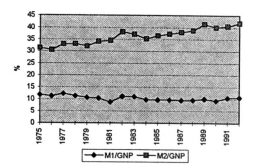

Figure 7.9: Korea - M1/GNP, M2/GNP ratios

As the 1970s came to a close, the policies were beginning to display some weaknesses. The economy began to exhibit signs of substantial excess capacity in particular industries due to the credit subsidies which had helped stimulate over-eager industrial expansion and the duplication of investment by competing companies. Large foreign borrowing, rapid expansion of monetary liabilities from accommodating policies, and expansionary fiscal policies helped to make inflation chronic and deep-seated. In 1978, the BOK responded to the inflationary pressure by increasing the deposit rate to 18.5 per cent with the objective of reducing domestic consumption. The increase failed to make long-lasting gains as expectations of inflation remained high (Kim, W., 1988). As monetary claims continued to grow and to stimulate aggregate demand, the Korean current account consistently deteriorated. As a fixed exchange rate policy was being adhered to in 1975-79, the implicit overvaluation of the won helped stimulate over-capital intensity, against the country's comparative advantage. The growth of the financial system remained stagnant during this time period and the $M2/GNP$ ratio actually declined from 33.9 per cent in 1970 to 31.6 per cent by the end of 1979 (Figure 7.9) (Cho and Khatkhate, 1989).

Financial Liberalization: Elements of Reform

With the onset of the second oil price shock and the substantial increase in world interest rates, Korea's balance of trade deteriorated further, inflation peaked, and the structural problems of over-capacity put many heavy and chemical industrial firms into financial payment difficulties. In response to this macroeconomic tribulation, the government adopted measures in 1979 aimed at economic stabilization. The measures reflected the policy priorities of price stability and economic growth. The BOK sought tighter control of monetary expansion and this was aided by reductions in fiscal expenditure. Although actual fiscal outlays had fallen, the government still allowed a counter-cyclical increase in the deficit at this time. A large devaluation of the won by 21 per cent in January 1980 was undertaken and was soon followed by a consistently managed downward float (Kwack and Chung, 1986). The exchange rate was from then on consistently managed as a tool to keep Korean goods competitive, thereby rescuing an export performance which had begun floundering in the throes of world recession.

The rapid devaluation had the immediate effect of increasing the foreign financing costs of the export industry. The increase in the cost of imported inputs, combined with higher world and domestic interest rates, pushed firms into greater indebtedness. Korea's external debt almost doubled between 1979 and 1983 from a manageable US$20.3 billion to a steep US$40 billion before reaching a peak of US$46.8 billion in 1985 (Kim, W., 1988). In June 1980, the government increased the discount rate by 1-2 per cent while the rate on loans to exporters increased by 6 per cent. Such attempts at pursuing a positive interest rate were, however, thwarted by inflation rates which rose from 18 per cent to 29 per cent p.a. (Collins and Park, 1989). Heavy indebtedness and squeezed profits pushed many firms into financial difficulty. Non-performing loans increased and banks found that large portions of their loan portfolios, including a substantial proportion of directed loans, were becoming inactive. In this fragile atmosphere, the government decided to attempt a more substantial liberalization of the financial system.

The first movements in financial deregulation came in 1981, when the government began a program of privatizing the nationwide commercial banks by divesting its share holdings. The rationale behind the move was an effort to increase the competitiveness of the banking sector and reduce the administrative and managerial influence of the government in the sector. As a result, most regulations governing bank management were abolished or amended, and bank budgets, personnel management, and organizational structures were made independent of government approval in a revision of the general banking act in 1982 (Park, 1989). Additionally, banks were allowed to offer new retail banking services including household chequing accounts, credit cards, and the payment of public utility charges through automatic transfers and automatic teller services (Lee, 1986).

In an effort to enhance the role of financial institutions as mobilizers of savings and to promote the development of short- and long-term financial markets, new financial institutions and products were introduced. The government authorized two new domestic banks and sixteen new foreign banks to begin operations.[15] Also, investment and finance companies were allowed to sell commercial paper at rates determined by the market. The higher interest rates these NBFIs were allowed to offer gave them a competitive edge over the commercial banks (Cho and Khatkhate, 1989). In compensation in 1982, banks were allowed to sell on the repurchase market Repurchase Agreement Bonds (RPAs), which they accepted from government and public utilities. In 1984, the commercial banks were permitted to issue Certificates of Deposits (CDs) at fixed discount rates which were higher than those on time deposits with comparable maturities (Lee, 1986).

The government also began moving slowly into the liberalization of

---

[15] During the 1980s, foreign banks have not exerted as much competitive pressure as they might have due to being handicapped by discriminatory regulation on the extent of their operations. Rather, foreign banks have been employed primarily to stimulate the inflow of capital from abroad (Lee, 1986).

interest rates. The unruly behaviour of inflation during this time made free market determination of interest rates unpalatable to the monetary authorities. However in June 1981, interest rates on interbank, call, and discount on prime commercial paper, were liberalized (Cho and Khatkhate, 1989). The BOK combined reserve requirements, open market operations in terms of forced placement of monetary stabilization bonds, and a contractionary fiscal policy, in a movement to bring down inflation. Also, the BOK simplified the complex structure of interest rates in 1982 by reducing the quantity of preferential lending rates and unifying the bank loan rate at 10 per cent.   However, it maintained all other interest-rate ceilings. The BOK moved further towards market rates in early 1984 when a narrow interest-rate band of 10-10.5 per cent was introduced to enable banks to charge different rates, depending on borrowers' perceived risk characteristics and the maturity of the loan (Kim, W., 1988).

Impact of Financial Liberalization

Despite the post-1982 success in controlling inflation, the financial liberalization of the early 1980s made only limited progress in changing the structure of the financial industry as these reforms did not alter the *de facto* pattern of financial control to any significant degree (Park, 1989). The key barrier to real financial change was the long-standing reliance of financial intermediaries on the government for both direction in lending operations and as a source of financial resources.   Continuing reliance on the government for support was necessary due to the prevalence of non-performing loans in bank portfolios. As the majority of these loans were extended under the auspices of government direction, the government had a moral, as well as practical, obligation to ensure the liquidity of the banking sector (Cho, 1989).   During this time the BOK was acting as a lender, often of first, but especially of last resort to the commercial banks. As banks still lacked sufficient credit evaluation skills, initiative, sound loan portfolios and freedom in competitively pricing deposits, the banks had little choice but to rely on the government for direction and control.

The continued hegemony of the government in the financial markets was underlined by the financial crisis of 1982. By 1982, the Korean economy was beginning to experience price stability, which had the primary subsequent effect of turning real interest rates substantially positive (figure K.2).   The high real interest rates dealt a harsh blow to many highly-leveraged Korean firms which could not withstand the profit squeeze. Such firms which were over-extended with debt-burdens, became unable to meet their financial contributions without the aid of distress borrowing. Many of these firms were concentrated in the heavy and chemical industries and were suffering from over-capacity at the time as a result of past policy direction. The tight monetary and fiscal policies slowed down the rate of growth of domestic assets of the banking sector from 37 per cent in 1981 to 13 per cent in 1984, implying that the previously elastic supply of credit to these firms was drying up. The reduction in available credit gave rise to a substantial volume of non-performing loans (Cho and Khatkhate, 1989).

The situation came to a head in May 1982 when a scandal on the UMM forced two large corporations into bankruptcy. The scandal caused a further contraction of loan availability from both official and unofficial money markets and succeeded in putting the solvency of the financial system into jeopardy. Fearing the consequences and costs of a collapse in the financial system, the government moved in with policies aimed at guaranteeing the solvency of the industrial sector. As a first step, the BOK began channelling funds through the banking sector to threatened firms, which reduced the quantity of non-performing assets. Next, the government began frequent downward adjustments to nominal loan rates in order not to aggravate the arrearage of firms with payment problems (Cho and Khatkhate, 1989). By actively managing interest rates, the BOK contributed in a substantial manner to the reduction of the corporate debt burden and strengthened the financial position of many firms (Cho and Khatkhate, 1989). Additional measures were used to bail out the problem firms including direct financial support from the government, tax allowances for writing off bad debts, concessional credit from the BOK and industrial restructuring measures (Park, 1989).

The industrial restructuring measures included a limited closure of unprofitable plants, the merging of duplicated investment projects and the postponement of other planned investments (Park, 1989). In undertaking the restructuring, the government ensured that social and political costs were minimized by mitigating the displacement from employment which such restructuring caused. To reduce the costs, the government essentially shifted the burden of adjustment to the commercial banks and, in so doing, avoided compounding the problems in the real economy with business failure (Layman, 1988). Hence, direct financial assistance from the government often took the form of forcing commercial banks to assume the debts of these troubled firms. In compensation, the BOK continued to provide liquidity to the banks at discounted rates, with an implicit guarantee to act as a lender of last resort should any bank ran into liquidity problems.

The immediacy of the non-performing loans crisis was gradually alleviated by these policies and by the onset of strong global and Korean economic performance from 1985. The legacy of the period for the commercial banks, however, was a further burdening of loan portfolios with the dead weight of more non-performing loans which limited their autonomy and effectiveness.   Faced with the problem of a highly dependent banking system needing continued support and control, the government shifted its liberalization gaze on to the non-bank financial sector (NBFI). The NBFIs during this period had most constraints removed concerning size and allocation of their funds to particular industries, and were either freed from, or able to circumvent, interest-rate ceilings on both services and use of funds.   The NBFIs and security markets were free to offer higher rates of interest than the banks and entry restrictions for NBFIs were removed, increasing the competitive nature of these markets.   The result of these much more significant changes was the extension of NBFIs and direct finance at the expense of the market share of the commercial banks.   The expansion of the NBFIs in the late 1980s is illustrated by the rapid growth of $M3$/GNP relative to the $M2$/GNP ratio (Figure 7.9).   The graph implies that the NBFIs have been largely responsible for most increases in intermediation which have occurred in the Korean economy (Cho and Khatkhate, 1989).   The expansion of non-controlled credits at the expense of controlled credits has made substantial inroads into the equalization of industrial borrowing costs, and helped ease access to credit for smaller industrial enterprises.

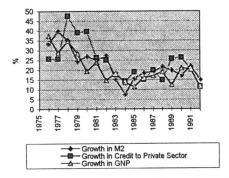

Figure 7.10: Korea - growth in M2, credit to private sector, GNP

The Korean experience with financial liberalization in the first half of the 1980s lacked a consistent keynote, with controls on interest rates and institutional restrictions at least being implicitly retained for the banking sector.   The effects of liberalization were rather insignificant and the government was constrained from fully pursuing its goals due to the weight of past policies on the existing institutions.   The extent of non-performing loans due to over-lending under government priority, external shocks and the attempts at liberalization made full-scale liberalization foolhardy. The government had little choice but to continue to supply credit to those firms which were having payment difficulties and to act as a lender of last resort to the banking system. Credit rationing was deepened as the amount of credit available to non-distressed firms dried up (Figure 7.10). Credit money remained endogenous and responded to the dictates of the financial crisis. The expansion of the NBFI sector served to decrease the extent of government intervention in the financial markets and expand the official credit market to encompass a greater number and type of firm. The ability of NBFIs to circumvent regulations concerning pricing and allocation further served to weaken direct BOK control over the money supply. The main lesson was the endogeneity of the money supply, and its importance to the real sector made the rapid increase and deregulation of interest rates impossible. As money plays a fundamental role in the economy, the rapid change in the conditions in which it was made available had a significant detrimental impact on indebted firms, which required subsequent monetary accommodation. The result was that little significant change was allowed and the government remained in firm control of interest rates - their true exogenous policy tool.

1985-1992: Recent Developments and Subsequent Measures of Reform

The Korean economy began to boom with the stimulus of a favourable world environment characterized by the three lows - low oil prices, a low value of the US$ against the yen, and low world interest rates. With global recovery Korean exports rebounded, and by 1986 the current account went into surplus which by 1988 had grown to US$14 billion. The strong export performance contributed to double figure growth rates (average 12 per cent) and to a reduction in unemployment to historically low levels (figure 7.10)(Park, 1989). The combination of strong economic performance and excess world liquidity stimulated a rapid accumulation of net foreign assets by the financial sector. Accompanying this growth in available foreign funds, the rise in domestic incomes increased savings and the private sector began to rapidly accumulate financial assets. The supply of funds to the business sector consequently underwent rapid expansion and the Korean economy was in danger of overheating.

In response, the BOK maintained its policy objective of stable prices by issuing massive amounts of monetary stabilization bonds. The extent of the bond issue was equivalent to more than a quarter of the increase in $M2$ for 1986. As inflationary pressures persisted into 1987, the BOK again drained liquidity by issuing vast volumes of monetary and foreign exchange stabilization bonds. By September the level of bonds outstanding in the financial markets had reached won 4.3 trillion (Layman, 1988). As these bonds were competitively priced, with interest rates around 12 per cent, issues of corporate bonds were crowded out and caused a credit shortage for industrial firms. Supporting these bond issues, the BOK reduced access to the foreign exchange swap facilities. The net effect of these policy moves was to increase the funding costs of foreign banks engaged in local currency lending and decrease the ability of these banks to lend.

The BOK stepped in to make lending to firms with debt-equity ratios exceeding 500 per cent (essentially all large firms) more prohibitive (Layman, 1988). The rationale was to wean these large firms off bank credit and encourage the growth of direct finance. To achieve these policy goals, access to the export loan rediscount facility contracted. Additionally, the BOK started to favour the small to medium-sized enterprises (SMEs) in the allocation of bank credit. As most small- and medium-sized enterprises had difficulties in borrowing from banks due to their lack of creditworthiness and collateral, the BOK felt it necessary to expand the credit guarantees offered by the Korea Credit Guarantee Fund. The BOK began to provide rediscounts to SMEs of up to 70 per cent of the value of commercial banks whilst limiting the amount to 30 per cent for others. The continued use of the rediscount facility during this period to allocate funds through the banking system, offset much of the contractionary effect of the monetary stabilization bond issues. The task of monetary control was also complicated by growing tightness in the labour market. The increasing cost-push pressure from manufacturing sector wages put pressure on monetary aggregates which therefore necessitated further efforts to sterilize the ever expanding flow of foreign capital. As the Korean government maintained its strict regime of capital controls, the policy scope for restricting the rise of net foreign assets was limited to the repayment of debt (Layman, 1988).

Fearing the adverse effects on competitiveness that domestic inflation would entail, and smarting from the financial crowding out that reliance on monetary stabilization bonds was having, the BOK sought to enhance their indirect monetary control methods. The prerequisite for more effective monetary control was seen to be a liberalization of the interest rate structure which was begun in earnest with the December 1988 plan (Kim, W, 1988).[16]

---

[16]The government was optimistic that liberalization could stabilize lending rates in the long run by decreasing firms' precautionary demand for funds. Corporations often borrowed additional funds for precautionary reasons prior to liberalization as they could not always

The reform package began by fully liberalizing all interest rates on loans from banks and NBFIs, excepting those interest rates on loans subsidized by government funds. Under these measures, 80 per cent of all bank loans and 99 per cent of all NBFIs loans were subject to liberalization measures (Kim, W. 1988). A prime rate system was introduced whereby each financial intermediary determined its rate after considering the rediscount rate at the BOK. The interest rate structure on a few financial market instruments - certificates of deposits, commercial paper, and corporate bonds - which had been subject to administrative guidance, was fully deregulated. Despite these moves, only the interest rates on a few of the deposits with the longest maturities were deregulated, owing to the BOK's fear that excess competition for funds amongst financial intermediaries would drive up interest rates to potentially destabilizing levels. Accompanying the deregulation of loan rates, the term structure of deposit interest rates was rearranged according to maturity and excessive differences in interest rates between banks and NBFIs were reduced. In all, 23 per cent of total deposits were liberalized, 29.8 per cent restructured and the remaining 47 per cent unchanged (Kim, W. 1988). The government's hesitancy in altering deposit rates was seen as a measure to help stabilize the financial market and to minimize portfolio movements of funds between liberalized and regulated financial assets after the reforms were implemented.

Although liberalization was now seen as possible, due to an increasing diversification of corporate sector financing, the aforementioned liberalization has not yet succeeded in significantly altering the financial system (Park, 1989).[17] The banks, which are still plagued by considerable non-performing assets, all feared abrupt fluctuations in interest rates and the effects this would have on corporate clients. The banks also lacked appropriate credit evaluation expertise needed for accurate loan pricing. As a result, the seven nation-wide commercial banks all agreed to keep deposit rates at their original levels. They jointly agreed to set their prime rate at 11 per cent and to have five different lending rates at 0.5 per cent intervals between 11 per cent and 13 per cent, reflecting credit standing and maturity

borrow from banks when they needed funds due to the strict credit control system (Kim, K., 1989).

[17]Bank borrowing, as a percentage of external financing fell from 40 per cent in 1985 to 26 per cent in 1987. This change was due largely to increases in NBFI and direct finance facilities. Improved business profitability since 1986 also stimulated an increase in internal and equity financing. Such sources increased from 15 per cent in 1985 to 39 per cent in 1987 (Kim, W., 1988).

(Kim, W., 1988). Such non-competitive behaviour reflects fears of the potential debilitating effect which financial liberalization can have on bank profitability. Even if the interest-rate spread between loans and deposits remains constant, the added costs of fund-raising from a sharp increase in deposit rates will exceed additional income from loan assets. The discrepancy is due to the large increase in the proportion of non-performing assets held by banks caused by such abrupt changes (Park, 1989). Thus, in the short run, interest rates will still not act optimally as a mechanism in the allocation of resources as the persistent high demand for bank loans and the needs of banks' portfolios dictate otherwise.

However, the BOK still expected some increase in short-term interest rates and this combined with the rapid appreciation of the won during 1987-89 (Figure 7.6), threatened to provide a profit squeeze for many of the SMEs (Kim, W., 1988).[18] In line with its shifting policy objectives, the government promised to offer aid if the increases in interest rates post-liberalization were large. The aid offer was administered by supplying the commercial banks with additional liquidity to bolster SMEs from monetary stabilization accounts. A second, small and medium industry discount facility was to be established to broaden the source and availability of funds for such firms (Kim, W., 1988).

In efforts to shore up control of the money supply, the BOK turned to more indirect methods of monetary control. As the quantitative control of bank credits and the mandatory underwriting of monetary stabilization bonds became ineffective in absorbing the large amounts of foreign liquidity, the government began issuing monetary stabilization bonds on an auction basis to reflect prevailing market conditions. To deepen the financial sector, the type of financial instruments available to be traded was diversified. The rediscount facility, which had been used so effectively in the pursuit of individual policy objectives, was redesigned to control liquidity. The change in priorities led the BOK to decide to gradually abolish the automatic rediscount facility for loans to export and heavy and chemical industries. The BOK also reinforced the position of required reserve ratios, and encouraged banks to sell securities holdings to make up for any acquired shortfalls. A 30 per cent marginal required reserve ratio on average increments of deposits from the year preceding, was included by May,

---

[18]With the large current account surplus, Korea was put under significant pressure to revalue the won/$ exchange rate in order to dampen its rising trade surplus with the US. The exchange rate peaked by 1989 and began to depreciate by 1990 as the BOK began managing it downwards.

1989.

The end of the last decade, then, saw the first tentative movements to liberalization of the interest rate regime and financial structure in Korea. A consistent theme running through this period has been the difficulty of liberalizing deposit rates and substantially changing the conditions under which credit is made available. Thus, the BOK has not allowed significant competition for funds to develop between intermediaries and has made explicit its commitment to supplying liquidity to firms experiencing financial difficulties. In acting as this lender of last resort, and as a risk-sharing partner, the BOK has ensured that credit money is created to serve the needs of the banking and real sectors. Money remains created by the needs of the productive sector and increments in its supply are largely determined by the financial needs of firms. Although the BOK reduced the amount of commercial bank lending automatically rediscountable, it continued to use judicious access to the window to lighten credit conditions for SMEs. As large firms, even though highly leveraged, are seen as having a higher credit standing by the banking community, the broadening of access to official credit markets to SMEs will have increased the amount of intermediation that occurs by official intermediaries. The deepening of the financial sector, including the growth in equity and the emerging inter-bank markets, implies banks can also diversify their sources of funds to satisfy existing credit demands and their reserve requirements. If the reform is to be maintained, indirect monetary control tools are required to be effective in limiting this response of money to real sector demand. However, it is the presence of real sector credit demand which necessitates this gradual piecemeal approach to liberalization and sets limits on the extent of change possible.

Issues of efficiency in resource mobilization and intermediation have played a subservient role to the need to minimize disruptions in the real sector on which Korea's development plans have rested. In 1990 alone, some 50 per cent of commercial bank lending went to rescue small and medium-sized companies poised on the verge of bankruptcy (*The Banker*, Mar. 1991).

With Korea entering the 1990s as one of the most successful of the recent developers, interest in investing in Korea remains large. Due to the bulk of foreign funds and Korea's desire to more fully integrate with the rest of the developing world, the BOK has continued with its liberalization of foreign exchange transactions. In 1992, Korea embarked on a capital market internationalization plan. The freeing of its capital controls and the closer integration of its domestic financial markets have been the two dominant themes in Korea's financial policy in the 1990s.

In terms of integrating the domestic financial market, the BOK introduced new legislation towards the end of 1990. Aimed at consolidation, the BOK wants the 32 short-term financial companies (STFC) set up in the early 1970s to absorb the UMM, to disappear or be scaled down (*The Banker*, Dec. 1990). The STFCs are seen to compete directly with banks by offering depositors better rates and funding corporate clients with easier access to short-term funds. The STFCs, which have benefited from less regulation and have performed better than the banks or the security houses, have been pushing up interest rates in competition for funds to levels higher than that desired by the authorities.[19] The broad speculation is that five or so of the Seoul-based STFCs will become banks, either independently or by merging, and the rest will merge with securities firms (*The Banker*, Dec. 1990). As the *chaebols* hold big equity stakes in STFCs either directly or through affiliates, it is likely that these moves will further concentrate financial power in their hands.[20] The consolidation moves are, however, likely to make it more difficult for SMEs to finance their working capital once the STFCs disappear. It is also of questionable judgement to consolidate the well-performing intermediaries in order to upgrade less efficient institutions.[21] The measure, however, is providing banks with some compensation for absorbing the costs of restructuring from the early 1980s.

The BOK has also taken steps to internationalize the capital markets and began by opening the stock market to foreigners in 1992. However, the free flow of capital in and out of Korea is only likely to be realized some time after 1997. The role of foreign banks in these plans, and in the financial system as a whole, is unclear. At present foreign banks complain of limits imposed on their major source of funding in domestic currency, the swap facility, and of lending limits and regulatory requirements which competitively disadvantage them. Given their branching restrictions, foreign banks must rely on a swap facility of foreign for domestic funds with the BOK as their primary source of domestic funds. Since the current account surplus in 1986, the swap facility has been reduced by almost 10 per cent

[19]Figure 7.10 illustrates the growth of these STFCs, especially in the late 1980s, as $M3$ has grown faster (30.3 per cent in 1989) than $M2$ (19.8 per cent in 1989).

[20]Any new banks which are established will be exempt from current regulations limiting individual equity stakes in banks to 8 per cent. The existing regulation is widely held to be circumvented through the use of holding companies.

[21]Commercial banks' return on equity in 1990 was placed at 5.66 per cent, which was far lower than the 14.38 per cent of the less regulated STFCs and the 10.42 per cent of security companies.

a year as part of monetary control measures. The foreign banks do, though, occupy a niche in the market as suppliers of foreign exchange and benefit from having the *chaebols* place some 90 per cent of their foreign exchange transactions with foreign banks.

Despite the movements to liberalize the financial system, Korea still retains a fairly primitive financial system compared to its sophisticated manufacturing base. The major deposit interest rates are tightly controlled by the government and the gap between official and market (UMM) rates remains wide. The interest rate structure still displays certain irrationalities. For example, prime rates are set at 10 per cent, whereas market determined yields on three year corporate bonds hover around 18 per cent, paradoxically making intermediated finance cheaper than direct. As a result, the profitability of both bankers and corporate customers is suffering. Financial institutions are still forced to buy monetary stabilization bonds from the BOK at 13 per cent and then sell them to investors at higher interest rates (*The Banker*, Dec. 1990). Interest-rate spreads on normal intermediation remain thin, often as low as 0.5 per cent, and at times even a reversed margin (*The Banker*, Mar. 1991). Hence, a key task for the remainder of the 1990s remains the liberalization of deposit interest rates. The BOK is likely to proceed slowly on this task as deposit rates are certain to rise to compete efficiently with the much higher priced corporate bonds. As this would cause a large increase in lending rates, the continued dependence of industry on bank finance would inevitably lead to financial difficulties in the productive and financial sectors. The ensuing inflation and reduction in economic growth are two concrete reasons why the BOK will proceed slowly in freeing interest rates from its direct control and guidance. As a result, deposit rate deregulation has been left until after 1997. This postponement is despite the announcement in May 1993 of the BOK's desire to deregulate all lending rates, excluding those charged on loans extended to companies strategically protected by the government (*The Banker*, July 1993). Even so, the government stresses that it is under no obligation to go forward with this plan. Any adverse developments in the term structure of interest rates would be sufficient provocation to cause the government to back off. Already borrowing costs are beginning to increase and cause some problems. It was estimated that the effective borrowing cost from banks in 1991 was close to 25 per cent.[22] By the end of the year, eight in

---

[22]The effective borrowing rate is higher than the nominal rate, as many banks require favours such as the holding of compensating balances, that is the company does foreign exchange or letter of credit business with them as a prerequisite for the provision of liquidity.

100 companies were going into bankruptcy and the situation did not improve much in 1992 (*The Banker*, Mar. 1992).   By the end of 1993, market interest rates were still expected to rise due to inflationary pressure and expected demand for credit from companies desiring to invest in capital facilities.

Although there have been efforts to wean the Korean corporate sector off bank finance, Korean firms remain heavily reliant on bank credit.   Debt-equity ratios of over 500 per cent are still far from uncommon.   The two biggest *chaebols*, Samsung and Daewoo, had debt-equity ratios of 675 per cent and 755 per cent respectively in 1990 (*The Banker*, Mar. 1992). Financial power and access to credit remains in the hands of the industrial *chaebols*.   40 per cent of banks loans during 1991 went to the top 30 *chaebols* and of that 46 per cent went to three core firms (*The Banker*, Mar. 1992).   Despite this, the top five *chaebols* suffer from a shortage of daily working capital.   The *chaebols* must, therefore, strengthen their treasury management skills as the 1990s promise to present them with more difficult borrowing conditions.   If the Korean economy is to continue its impressive industrialization process, the *chaebols* will have to more effectively tap direct sources of finance.   The banks will have a large part to play in the transition by diversifying their lending to include new types of business.   At present, loans for non-industrial purposes have been severely limited by the BOK, which fears the inflationary potential of such lending on the economy. If liberalization proceeds, banks will need to exploit such additional business and develop the personnel skills necessary to do so.   Standing in the way of such diversification remains the continued hegemonic presence of the government in the affairs of the commercial banks.   The lack of bank autonomy, and use of the banking sector to control the private sector, hindered competition between banks and removed much of the spur to innovations.

MALAYSIA

Financial Policy prior to Reform and Macroeconomic Background

The backbone of Malaysian economic policy during the last two decades has been the New Economic Policy (NEP) of 1969. The NEP called for the eradication of poverty, irrespective of race, and a broad restructuring of economic policy in society to favour the *Bumiputera*, or indigenous Malay population.   A prevalent consequence of the pursuit of policy goals during the 1970s was a chronic government deficit of around 6-7 per cent of GDP (Cho and Khatkhate, 1989). Government spending was concentrated in undertaking large development projects and subsidizing public enterprises.

The Malaysian currency, the ringgit, was pegged to a composite basket in 1973 which was then managed as a primary tool for domestic stabilization (Figure 7.11).

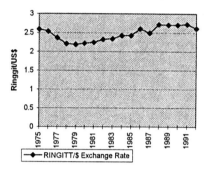

Figure 7.11: Malaysia- ringgit/$ exchange rate

At the same time, a large proportion of foreign exchange controls were lifted making the Malaysian economy highly open. The openness of the economy and the possibility of large-scale capital flows required the authorities to introduce a new interest-rate package in 1974. The package included both higher interest rates to discourage capital flight and the imposition of a credit growth rate ceiling to control the money supply. The ceiling excluded freshly created priority areas which concentrated on the policy goals set out in the NEP - the *Bumiputera*, manufacturing and exports.[23] The ceilings functioned throughout the 1970s and were quite effective in providing a large amount of monetary and price stability. As a result of these policies, made necessary by the open capital account, the rates of interest on borrowing were not at unduly low levels for any significant period during the 1970s (Figure 7.12). The stable and low rates of inflation throughout this time allowed returns on savings to remain positive. Both *M*2 and *M*3 increased as proportions of GDP as Malaysia's

---

[23] At least 25 per cent of new credit extended within the new 20 per cent credit growth ceiling had to be directed for productive investment in the manufacturing sector. It was estimated that during this period, 30 per cent of all bank credit was extended under such programs (Cho and Khatkhate, 1989).

financial sector deepened considerably and developed a sophisticated array of financial intermediaries and instruments (Figure 7.13).

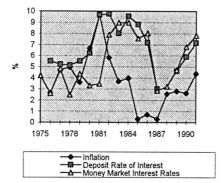

Figure 7.12: Malaysia - inflation and interest rates

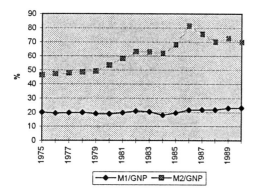

Figure 7.13: Malaysia - M1/GNP, M2/GNP ratios

The policy to stimulate domestic economic activity did contain an element of large government participation. The government's intervention was given further impetus as the Malaysian economy began to develop significant balance of payments imbalance during 1977-78. As the terms of trade underwent a continued deterioration, the government began to suspect that growth would have to be based on domestic sources (Bank Negara Malaysia, 1989). Economic policies were then reappraised in the context of the need to revive and sustain domestic demand at a high level. The element of aggregate demand policy makers were most keen to encourage was private fixed investment (Bank Negara Malaysia, 1989).

In January 1977, the Central Bank, Bank Negara (BN), introduced new credit facilities to assist the further development of priority sectors in the economy (Bank Negara Malaysia, 1989).   As a cornerstone, the BN arranged for the rediscounting of bills of credit to finance the production of manufacture and exports at preferential rates. The rediscounting of export bills was done through the export credit refinancing (ECR) facility which statutorily required the BN to refinance credit extended by commercial banks to exporters of goods manufactured in Malaysia. A low-cost housing scheme financed at preferential rates was also introduced to stimulate the domestic non-tradable sector.   Such intervention exerted a considerable impact on the direction of credit allocation as Malaysia's conservative banking establishment would not lend in such areas without coercion.

As in other developing countries, monetary policy was the handmaiden of development policy and credit was allocated in accordance with policy goals. The money supply did respond endogenously to credit demands determined by the NEP. However, the existing corporate bodies (usually Chinese-owned) were not favoured by preferential access to credit (Somogyi, 1991). Rather, the Malaysian policy makers sought to use the financial system as a tool to increase the economic participation of indigenous Malays. As a result, Malaysian firms remained modestly leveraged, with debt-equity ratios in the range of 100-150 per cent (Cho and Khatkhate, 1989).   The industrial structure in which reform was to take place was, therefore, largely free of the distortions which have served as the primary barrier to change in other countries.

Financial Liberalization: Elements of Reform

Financial liberalization came relatively early, and in more favourable circumstances, for the Malaysian economy than for most other developing countries. As part of its ongoing restriction plan, the BN announced a new interest-rate regime in October 1978. From that period onwards, banks were allowed to determine the interest rate offered on deposits and lending charged to prime customers for loans and advances. In this regime, the maximum rate of interest to be levied by the banks on loans to priority sectors continued to be regulated. Priority sectors during this time remained Bumiputera loans not exceeding RGT500 000 each, small-scale enterprise loans not exceeding RGT250 000, and housing loans not exceeding RGT100 000 each (Cho and Khatkhate, 1989). The banks were also required to continue with the preferential interest rate system on loans extended to the government to fulfil their statutory requirements. A slight modification was added late in 1981 which allowed commercial banks to peg their lending rates to a base lending rate (BLR), based on the cost of banks' funds. The margin to be charged for each customer over the base rate was to correspond to perceived creditworthiness. By November 1983, all interest rates on loans and advances, apart from priority sector lending, were linked to the base rates of the respective banks (Bank Negara Malaysia, 1989).

In the period prior to reform, the primary tools of monetary policy involved the active use of reserve ratios and rediscount operations (Bank Negara Malaysia, 1989). An additional aim of the reform was to deepen money markets in order to pave the way for more indirect methods of monetary control. To diversify its policy tools, the BN introduced new money market instruments, most notably bankers' acceptances and negotiable certificates of deposit.

Impact of Financial Liberalization

Financial liberalization in Malaysia was not an abrupt change from the past, but rather a smooth evolution necessitated by the growing ability of institutions to circumvent existing regulation. As existing interest rates were significantly positive, Malaysian enterprises not benefiting from credit with a substantial subsidy component did not become particularly highly leveraged. The average pre-liberalization lending rate was about two percentage points above the prime rate and served to discourage an over-reliance on credit by the Malaysian business sector (Cho and Khatkhate, 1989). The immediate response to the reforms was, therefore, muted, with few initial repercussions. This muted response was largely due to the initial conditions of policy which allowed banks to charge higher interest rates to non-priority borrowers depending on liquidity conditions in the market. Additionally, the policy only directed credit towards small borrowers, which helped diversify the banks' loan portfolios. The greater initial play of market forces in the financial system prior to liberalization implied that the worst distortions of repression, which undermined reform elsewhere, were largely absent. As a result, the immediate effect of liberalization was small. Despite the liberalization, lending rates remained more or less state controlled as the rates set by the two major banks in the country determined the rates at which the remaining banks could effectively compete. Of these two major banks, one is the wholly government-owned Bank Bumiputera, and the other is the Malayan Bank which is 55 per cent owned by government agencies.

However, the longer term implications of a deregulated financial sector with market-based interest rates were to be felt, starting with the deleterious shocks to the Malaysian economy of 1979. Initially, the reduction in terms of trade and severe global inflationary pressures were viewed by Malaysian policy makers as a short-term problem (Ariff and Semudran, 1989). The government thus decided that the economy had enough freedom to pursue an optimistic counter-cyclical (expansionary) fiscal policy. The large increments in government spending were aimed at stimulating domestic demand, particularly investment, to provide an atmosphere in which economic goals could be met.

By 1982, it became increasingly clear that the global downturn was more severe and prolonged than initially thought. The central position the government had given to fiscal stimulus began to cause a large external imbalance, as a significant proportion of fiscal spending involved the import of foreign capital (Figure 7.14) (Somogyi, 1991). The continued import of physical capital which increased domestic capacity, and by extension domestic incomes, caused inflationary pressure alongside growing deficits in the balance of payments and fiscal budget. Policy makers also had to worry about increases in the amount of external debt.[24]

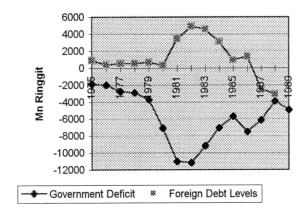

Figure 7.14: Malaysia - government deficit and foreign borrowing

[24]The fiscal deficit grew to 19.8 per cent of GNP by 1981 which led to a tripling in foreign debt from RGT10 billion in 1980 to RGT31 billion by the end of 1983, or 48.5 per cent of GNP (Sheng, 1989).

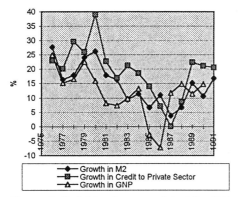

*Figure 7.15: Malaysia - growth in M2, GNP, credit
to the private sector*

In this worrisome atmosphere the government undertook a policy shift which featured a consolidation of and reduction in government spending. By the middle of 1982, a stringent austerity program began to bite and liquidity in the financial markets tightened significantly. As the BN actively reduced access to the discount window in support of these policies, financial institutions were left to compete aggressively for deposits. The most successful were the co-operative and illegal credit companies which succeeded in attracting funds away from the banking system with much higher interest rates. In the period 1982-86, this competition pushed up the level of deposit and lending rates to amounts substantially higher than those previously experienced. The real interest rate climbed to 11.8 per cent a year. in 1985 (Cho and Khatkhate, 1989).

The Malaysian economy was granted a slight reprieve with temporary recovery of commodity prices in 1983-84 (Figure 7.15). The recovery was short-lived and Malaysia again suffered from a collapse of commodity prices. The terms of trade deteriorated by 4.5 per cent in 1985 and by a further 15.5 per cent in 1986. As the ringgit plunged to 16.7 per cent against its composite, the private sector suffered a reduction in its total export income of 2.6 per cent in 1985 and 5.9 per cent in 1986 (Sheng, 1989). Compounding the difficulties was the fiscal austerity program which saw public expenditure falling enough to allow a reduction in the deficit, despite a large recession-induced fall in government revenues. The result of these aggregate demand shocks was a sharp contraction in cash flow which damaged many companies still committed to a large cash outlay, particularly in regard to property holdings secured by debt.

By mid-1985, the combined reduction in income, tight liquidity, low inflation and a sharp decline in share and property prices illuminated the financial over-commitments of many entrepreneurs (Sheng, 1989). The problem was that in the years after financial liberalization, the financial climate was characterized by highly liquid financial markets. The ease of credit and buoyant demand conditions created by government expenditure fostered a climate of entrepreneurial optimism. Part and parcel of this boom mentality was the speculative acquisition of shares and properties financed largely through bank credit. Such increments in credit increased the gearing of many firms, putting them into financially fragile positions. These fragile positions were quickly exacerbated by the shocks of a sharp decrease in income and a rising debt service cost triggered by the tight liquidity of banks forced to compete for deposits. As payment commitments of firms began outstripping actual cash flows, the economy was faced with an impending debt deflation and asset values began to collapse.[25]

For the private sector, this initial inability to reduce expenditure to account for its shortfall in income represented a bind on further operations. As operating losses mounted, many firms faced financial ruin. Such firms either engaged in distress borrowing at very high interest rates or suffered substantial capital losses in disposing of assets to meet cash payments (Sheng, 1989). The loss of capital stock and/or increases in debt reduced the ability of these firms to meet existing payment commitments and succeeded in turning short-term liquidity problems into a full-blown solvency crisis.

The reckless expansion of credit in the deregulated financial markets which helped fund the speculative boom (Figure 7.15) left banks highly exposed to a concentration of risk. The ensuing fiscal and monetary contraction engineered by the BN meant these banks could no longer satisfy firms' credit demands, which had increased with their cash-flow problems. The inability of these firms to increase their borrowing eliminated their repayment abilities, resulting in large amounts of non-performing loans in banks' loan portfolios. Bad debt provisions grew during this period from around 3.5 per cent of total loans to the system to 14.5 per cent by the end of 1988 (Sheng, 1989). The most severely affected official institutions were

---

[25]The first sign of financial instability was the failure of a small credit leasing company, Seita Timor Credit and Leasing, followed later in 1985 by the failure of a large public-listed company in Singapore, Pan Electric. The Pan Electric failure closed the Singapore and Kuala Lumpur stock exchanges and caused a run on several related financial institutions. The runs were stopped only after Bank Negara stepped in as lender of last resort and provided the necessary liquidity to bolster the failing institutions. The instability uncovered by the Pan Electric failure ushered in sporadic episodes of runs throughout 1986 which led to the failure of deposit-taking co-operatives in July and August (Sheng, 1989).

four medium-sized domestic commercial banks into which the BN was forced to inject fresh capital and a new management team. Similar treatment was necessary for four finance companies which became insolvent due to the losses on their loan portfolios.

The banking system made the situation worse by being unwilling to reduce its lending rates, even after the BN eased the liquidity situation and deposit rates started falling. During this period, the BN reduced the statutory reserve requirements by 1.5 per cent in 1985 and 1986, and the minimum liquidity requirements from 20 per cent to 17 per cent in October 1986. The widening spreads reflected both the oligopolistic market forces in the financial markets and a desire by banks to cover the losses they were making from non-performing loans, interest in suspense and higher bad debt provisions. In this regard, the BN attempted to apply moral suasion on the banks to bring down the ever widening margin. The limited success in lowering loan rates served to compound the financial problems of many firms (Bank Negara Malaysia, 1989).

In 1986, the BN responded to the problems by undertaking the liberalization of access to the discount window. A negative list of ineligible goods replaced the positive list of product eligibility, thereby widening access to the facility. The BN also undertook packages to restore credit to the financial markets with the creation of a New Investment Fund (NIF) in September 1985. The NIF ensured bank credit was to be available at a reasonable cost for the financing of preferred productive activities (Bank Negara Malaysia, 1989). The BN also undertook to strengthen capital adequacy requirements and banking supervision. The solvency of banking institutions which were strongly hampered by non-performing assets, was assisted with significant injections of new capital and the replacement of existing management teams.[26] These measures were successful in restoring stability to the financial system and banks were able to make RGT794m pre-

---

[26]The first three banks (United Asian, Periwara Habib, and Sabah Bank) that failed in 1985-86 incurred combined losses of RGT1.2 billion. The Central Bank responded by injecting RGT3.5 billion in fresh capital and RGT556m in temporary liquidity funds placed with institutions facing deposit runs. The Central Bank also pumped in RGT672m in a rights issue subscription and granted RGT401m in subordinate loans. The largest losses accrued to the state-owned Bank Bumiputera which reported losses of RGT1.06 billion for the year ending 1986 (*The Banker*, June 1990).

tax profits by the end of 1987.[27]   However, non-performing loans still comprised 33 per cent of banks' portfolios and provisions mounted to RGT577m, although this was down from the peak in 1986 of RGT1 270m (Loong, 1989).

The most scandalous failures, however, were amongst the deposit-taking co-operatives (DTCs) and illegal deposit-taking institutions (DTIs) in the informal market.   The lack of regulation allowed the DTCs to continue taking deposits, even after they encountered severe financial difficulties. The DTCs were able to sustain a Ponzi-style game whereby they solicited new deposits to meet deposit withdrawals and interest payments or to cover their mounting losses. The ultimate failure of one of the major DTCs had widespread contagion effects and left depositors with large losses and no deposit insurance.   Although of undoubted importance to the stranded depositors, the affected institutions were small with total assets not exceeding RGT5 billion or 2.5 per cent of total assets of the financial system (Sheng, 1989).[28]

1985-1992: Recent Developments and Subsequent Measures of Reform

Strong economic performance has helped the Malaysian financial sector recover. The external current-account balance began to show a surplus in the late 1980s which allowed the ratio of foreign debt to GDP to fall, reaching 43 per cent by 1989 (Figure 7.14).[29] Economic activity has further accelerated during the 1990s, underpinned by accommodative financial policies, an increase in foreign direct investment, and the slight strengthening of petroleum prices helping to restore a battered terms of

---

[27]The main reason for the recovery of banks was the cartel present in the industry. The banks paid no interest on the majority of current accounts and levied service charges on non-interest-bearing accounts. By the end of the 1980s, corporate borrowers in Malaysia were paying some of the widest interest margins in the world (*The Banker*, June 1991).

[28]A problem with these institutions was that they were informal and therefore ineligible for lender-of-last-resort facilities from the BN. This represented a dilemma for the BN as there existed a danger of contagion from failing UMM intermediaries infecting the official markets and triggering a more widespread financial crisis. The Central Bank ended up bailing out a number of deposit-taking co-operatives, assuming control of four finance companies and more than two dozen co-operatives (Lowenstein, 1989).

[29]Malaysia has consistently exported more goods than it has imported since 1981. The total current account showed large surpluses in 1987 (US$2.6 billion) and 1988 (US$1.82 billion).

trade.[30]

The financial sector has received help largely from two areas. The first is the huge inflow of foreign investment (RGT5 billion in 1989) which helped to stimulate a rapid increase in corporate investment to RGT5.4 billion (*The Banker*, June 1990). This source of profitable business for the banks has helped them surmount the problems with non-performing assets. As foreign direct investment has served to bring new financial wealth into Malaysia (foreign currency), the domestic monetization of that wealth has increased domestic income and helped swell liquidity in the financial sector. The now highly liquid banks have been able to start reducing loan and deposit rates, which has consequently helped reduce the size of intermediation margins. The net effect of these developments, in a macroeconomic sense, is that large aggregate demand pressures have arisen which have been reflected in growing domestic inflation.

The second area assisting the recovery of the financial system has been the upturn in property values which has turned a large number of non-performing loans into performers. This rebound in asset values has significantly improved the net worth of many banks' loan portfolios.

In response to the problems of the mid-1980s, the BN introduced the Banking and Financial Institutions Act in 1989. The act aimed to set out guidelines for the closer supervision of the financial sector. The new rules included a risk-weighted capital adequacy ratio target of 7.25 per cent for commercial banks and finance companies. The increase in regulation has caused some consternation amongst Malaysia's bankers who now complain of over-regulation leading to greater uncertainty. The problem with the rules of the new act is that they are vague and insufficiently promulgated, requiring the commercial banks to check with the BN to ensure the legality of their activities (*The Banker*, June 1991). The BN, for example, insists on having a say in the pricing and issuing of any new products the banks may wish to offer.

However, the most pervasive intervention remains in the area of priority sector loans, which was not substantially altered in the new development policy unveiled in 1991. Banks are still expected to extend 20 per cent of their loan portfolios to priority sectors, which mainly compromise small enterprises and housing (*The Banker*, July 1991). The biggest recipient is

---

[30]The recovery has been helped by a steady downward management of the ringgit. In response to the real appreciation of the ringgit in the early 1980s, the BN has managed the exchange rate to maintain Malaysian competitiveness. The real exchange rate of the ringgit declined by 35 per cent between the latter part of 1984 and the beginning of 1989 (Somogyi, 1991).

still the Bumiputera who continue to benefit from concessional rates, levied just above the base lending rate. As such Bumiputera projects have below average success rates, banks are loath to offer them credit on an uncoerced basis. The government compensates by acting as a risk partner through the Credit Guarantee Corporation (CGC) which guarantees to honour 65 per cent of any claim arising from such lending (Bank Negara Malaysia, 1989). The CGC attempts to apply stringent project appraisal to help increase repayment rates and encourages banks to lend to higher risk borrowers. Banks still risk a penalty for failing to meet their quota which usually entails the placement of undisbursed funds with the BN. Such funds are then made available for priority lending through the discount window, and eventually returned to the bank free of interest. Since such lending does not encourage an over-reliance on credit by the dominant firms in the economy, it is not seen to be inherently destabilizing, nor does it largely increase the susceptibility of the financial system to adverse shocks.

A similar innovation was the creation of the Malaysian Export Credit Insurance Board (MECIB) which functions in the same way to provide loan guarantees to exporters exploring new markets. The policy reflects a desire to diversify Malaysia's export markets and reduce their reliance on western markets.

The recent developments tend to suggest an increase in government participation in the financial system, a direction opposed to the general spirit of liberalization. The lesson that has been learnt is that increased supervision and regulation is necessary to ensure that development policy goals are reached and that stability in the financial markets is maintained. A more liberalized system may weaken the resilience of the financial sector, and the real economy, to adverse external and internal shocks.

THE PHILIPPINES

Financial Policy prior to Reform and Macroeconomic Background

Modern Philippine economic history is clouded by the large impact that the Marcos administration had on all facets of economic life. The domination of the economy by the Marcos regime can be traced back to 1972 which saw the declaration of martial law and a shift in development policy to encompass a much broader role for the government in the economy.[31]

The external shocks of the early 1970s left the Philippines with a deterioration in its terms of trade and a slow down in the growth of external and domestic demand. To ensure continued economic growth, the government relied on expanding aggregate demand through increments in its own investment expenditure. Government expenditure turned expansionary and increased in real terms by 17 per cent in 1973 and 40 per cent in 1975 (Dohner and Intal, 1989). The rapid expansion of national government expenditure was not, however, matched by corresponding increases in revenue generation through taxation. By the end of the 1970s, total expenditure by national government and public corporations was exceeding 18 per cent of GNP, whereas domestic revenue mobilization by the government lagged behind at 13.5 per cent of GNP. The remaining substantial resource gap had to be closed by borrowing. The government ended up pursuing a foreign borrowing strategy which saw a rapid build-up of foreign debt between 1975 and 1982. The public sector did most of this borrowing and held two-thirds of the debt of the non-banking sector by the end of that decade (Dohner and Intal, 1989).

The rapid expansion of the government into the economy had the added feature of allowing the entrenchment and consolidation of the power base of the existing regime, by providing an institutional mechanism for the distribution of patronage. As entrenchment became more important to the regime, the allocative role of government policies grew to foster the development of 'crony' capitalism. Philippine financial policy increasingly fostered a small group of politically connected businessmen who were additionally favoured with direct subsidization, or who were the recipients of monopoly rights. The direction of such influence building often helped form priorities that determined development policy goals. During this period, import substitution became the key element of industrial policy and this often involved the nationalization of foreign-owned industries (Sicat, 1985).[32]

---

[31]The Marcos regime first came to power in 1967. The first regime put through policies geared towards economic stabilization, including a devaluation in 1970 and tighter monetary and fiscal policies. A deteriorating political situation led the regime to declare martial law in 1972 and change their regime to a more expansionary one (Dohner and Intal, 1989).

[32]To put this in context, the Philippines were granted favoured nation trading status by the US which was largely aimed at encouraging the sale of traditional Philippine exports to the American market. Many Philippine policy makers saw this as pseudo-imperialism and reacted by trying to diversify their industrial sectors, away from their comparative advantage. The

To further encourage investment in the areas favoured by policy, notably manufacturing, energy and agriculture, the government undertook a high degree of participation in the financial sector and largely determined the flow of funds to the projects or individuals they favoured. Interest rates at which the banking system could disperse funds were set low, often resulting in negative real rates. The result was that borrowing from government-owned financial institutions was a very lucrative proposition available to the well-connected. The category of loans, 'projects under government behest', became very large and dominated the portfolios of the banking institutions (Okuda, 1990). The corporate bodies which grew up in this atmosphere were built heavily on borrowing from government-owned financial institutions, or from the private-sector money markets on the strength of their association with the regime. As a result, the corporate sector became highly leveraged with debt-equity ratios estimated at between 350-450 per cent during this period (Cho and Khatkhate, 1989). The demand for credit in this period was very high due to the fungibility of the funds which made the enrichment of individuals possible on the back of low-cost development loans. Often, funds acquired were diverted to consumption or channelled to the money market which had the attraction of much higher interest rates. Such arbitrage and corruption exacerbated the leveraging of the politically connected elite which had access to official sector funds. The elastic supply of credit to these politically favoured enterprises, ensured that the supply of money responded to their expenditure decisions.

The character of finance in the Philippines during this time was influenced by the systematic failure of financial intermediaries to mobilize sufficient resources. Despite the high rate of investment in the Philippines, the country had one of the lowest rates of financial mobilization amongst south-east Asian countries (Dohner and Intal, 1989). The inability of the banking system to mobilize resources left it particularly dependent on the government for the funds needed to satisfy credit demand. With this situation, the financing of corporate firms came primarily from foreign loans, equity contributions and net lending from the national government, which took up an increasing share of national government outlays. The last category of funding was primarily extended through the discount window of the Central Bank, the Central Bank of the Philippines (CBP), which also served to restrict access to those sectors and projects favoured by the government (Okuda, 1990). As time passed, the amount of specialized target lending

government then undertook policies of exchange and import controls and protection to encourage import-substituting industries (Sicat, 1985).

programs increased and dominated the activity of the commercial banks. Even private banks were strongly influenced by government economic plans and industrial policy as much of this lending was seen to carry an implicit guarantee. Additionally, many banks originated as procurement divisions for local *chaebol*-like business groups, providing a further supply of credit to the corporate elite bodies.

The banks were also subject to credit allocation legislation, such as the 'agriara' law which required banks to allocate at least 25 per cent of their loan portfolios to agricultural projects and the beneficiaries of agrarian reform (Tolentino, 1989). Commercial banks were required to allocate at least 25 per cent of deposits generated in a given geographical region to loans in the same region. The effect of such legislation was to increase the risks in the financial system by forcing bankers to finance projects normally rejected by the banking system (Tolentino, 1989). To compensate for such risks, bankers would often only lend to those firms with enough political influence or physical collateral.

Foreign borrowing was also allocated on the basis of government policy as the Philippine private sector had difficulty in raising capital abroad directly. The extensive foreign borrowing which took place relied on the intervention of government financial institutions to extend an official loan guarantee. Again, the only firms with access to such guarantees were those favoured by development objectives or those with political connections (Okuda, 1990). As only particular firms were able to get subsidized foreign exchange and import licences, those who did borrowed heavily. The industrial structure which was created was fed largely on imported raw materials and became increasingly dependent on continued access to subsidized credit and foreign exchange (Sicat, 1985).

Thus during the 1970s, financial policy was completely subordinate to the regime in place. The credit demands of firms with access to subsidized official market credit determined the quantity and allocation of the money supply. The large-scale corruption involved meant that although the necessary creation of money occurred to create incomes, it was not fostering the development of productive capacity or output. The expectations of the continued receipt of patronage served to create a financial climate and industrial structure which was weak, had over-extended itself, and was not creating the necessary revenue to finance the existing structure of debt (Tolentino, 1989).

As the extensive government intervention in the financial system began showing these strains by the late 1970s, most of the investments began performing poorly. The large inefficiency and the monetary disequilibrium associated with CBP accommodation stimulated capital flight. Such capital flight had become a virulent tide by the early 1980s and foreign debt problems reared their oppressive head. The problems reached a zenith with the adverse foreign shocks of the early 1980s. The weak and gluttonous industrial sector was ill prepared to deal with the triple shocks of higher oil prices, higher world interest rates and the world-wide recession. As the terms of trade deteriorated and export earnings fell, firms found they had to face both a cost and revenue shock. The large net reduction in firms' current income was reflected in a growing inability of firms to meet existing payment obligations. The squeeze in foreign borrowing which occurred simultaneously then led to a domestic financial crisis. During this crisis, a series of major companies failed and had to be bailed out by the government at great expense. The inability of the Philippines to translate investment into true productive capacity became a binding constraint on its ability to service its more expensive debt obligations. In October 1983, the Philippines became the first and only Asian country to declare a debt moratorium, and access to foreign capital markets for the country effectively dried up (Blejer and Guerrero, 1988).

Financial Liberalization: Elements of Reform

With the onset of their debt moratorium, the foreign currency-starved Philippines turned to the IMF/World Bank for new borrowing. The ensuing financial rescue program was made dependent on the standard conditionality, which included a package of financial reforms aimed at liberalizing the financial system. The reform package which was initiated in January 1983, aimed at a gradual abolition of legal ceilings on interest rates (Tolentino, 1989). The government made moves to remove interest-rate ceilings on savings, fixed-term savings, deposit substitutes and loans with maturities of more than 730 days. Although some specific ceilings remained on preferential credit programs, interest rates became more widely market based (Okuda, 1990). In 1985, the CBP aligned the rate of discounting on preferential loans to the market rate, thereby eliminating one of the last bastions of highly subsidized credit.

The package also sought to reduce specialization amongst the types of banking institutions. This element of reform complemented the amendment to the banking laws of 1980 which permitted the adoption of universal banking laws. The legislation allowed banks to move into near banking activities, such as those carried out by investment houses and finance companies. Nine commercial banks initially opted to extend their activities and became universal banks, although difficulties led to one bank abandoning its universal status (Cho and Khatkhate, 1989). To foster growth in the securities market, financial institutions were encouraged to hold stock and conduct underwriting and trading activities (Okuda, 1990).

At this time, the Philippines was generally seen to be vastly over banked with a preponderance of very small banks. The smaller commercial banks, for instance, were too small to achieve economies of scale and could manage to secure only about 5 per cent of the assets of their top-ranked competitors. New legislation was enacted to rationalize the banking system and encourage consolidation. The government raised the minimum capital requirements by requiring capital adequacy to be 10 per cent of the capital-to-risk asset ratio for banks capitalized at less than P500m (Cho and Khatkhate, 1989). The CBP also approved 100 per cent investment by commercial banks in regional savings and agriculture banks, and introduced a system whereby regulations were eased in proportion to the scale of business. Despite this movement towards consolidation, mergers rarely took place and the number of commercial banks declined from 30 in 1980 to 29 in 1988 (Okuda, 1989).

Although they were not abandoned, the reforms made moves towards the closure of allocative, low interest rediscounting and seed-funding windows. Although the CBP sought to eliminate a large majority of the categories eligible for loan rediscount, access to the rediscount window was widened for non-bank financial intermediaries. The rationale of this policy move was to encourage the supply of long-term capital. In conjunction, ceilings on commercial bank long-term lending and securities investment were removed.

Impact of Financial Liberalization

The first round of financial liberalization can only be judged in the context of the economy-wide setting of the Philippines. The liberalization was an aspect of a general IMF-sponsored stabilization package which included a large devaluation of the peso in 1983. The devaluation was not combined initially with monetary contraction and the resulting accommodation of the price shock created an escalation in domestic inflation from 19 per cent in 1983 to 50 per cent in 1984 (Figure 7.16). To counter this inflation, an aggressive contractionary monetary policy was followed in conjunction with a second subsequent devaluation of 28 per cent in June 1984 (Blejer and Guerrero, 1988). The CBP began selling high-yield financial instruments which pushed nominal interest rates on these bills from 14-15 per cent up to 39-44 per cent. The portfolio reallocation of savers caused by the very high rates on these instruments led to a full-scale run on the banking system. Many private banks suffered liquidity shortages as depositors withdrew time deposits and converted their savings into high-yield risk-free CBP bills.

With banks competing for liquidity, commercial bank deposit rates shot up after 1984, leading to a squeeze on their profitability (Cho and Khatkhate, 1989).

The highly-leveraged corporate borrowing sector soon became enmeshed in financial difficulties and was forced into a situation of borrowing to meet its debt obligations. The higher debt burdens had the consequence of increasing leveraging, as firms doubly-increased costs through undertaking distress borrowing at high rates of interest. The ratio of total liabilities to total assets for the top 1000 corporations rose from 78 per cent in 1979 to 84 per cent in 1985, equivalent to changes in their debt-equity ratios of 315 per cent to 412 per cent respectively (Cho and Khatkhate, 1989). As additional credit to the private sector dried up due to the government's contractionary measures, firms in severe payment difficulties were forced to default on their loan commitments or undertake a divestiture of capital assets. The latter action often contributed to insolvency and bankruptcy by decreasing their ability to generate income thereby reducing the repayment ability of the firms.

As growing numbers of firms defaulted on their loan commitments, banks found their portfolios deteriorating. Non-performing assets and arrearage rates had quickly increased to 30-90 per cent of total assets (Cho and Khatkhate, 1989). The CBP had to intervene in its role of lender of last resort to bail out several of the banks. The result of this instability was that in the period 1980-86, the banking system experienced a contraction of real assets of some 44 per cent, and credit to the private sector contracted by 54 per cent (Figure 7.17).

In 1986, the stresses exposed in the financial system came to a head with the *de facto* insolvencies of the state-owned Philippine National Bank the largest commercial bank, and the Development Bank of the Philippines. Fearing that a general financial collapse would occur if either failed, the CBP aided the government in rehabilitating these banks. A transfer of non-performing assets amounting to 80 and 90 per cent of total assets respectively, to the government-owned asset privatization trust, was arranged. The government was also instrumental in installing new management teams in these banks (Polvorosa, 1988). For smaller and rural banks in difficulty which were not of a sufficient size to threaten the stability of the financial system, the CBP often refused to come to their rescue in a similar manner. Thus, during the period 1980-87, three commercial banks, 147 rural banks and 32 thrift institutions were allowed to fail completely (Cho and Khatkhate, 1989). The plight of banks was especially bleak as the government was responsible for contributing the majority of their liquidity and often took an effective role in running almost all aspects of bank operations and decision making. Changes in government policy towards these banks, then, had a significant impact on their ability to continue operations. The large reliance of banks on the CBP meant that the latter could substantially affect the financial system and the ultimate flow of credit.

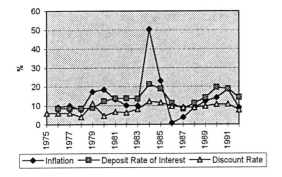

Figure 7.16 The Philippines - inflation and interest rates

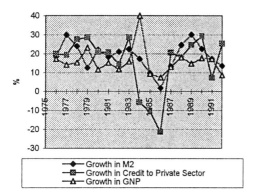

Figure 7.17 The Philippines - growth in M2, credit to the private sector, GNP

Finally recognizing the funding and financial problems these banks were in, and its own moral responsibility, the CBP launched a rehabilitation program in April 1987 to strengthen the rural banking system and place it in a more viable position (Polvorosa, 1988). The program included a capital build-up, a debt-conversion scheme, and a plan of payment for rural banks experiencing financial difficulties. The government was able to undertake the program as monetary policy in 1987 was relaxed in the face of reduced inflationary pressure. The slightly more relaxed monetary stance allowed a greater availability of credit to the private sector and contributed to a renewal of growth in economic activity.

Despite the attempted liberalization, the share of policy-directed lending in total loans increased during this period. Formal government intervention remained large in areas such as agricultural finance. Official economic plans and industrial policy continued to have a strong signalling effect on private lending decisions. The reason for this continued influence was the important role rediscount financing from the CBP played as capital for Philippine private banks. The reliance on rediscounting, as a source of liquidity, combined with informational deficiencies and unsound management practices, meant policy retained its overbearing allocative role. The importance of the rediscount rate was only slightly reduced in 1987, as the liquidity position of financial institutions was enhanced with the relaxation of monetary policy. The total outstanding credits of the CBP rediscount window increased by only P0.1 billion to reach the level of P7.7 billion at the end of 1987, equivalent to 5.12 per cent of total liabilities of the financial system (Polvorosa, 1988). Thus, the financial reform which was implemented did not succeed in changing the fundamental role of the government in determining the allocation of credit. By increasing the size of the formal financial system, the relative importance of the government's allocative function increased and other policy-directed financing was largely left untouched.

The problems in the financial system mirrored the problems of the economy, which stagnated against the background of political turmoil during 1984-87. Reflecting the uncertainty of the macroeconomic environment, the maturity of capital shortened and policy makers found it exceedingly hard to build interest-rate structures with the relevant incentives to increase long-term lending (Okuda, 1990). Rather, financial institutions posted substantial excess reserves (21 per cent between 1987 and 1990) on most deposits.[33]

1985-1992: Recent Developments and Subsequent Measures of Reform

By mid-1989, the CBP was still concerned about the number of banks in the economy and tabled a series of incentives aimed at encouraging a minimum size. Mergers and consolidation were encouraged as weak banks were seen

---

[33]The presence of high reserve requirements and substantial excess reserve holdings by banks has stymied the growth of the capital markets by constraining the long-term provision of finance.

as having higher operating costs, reducing the overall efficiency of the financial system. The presence of many weak banks with poorly performing loan portfolios also made the financial system prone to instability in the event of an economic downturn. As an opening salvo, the CBP announced its intention to revoke lender-of-last-resort facilities to weak banks, except in times of general financial emergency or if the given bank was facing problems of liquidity rather than solvency (Lowenstein, 1989a). Despite this suasion, few mergers have taken place and the Philippines remains over-banked.

Attempts at increasing competition in the Philippine banking system have met with little success as the banks have clubbed together in cartel-like fashion. The government, in its desire to reduce the number of institutions, may have encouraged the increasingly monopolistic behaviour of its commercial banks. The banks have benefited from this near cartel nature of decision making, pricing interest rates so as to enjoy a wide margin between loan and deposit rates. Ordinary prime rates in 1990 were around 25-26 per cent, with super-prime for blue-chip borrowers a few percentage points lower. This was despite the fact that bankers were only paying around 6 per cent for savings deposits (*The Banker*, Sept. 1990). The result of the exaggerated margins has been bumper years of profitability for Philippine banks throughout the early 1990s. Bankers still do not appear to face real competition as yet, being shielded by *de facto* barriers to entry and strict limits on the opening of new branches. The restrictions on foreign banks prohibiting them from universal banking and from opening up branch networks, which has hindered the competitive pressure such banks may exert, are beginning to be lifted. In May 1993, the CBP liberalized the procedures for foreign banks opening new branches in the hope that their entry will increase the efficiency in the financial system (*The Banker*, July 1993). It is also hoped that the adverse consequences of spread reduction which such competition will foster will be offset by an increase in the amount of banking transactions.

The lack of competitive pressure has allowed low interest rates to be paid to depositors and this has had a predictably adverse effect on savings mobilization. The ratio of $M2$ to GNP decreased between 1985 and 1989, which indicates a small supply of loanable funds. The shortage of funds has allowed bankers to charge high loan rates and these rates have done much to discourage investment. High interest rates persisted until 1991 with the implementation of an IMF stabilization plan, ensuring lending remained low, and adding to the stagnation of investment. Capital formation has been particularly ravaged, as the high rates of interest have made such investment seem relatively unattractive.

A pervasive problem for the financial system in the early 1990s has been the chronic shortage of foreign exchange, exacerbated by the continuation of large fiscal and balance of payments deficits. The foreign exchange shortage became acute with a sharp depreciation of the peso in late 1989, which further deteriorated the balance of payments situation and made debt-service more costly. The CBP was put under pressure by the government to set aside all available foreign exchange for oil and other essential imports (*The Banker*, Dec. 1990). The foreign exchange shortage reduced the ability of banks to engage in foreign exchange related fee-earning activities, as well as their ability to service corporate customers effectively.

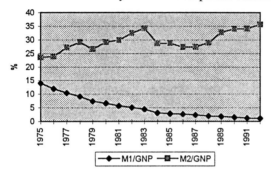

Figure 7.18 The Philippines - M1/GNP, M2/GNP ratios

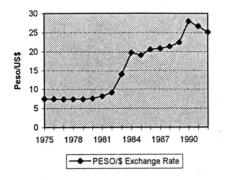

Figure 7.19: The Philippines - Peso/US$ exchange rate

The acuteness of the foreign exchange shortage was heightened by the continued negative impact that large foreign debt levels were having on the economy. By a combination of poor debt management and bad advice from international institutions, the Philippines suffered from current account external deficits with magnitudes reminiscent of the early 1980s. The country, by 1991, owed US$28 billion to foreign creditors despite the fact that more than US$1 billion of commercial debt was successfully swapped at half-price discount using a debt-equity swap facility. External debt service swallowed an average 8 per cent of GDP annually, leaving the economy worse off by 2 per cent per year on average (4 per cent in 1990) and reducing domestic per capita income by 4.5 per cent a year during 1986-90. Calls in the increasingly hostile legislature for another moratorium on debt service began ringing out. The IMF (Brady Plan) stepped in again and worked out a standard economic stabilization programme with Manila late in 1990, introducing the usual tight monetary and fiscal conditions.[34] Early in 1991, the IMF approved an 18-month stand-by facility of around SDR 205m, although a quarter of that was to be used solely for reducing the country's external debt (*The Banker*, May 1991). However, internal and external debt servicing still manage to swallow 40 per cent of the government budget and the fiscal deficit has topped 5 per cent (Figure 7.20).

Adding to the difficulties of the financial system has been the poor performance of the CBP. The troubled economy has placed the CBP in a position of not being able to implement effective monetary policy, due to losses averaging P18.8 bilion a year between 1986 and 1992. In response, a new Central Monetary Authority (CMA) has been set up to replace the CBP and started operations at the end of 1993 (*The Banker*, July 1993). The CMA started with a clean balance sheet and took over functions limited to monetary management and the supervision and regulation of the financial system. The primary objective was to maintain price stability and to improve regulation and supervision.

The future of financial liberalization is such that any change which comes will be partial and slow. Powerful interest groups such as the local banks and owners will make sure change will be limited and the enthusiasm of policy makers for big bangs is waning. The continued reliance of corporations on debt finance, and the remaining large debt levels, make any larger moves to liberalization unlikely. It is doubtful if banks have significantly improved operations and it appears that the fundamental weaknesses in the financial system have yet to be redressed.

---

[34]The Brady Plan worked out with the Philippines aimed at general foreign debt reduction. It included the rescheduling of existing debt, and debt-equity swap facilities.

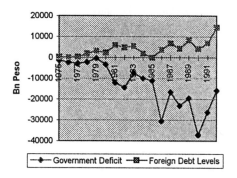

Figure 7.20: The Philippines - government deficit and foreign borrowing

POLICY IMPLICATIONS

The history of these countries' experiences in developing their financial systems has been full of episodes with varying degrees of enthusiasm for liberalization. What is immediately striking is the broad similarity of policies pursued before, during and after liberalization. Through all these phases, the respective governments have played decisive and visible roles in determining the content and complexion of financial policy. A few striking conclusions emerge.

1. **The policy regime in place prior to liberalization created an institutional structure which determined the adjustment consequent upon financial policy changes. In all these countries, the direction and quantity of credit responded to the dictates of development policy objectives.**

In Indonesia, Korea, and the Philippines, the direction and price of credit was determined by the government to the benefit of large firms in the industrial and export sectors. The elastic supply of subsidized credit to these priority industries served to create an industrial base characterized by large firms with an excessive debt reliance and high leveraging. As the respective Central Banks relied on guidance through the discount window to achieve the policy goals, the ensuing accommodation of credit demand made monetary control more difficult. The Central Banks were then forced to rely on direct quantitative controls on non-priority lending to rein in liquidity. The direct quantitative controls enforced a large degree of credit rationing by constraining banks' lending ability. The tools of such monetary policy included the extensive use of reserve ratios, credit ceilings and selective rediscount. The resulting policy regime was one of 'financial repression', which can be viewed as the logical response of monetary policy subservient to the credit demands engendered by development policy. As credit responded endogenously to the dictates of development policy, the monetary authorities had to resort to repression.

In Korea, firms which benefited were in the manufacturing industry and exports and led to the formation of *chaebol* and *chaebol*-like corporate bodies. In Indonesia and the Philippines, the links to the government were more direct and led to industrial structures dominated by state and quasi-state-owned enterprises. The only exception was Malaysia which had a development policy determined to widen economic opportunity for a relatively disadvantaged group of economic agents. As a result, credit policy and accommodation was limited to relatively small-scale borrowing which did not unduly threaten monetary and price stability. Thus, Malaysia benefited from having less pre-reform repression and did not suffer from having a corporate sector burdened by imprudent levels of debt. Nevertheless, the institutional structure in each country which was created by past policy incentives served to determine the nature of the responses to financial liberalization.

2. **In terms of liberalization, the background against which reforms were undertaken was quite similar across countries, being generally adverse.**

Malaysia benefited from the most fortuitous circumstances for reform, beginning liberalization before the macroeconomic imbalances of the 1980s became apparent. For the remainder of the countries, the adverse macroeconomic shocks of deteriorating terms of trade, increased world interest rates, and a world-wide recession became increasingly debilitating. Achieving macroeconomic stability grew increasingly elusive and the developments made some package of reforms inevitable.

3. **When reforms did come, the elements of reform displayed broad continuities across countries.**

Table 7.1 outlines the various policy elements of each country's reforms.

Table 7.1: Elements of reform

Instrument of reform:	Country:
Domestic	
Removal of interest-rate ceilings	Indonesia (1983, 1988)
	Korea (1981, 1989)
	Malaysia (1978)
	Philippines (1983)
Removal of credit ceilings	Indonesia (1983, 1988)
	Korea (1981, 1989)
	Philippines (1983)
Rationalization or removal of access of priority loans to rediscount facilities	Indonesia (1983, 1988)
	Korea (1981, 1989)
	Philippines (1983)
Introduction of new financial instrments	Indonesia (1983, 1985)
	Korea (1984)
	Malaysia (1984-85)
	Philippines (1982)
Privatization of commercial banks / change in structure of ownership	Korea (1981)
	Philippines (1983, 1989)
International	
Devaluation	Korea (1980)
	Philippines (1983, 1984)
	Indonesia (1985)
Removal of credit controls	Indonesia (1988)
	Korea (1993)

More often than not, domestic financial reforms were combined with international elements of adjustment - exchange-rate depreciations in particular.

4. **The short-run costs to liberalization were very high as liberalization entered the economy as a severe adverse shock. Such high costs encouraged large slippage from the reforms.**

5. **Interest rate structures, when freed, showed either a great deal of short-run volatility or a great deal of long-run insensitivity to policy action.**

Perhaps more interesting than the similarity of tools is the broad congruence of results in the short run. The similarity of results suggests that when liberalization did come, it was implemented at a particularly high cost and the majority of elements, particularly interest-rate liberalization, could not be sustained due to these costs. The high cost of liberalization was borne mainly in terms of large increases in non-performing financial assets (loans). In the post-liberalization atmosphere, interest rates rose due both to high world interest rates and the fact that liberalization was accompanied by tight monetary and fiscal policy (necessitated by the need for stabilization). Additionally, ensuing volatile behaviour of interest rates meant that funding costs to such highly leveraged firms was considerable. With firms payment obligations far exceeding expected receipts, they borrowed increasing amounts to cover required payments. Since these increments in spending caused a further increase in outstanding debt, firms found themselves in a bind of increasing costs (a Ponzi-game).

The response of banks during this time was to be increasingly drawn into a vortex of moral hazard. The moral hazard had two complementary elements. First, since banks were lending under the auspices of development policy, many expected the government to fulfil its 'moral' obligation of guaranteeing their solvency through the provision of lender-of-last-resort facilities. Second, as many banks were highly exposed to the firms experiencing payment problems, it was in their interests to continually prop up these firms. As a result, the financial positions of firms and banks deteriorated dramatically in the immediate post-reform atmosphere.

As large parts of the industrial and financial sectors of these countries came under increasing pressure to survive, the governments and Central Banks had two options: either continue with the reforms and risk the collapse of the financial system and widespread industrial bankruptcy, or reverse the elements of the reform causing the most difficulties - interest rate and discount policy reform. In general, the latter option was chosen as very few Central Banks were willing to risk the stability of the financial system. Rather, Central Banks retreated from interest and discount policy liberalization, with these two elements of policy showing the greatest slippage.

These short-run responses were particularly acute in Indonesia, Korea and the Philippines which had all attempted 'big bang' packages of liberalization and were then forced to repeal the reforms in the face of growing instability. In these three countries, the post-liberalization financial system was characterized by an increased level of government intervention. Governments were forced to restructure industrial firms, banks and debt liabilities by writing off exhaustive chunks of outstanding debt. Governments achieved this by re-entering the financial systems to absorb the credit risks prevalent in the economies. The resulting increase in government participation could be said to be diametrically opposed to the spirit of liberalization. The inherent unsustainability of reforms in the short run had thereby the perverse outcome of increasing the level of repression in the economy.

The country which did not suffer pervasive financial crisis in the immediate aftermath of liberalization was Malaysia. Malaysia, which had an already relatively liberalized financial policy, had a very modest initial reaction to liberalization. Industrial debt levels were not excessive and the liberalization did not coincide with a period of stabilization entailing sharp reductions in demand and tight liquidity. Hence, interest rates did not increse rapidly and firms were not placed into a debt-cost cycle which would call the stability of the financial system into question. However, these free interest rates showed short-run stability, they also demonstrated long-run inflexibility.

The long-run inflexibility of interest rates in Malaysia demonstrated how governments lacked the ability to influence interest rates by indirect measures. In not being able to influence interest rates, even after changing the liquidity characteristics of the economy, interest rates were allowed to rise to levels in excess of what would normally have been prudent. As banks were displaying cartel-like behaviour, the Malaysian government could not engineer a reduction in interest rates when it desired. The time lag to convince banks to lower their rates worsened an already growing financial crisis in 1985.

6. **Banks, when freed, often lacked the ability to properly assess risks and understand exposure. Thus, the quality of portfolios did not improve in the post-liberalization period.**

The genesis of the Malaysian financial crisis is also interesting in showing the failure of relatively free banks to improve the quality of loan portfolios. In general, banks in these countries lacked the ability to assess risk and understand the extent of exposure. As a result, bank credit increasingly fuelled a boom on the property market and Kuala Lumpur stock exchange. The rapid overheating of the economy led to an increase in the financial vulnerability of many Malay firms which participated in the boom. Similar developments occurred in Indonesia in 1988 when it underwent its second bang at reform. The increase in risk preference in post-liberalized financial institutions, as funding went into Jakarta's speculative markets, increased the likelihood of asset failure. Once the macroeconomic situation turned adverse and interest rates rose, the firms which had extended themselves on debt to pursue speculative activity ran into problems and were besieged by payment difficulties. Ponzi-games were played out in both countries and led to a full-scale financial crisis in Malaysia (1985-86) and Indonesia (1991-92). Again, authorities in Indonesia and Malaysia retreated from the reforms and restructured the debt claims in the economy by undergoing some form of pervasive action. In both countries, the experiences with liberalization placed a premium on increasing the regulation and supervision of the financial system.

7. Regulation and supervision of financial markets is now seen as being as important, if not more so, than liberalization.

As these countries prepare to meet the remainder of the 1990s, it would appear that only a few fundamental changes have been wrought in their financial systems. Indonesia, which has been the most reform minded of all the countries, is still reeling from its last attempt which went too far, too fast. The post-reform blues have led them to move into a period of re-regulation and increased supervision. Korea is acknowledged to still have a very unsophisticated banking system in comparison with its industrial base. Its banks are still highly protected, favoured, and operate with oligopolistic control. Deposit rates are still controlled by the BOK and the pervasive capital controls are only now being reduced.

Malaysia's bankers are beginning to recover from the spate of bad debts which plagued their portfolios in the late 1980s. Its banking sector is modest and very conservative, and is now complaining of being over-regulated and over-supervised with very little freedom of action. Malaysian policy makers are showing little enthusiasm for letting their bankers have the greater freedom they want. The Philippines still recognizes the need for reform of a system which retains some features of repression. The policy makers have ruled out any big bangs, preferring a slow, gradual, advancement of policies. The trials and tribulations of past liberalization attempts have instilled in them a patience to which maintaining regulation and supervision is integral. No enthusiasm for big bangs exists and the inert forces of oligopoly will be a constraining force against change.

Questions and tasks for change remain ahead for all of these countries' financial systems. The tepid results of liberalization, especially when contrasted with these countries' strong overall performance, lead to questions regarding the rationale of liberalization. If liberalization has been so haltingly applied in these relatively successful developing countries, what chance will it have in less dynamic economic circumstances? Also, as some of these countries have been very successful without a liberalized financial regime, is strict liberalization really necessary?

The latter point is simply a recognition that credit is important and that it plays a central role in developing economies - a role too important to leave entirely to either the market or the government. For financial policy to be successful, both elements must be present, with the market tempering the government's intervention and vice versa. Since the behaviour of financial markets in developing countries, even after periods of reform, is far from that of an allocative ideal, to allow these markets such freedom would seem misguided. The weaknesses imply that some degree of government intervention is necessary and desirable.

Theoretical Implication of the Case Studies

The implication that these case studies hold for economic theory is that for a model (theoretical or empirical) to assess accurately the dynamic impact of changes in monetary policy, the full transmission mechanism must be included. In all of these economies, the credit demands of the economy and the ability of the banking sector to satisfy that demand have been the dominant features of the adjustment process. Thus, a proper specification of the full transmission mechanism must encompass the behaviour of the banking system and the determinants of credit demand. Both of these features are crucial in determining how the economy will react to a given policy change.

The cases graphically illustrate how dominant a presence the government and the Central Bank have in the financial system. This dominant presence comes from being the primary source of funds on the margin for the commercial banks, and it coloured the interaction between the actors in the financial system prior to reform. This position, created by the policies of repression, gave the various Central Banks great leverage in altering the flow of credit in these countries. As a wide-scale change in policy such as liberalization had such a disruptive impact on credit flow, the bulk of the adjustment was felt by those agents who were the recipients of credit supply. As illustrated by the cases, the recipients of credit were those firms with access to credit under repression. The determinants of these firms' credit demands were the price of inputs (particularly imports), desired firm investment, the level of financial repression (or the scope of the interest-rate subsidy), and the level of outstanding debt repayments. Changes in any of these elements were enough to stimulate changes in credit demand, thereby sparking off an adjustment period. The financial liberalization inevitably increased the demand for credit more than it reduced it, by causing large increases in outstanding debt repayments. Thus, the adjustment costs of liberalization came about because of a reduction in credit supply combined with increasing credit demand. The necessary outcome was a debt-deflation and a consequential reduction in investment spending by firms.

The general absence of these features from most models of financial liberalization is why such models do very poorly at predicting the outcomes of most liberalizations. When the determinants of credit demand and the ability of the banks to create credit are explicitly modelled, money will then be endogenously determined by that model. The theoretical model will, therefore, be much richer and able to capture fully the dynamic response of the system to a financial liberalization.

8. Conclusions and Policy Directions

CONCLUSIONS OF THE TEXT

The book has dealt with the theoretical and empirical aspects regarding financial liberalization and the use of monetary policy in developing countries. The main premises which have been presented are:

1. Under a regime of financial repression, government intervention through the Central Banks plays a key role in the creation and allocation of credit. The Central Bank acts as a net supplier of wealth to the financial system. As a result, the Central Bank has a large potential to disrupt the flow of credit in a developing country.
2. The interaction of development policy and monetary policy has created financial sectors which, prior to reform, are dominated by firms with very large outstanding debt loads. Commercial banks possess loan portfolios over-exposed to these large borrowers.
3. Monetary policy works by altering the flow of credit money. The key adjustments to changes in monetary policy occur in the 'real' economy amongst firms which find their access to credit altered. An abrupt change in the conditions under which credit is supplied - either the price or quantity - will therefore have potentially severe effects for both productive and financial institutions.
4. A financial liberalization is an abrupt change in the conditions under which credit is supplied.

Conclusion One

With initial conditions in the economy conforming to those created by a prolonged period of financial repression, financial liberalization is not sustainable as a practical policy option. In these circumstances, the large costs associated with a failed attempt at liberalization are higher than those associated with the continuation of financially repressive policies.

Conclusion Two

Theoretically and empirically, money should be modelled as an endogenous variable, responding, though not passively or completely, to changes in nominal income. The determinants of credit demand must be specified, as well as the institutional features which determine the ability of commercial banks to create credit and satisfy that demand. Any model missing these features will not be able to capture the true impact of a policy shock on the economy. The bulk of the liberalization literature has missed these central elements of the monetary policy transmission mechanism.

5. A fifth premise presented is that in a paradigm of development, the weaknesses and flaws inherent in markets and the inability of markets to always produce the socially desirable outcome, leave scope available for constructive government intervention.

Conclusion Three

Financial liberalization is not a desirable policy program in a paradigm of development. Monetary policy should be subjugated quite rightly to the needs of development policy. However, any intervention must seek to redress specific market failings and encourage the successful realization of private enterprise if that intervention is to be successful.

POLICY DIRECTIONS

The questions that beg to be asked following the above conclusions are then: If a liberalization policy is undesirable, down what policy road should developing countries travel? What policy options remain open to these countries? The remainder of this chapter will use the preceding ideas in a prescriptive role to view policy directions. The central theme of this section is that developing countries need an optimal mix of markets and government intervention. Successful policy will be aimed at redressing market failure and not at replacing markets with obstructive government control. The government will then be taking the role of a market 'fixer' rather than that of a surrogate market. Policy makers will focus on fostering entrepreneurial incentives, as such incentives will be the key to development.

Finally, it will be presupposed that the government has already formulated a coherent development strategy. Such concerns are beyond the scope of this book. Suffice it to say that the goal for the government is not to formulate a rigid, over-bureaucratic, centralized plan. Rather, it needs a coherent view of the direction in which the economy should be going, and then move to ensure that the tool of finance is used to stimulate an entrepreneurial climate along those lines whilst discouraging over bureaucratization of the financing of the development process. Any controls that are in place will need to be simple and easily administered. Otherwise, the 'entrepreneurial will' will be drowned in a sea of government bureaucracy and obstruction. Government should have a vision and finance will be the lubricant which will help private enterprises achieve those goals.

Interest Rate Policy

At the heart of the financial liberalization debate is the question of whether interest rates should be 'free', that is market determined, or should they be under direct control of the government? The short answer would be neither. What is required is a 'managed' interest rate, that is one which is controlled by the government but tempered by the market. Under such a regime, the government would directly control interest rates, but do so in a way that responds to the liquidity conditions of the financial markets. Such a managed regime would give the government the ability to directly influence the interest rate during those stages of development when it has difficulty altering liquidity through indirect control measures. Until financial markets develop sufficiently to allow open market operations to work efficiently, the limited scope for the government to pursue desired policy changes must suggest that the managed rate system would be preferable.

In general, counter-cyclical interest-rate policy should be pursued so that the economy does not experience broad swings in the business climate. This is not to suggest a 'fine-tuning' mechanism, but rather a recognition that changes in interest rates should be determined by conditions in the market. If the market is highly liquid, it would be expected that interest rates would increase to soak up the excess. The focus on managing the interest rate would revolve around keeping the interest rate positive in real terms. The monetary authority could be set a statutory target to keep the real interest rate on deposits within some broad band (for example 2-8 per cent). Otherwise, disincentives to efficiency will be dominant and the economy will suffer from disintermediation. The real interest rate on loans should, however, still be used to reflect government development priorities. By setting positive but lower rates on favoured sectors, the government can deflect entrepreneurial enthusiasm into those pursuits deemed most responsible for growth and development. As long as interest rates remain positive, credit will not carry an implicit subsidy and firms' over-reliance on credit will not be encouraged. The categories of discriminatory interest rates, however, should be simplified with broad bands of eligibility set up to minimize bureaucratic obtuseness (for example, one preferential rate for export credit).

A benefit of such a managed interest-rate regime, in the short run, is that the government would be able to avoid the large cost-shocks associated with a fully fledged financial liberalization. If real interest rates are significantly negative, a gradual upward adjustment of the rates would be needed. The most significant factor here, however, will be the price level. Once the inflation rate is brought under control, the ability to maintain a positive interest rate in a managed regime will be much easier.

Beyond the period of adjustment, a further gain to a managed regime is that in retaining control of the interest rate, albeit in a much more dynamic and active manner, the authority can guard against adverse developments in the interest-rate structure caused by either excessive competition or excessive concentration in the financial markets. Excessive competition amongst banks, in a purely liberalized regime, can result in competitive institutions bidding for deposits when the market is short of liquidity. If loan rates are pushed up unduly in a scramble for liquidity, the precariousness of the financial system will be increased. As a result, it is likely that if deposit rates in a developing country are to be liberalized, they will by necessity be the last interest rates freed from direct control. If deposit rates are free in a fragile, but competitive, banking environment, problems ensuing from the competition for funds can be large.

However, if the banking market is over-concentrated with market power in the hands of a few dominant institutions, the scope for cartelized pricing of interest rates may allow banking spreads to grow too large. Managing both deposit and loan interest rates in tandem would allow the government to ensure spreads remained at prudent levels, and that the profitability of the banking sector is not at the expense of a beleaguered productive sector.

Monetary Policy

Price stability is an essential goal for competitiveness, business confidence, reduced uncertainty and the maintenance of positive interest rates. Also essential are the government's development goals for social progress and the enrichment of the country. The trick for the developing country is, then, to maintain price control while ensuring that credit is created to support the development process. If price stability is not maintained, cost-push effects occurring through wage indexation mechanisms will be likely to take over and erode any growth in national income. It is also likely with policies encouraging inflation that the IMF will enter the policy-making process, and most developing countries dislike such outside interference in the management of domestic economic affairs. However, if the development policy is decimated in a quest for the golden chalice of stable prices, growth will grind to a halt and the fall in investment spending will lead to a cumulative fall in development ability. The policy maker is, then, in search of the optimal policy trade-off.

It would seem that the basic requirement for price stability in a developing country is fiscal responsibility. The use of inflation as a means of financing budget deficits in the past has been the main cause of monetary disequilibrium in developing countries. It is, therefore, unlikely that the statutory discounting of large government deficits will be in the best interest of the economy. The large increases in aggregate demand emanating from such a policy will almost always be reflected in accelerating price levels. Policy makers in developing countries must realize that it was such fiscal excesses, requiring monetary incontinence, which initiated the purges of the liberalizers in the first place.

What else should the government do then to supplement their new found fiscal responsibility? In an ideal world a monetary authority would accommodate the needs of trade but would not accommodate increases in the price level. A policy structure approximating this ideal would start with the recognition that the monetary authority should not target any specific monetary aggregates. Such aggregates tend to be very elusive and the key nexus in developing countries is not on the bank liability side. Rather, it is on the banks' asset or credit side. Thus, the focus of the government's monetary targeting should be in ensuring only the gradual expansion of credit. By targeting credit, the monetary authority can seek to reduce, or encourage, investment expenditure when it deems most prudent.

A central proposal to such credit targeting would then be to switch reserve ratios from the liability side to the asset side. Thus, instead of being forced to hold reserves against deposits, banks would then be forced to hold reserves against loans. In pushing up such reserve requirements, the Central Bank could effectively alter (reduce) the flow of credit. Thus, the Central Bank will be able to manipulate credit more directly, without needing to resort to the maintenance of ceilings.

Further, discriminatory rates could encourage lending in certain areas such as investment and export trade. At the same time, the monetary authority could discourage lending to less desirable activities such as consumer spending, or the speculative purchase of goods (for example, property and stocks), by making the reserve requirements on such lending prohibitively high. Thus, the use of discriminatory required reserves on bank assets can ensure that credit will be issued to support a development plan.

Monetary Policy: the Discount Window

In conjunction with this, the government will need to maintain access to the discount window but should rationalize eligibility. Importantly, the government should replace positive lists specifying which specific areas are eligible for rediscount, with negative lists specifying which sectors are ineligible for rediscount. A positive list is far too confining and encourages rent-seeking by those fortunate enough to be on the list. Such listed firms also have an incentive to discourage other sectors from being admitted to discount facilities, which serves to reduce the dynamism of the economy. A negative list, however, allows newer and dynamic areas undergoing unforseen expansion, to be eligible for rediscount. As such, the growth of new sectors will not be discouraged by a lack of access to official credit markets, provided the new growth sectors fall broadly within the government's policy goals. The negative lists also gives banks more autonomy in deciding the allocation of credit. Of course, this autonomy will be bounded by the general development orientation of the economy, but banks will still need to assess creditworthiness and will make the final credit allocation decision amongst a broader selection of potential candidates. It is essential, however, that discount and reserve policy be used together to discourage lending either for personal consumption or for speculative purposes.[1] If this is accomplished, the combined use of these tools can be used to retain monetary (price) stability and at the same time foster their development goals. To minimize bureaucratic overhead, broad categories of eligibility should be defined, such as export credit or credit for those supplying inputs to export industries. The key to all this is that the government should be visible and guiding, not overbearing and stifling.

---

[1]The argument is that banks must be stopped from fuelling consumption, rather than an argument for the direct encouragement of savings. The reason is that the increase in aggregate demand from a large increase in investment spending will be quite large. The multiplied effects on consumption imply that any other increase in consumption, especially one due to bank credit, will be largely inflationary.

Monetary Policy: Open Market Operations

The monetary authority should also begin the use of open market operations with the use of competitive, rather than captive, auctions. Open market operations are desirable as they influence the liquidity positions of banks, making the achievement of monetary policy goals more likely. Also, the use of open market operations fosters the development of primary and secondary bond markets, which pave the way for a future transition to more indirect methods of monetary control. Such a transition will probably be desirable in the indefinite future, once the economy has developed sufficiently to make direct methods impractical.

Issues in Liberalization: Debt-Equity Ratios

The biggest limit to monetary policy change are the large debt-equity ratios, which pose a constant threat to macroeconomic stability. Governments will want to wean those highly-leveraged concerns off their over-reliance on credit. The easiest way to accomplish this is to first reduce the access of these firms to credit by limiting their eligibility to the discount window and by increasing the reserve requirements on that lending. Such policy measures will force firms to become more imaginative in fund raising. At the same time, the outstanding debts of firms to commercial banks will begin to be reduced, and the firms will become more accustomed to doing without implicit credit subsidies. Once this initial adjustment is under way, interest rates on past loans can be slowly adjusted upwards in real terms. Again, the rate of interest should never rise so high as to discourage investment or destroy the incentive of entrepreneurs. Once debt-equity ratios are adjusted downwards, freedom for the authority to undertake changes in monetary policy will be enhanced.

Alternatively, the Central Bank may wish to engineer a limited liberalization in which interest rates are raised to positive levels. However, to maintain the stability of the financial markets during the reform, the Central Bank can legislate that the new interest rates will not apply to outstanding debt. As outstanding debt will be repaid at the interest rate at which it was contracted, no severe cost shock will be present and no Ponzi-boom will be stimulated. New expectations formulated under the new policy regime will succeed in changing the borrowing behaviour of firms in the way desired by the policy makers, but the adjustment costs will be largely reduced.

Issues in Liberalization: Regulation and Supervision

The monitoring function of the Central Bank will be very important to ensure that credit risks do not become over-concentrated in a particular activity. Given the susceptibility of these economies to shocks, imprudent risk taking by financial intermediaries will leave the economy susceptible to too many financial problems. The regulators must make sure banks are not taking too many risks resulting in the over-exposure of their portfolios. Any large over-exposure leaves the banks, and the financial system, vulnerable to adverse shocks affecting these pursuits. Prudential regulation and supervision will be more important than liberalization in ensuring the unproblematic functioning of the financial system.

Issues in Liberalization: Competition

It is certain that the economy does not want to be over-banked with a plethora of small banks cluttering up the financial playing field. It would seem that competition is perhaps over-rated in this field as potential economies of scale, in areas such as maturity transformation and risk pooling, are best achieved by large, centrally placed institutions. Competition is also undesirable if it leads to the encouragement of risk taking or over-competition for funds. Either can increase the likelihood of bank failures, endangering the well being of the financial system through contagion effects. It is also much easier to monitor a small group of large banks, than a myriad of tiny institutions. However, there should be enough large institutions for cartelized behaviour to be unlikely. The easiest way to accomplish this is to set minimum capitalization requirements at high enough levels to ensure a minimum size for all banks.

In this regard, the monetary authority will probably wish to discourage the close competition of the different categories of financial institutions - finance houses, development banks and commercial banks. Restricting competition between categories of intermediaries makes it both easier to monitor each category and stops unequal competition between intermediaries with different regulatory status. Also, it will be easier to control the creation of credit by sectors if classes of institution are highly separable and liquidity does not flow between them rapidly.

The separation of activities amongst institutions is also likely to be desirable for other reasons in a process of development in particular, the creation of intermediaries designed to provide small savers/borrowers with access to banking and credit facilities. Such institutions could acquire the expertise required to profitably extend such credit, whilst reducing the official market rationing of those borrowers. Given the small returns on such lending, these institutions would benefit from a risk-sharing relationship with the government. However, the government's risk-sharing role should not be large enough to create a moral hazard which discourages prudent credit assessment. The government would then not need to force reluctant commercial banks to undertake lending for which they are ill suited.

Issues in Liberalization: Collateralized Contracts

The presence of collateralized contracts is still likely to be very important in that banks can manipulate and reduce risk behaviour of the entrepreneur. An even more advantageous policy, however, is to encourage and provide a very close working relationship between banks and industry. To do this, policy makers will want to tie in the long-term success of the financial institution with the long-term success of the firm. An element of such a policy is to encourage a framework of corporate control whereby the commercial banks play an active role advising firms on matters of finance, and ensuring that the firms do not engage in financial mismanagement. Such policies will discourage the control of corporations through the stock exchange, thereby undermining short-termism and allowing firms to function with much longer time horizons.

SUGGESTIONS FOR FUTURE RESEARCH

The policy recommendations have all sought to use intervention as a salve for market imperfections. The recommendations also try to embody the principle that a mix of markets and government intervention is the key to any successful development strategy. Future research in this area, on the mechanism for the co-ordination of government and industry, would be insightful. In particular, a rigorous theoretical approach to mixing markets and governments would provide the formal basis from which such policy application might arise. More specific to this thesis, estimation of a fully coherent macroeconomic model embodying the principle of post-Keynesian economics would be fruitful. Data limitations are always going to make such a task difficult.

Finally, it must be stressed that all future research, whether into monetary aspects or not, must seek to recognize and embody the institutional characteristics of developing countries. For too long, the developing world has suffered under policies suggested by theoretical paradigms divorced from the situation of development. If such failings can be rectified, economics and economic policy will be much more successful in their bid to push those countries along the path to prosperity and development.

Bibliography

Abbott, G. (1985), 'A Survey of Savings and Financial Development in Asian Developing Countries', *Savings and Development*, Vol.9(4), pp.395-421.

Abidin, A.Z. (1986), 'Financial Reform and the Role of Foreign Banks in Malaysia', in Cheng, H. (ed.), *Financial Policy and Reform in Pacific-Basin Countries,* New York: Lexington Books, pp.305-9.

Achan, (1986), 'Financial Reform in Indonesia', in Cheng, H.(ed.), *Financial Policy and Reform in Pacific-Basin Countries*, New York: Lexington Books, pp.221-23.

Ahmed, E. and Stern, N. (1989),'Taxation for Developing Countries', in Chenery, H. and Srinivasan, T. (eds.), *Handbook of Development Economics Vol. II*, New York: North-Holland, pp.1007-92.

Ahn, C. and Bing, W. (1985), 'The Choice of a Monetary Instrument in a Small Open Economy: The Case of Korea', *Journal of International Money and Finance*, Vol.4(4),pp.469-84.

Alesina, A. and Drazen, A. (1991), 'Why are Stabilizations Delayed?', *The American Economic Review*, Vol.81(5), pp.1170-87.

Alm, Bahl, and Murray. (1991),'Tax Base Erosion in Developing Countries', *Economic Development and Cultural Change*, Sept., pp.848-56.

Antiporda, T.D. (1986), 'Privatization in the Philippine Banking Sector', *The Philippine Economic Journal*, Vol.25(1&2), pp.7-16.

Arestis, P. (ed.)(1988), *Post-Keynesian Monetary Economics*, Aldershot: Edward Elgar.

Arestis, P. (1988), 'Post-Keynesian Theory of Money, Credit, and Finance', in Arestis, P. (ed.), *Post-Keynesian Monetary Economics*, Aldershot: Edward Elgar.

Arestis, P. and Driver, C. (1988), 'The Macrodynamics of the US and UK Economies Through Two Post-Keynesian Models', in Arestis, P.(ed.), *Post-Keynesian Monetary Economics*, Aldershot: Edward Elgar, pp.11-41.

Arida, P. and Taylor, L. (1989), 'Short-run Macroeconomics', in Chenery, H. and Srinivasan, T. (ed.), *Handbook of Development Economics Vol. II*, New York: North-Holland, pp.856-82.

Ariff, M. and Semudran, M. (1989), 'Malaysia', in Page (ed.), *Trade, Finance and Developing Countries*, London: Macmillan, pp.23-55.

Arize, A. (1989), 'An Econometric Investigation of Money Demand Behaviour in Five Asian Developing Countries', *International Economic Journal*, Vol.3(4), pp.79-93.

Arndt, H.W. (1988), '"Market Failure" and Underdevelopment', *World Development*, Vol.16(2), pp.219-29.

Arndt, H.W. (1987), 'The Financial System of Indonesia', *Savings and Development*, Vol.11(3), pp.305-315.

Arrieta, G.C. (1988), 'Interest Rates, Savings and Growth in LDCs: An Assessment of Recent Empirical Research', *World Development*, Vol.10(5), pp.589-605.

Atesoglu, A. and Tillman, J. (1980),'Money, Autonomous Expenditures, Income, and Causality in Korea', *Journal of Monetary Economics*, Vol.6, pp.527-34.

Bain, A.D. (1981), *The Economics of the Financial System*, Oxford: Martin Robertson.

Balino, T. and Sundararajan, V. (1986), 'Financial Reform in Indonesia: Causes, Consequences, and Prospects',in Cheng, H. (ed.), *Financial Policy and Reform in Pacific-Basin Countries*, New York: Lexington Books, pp.191-218.

Ball, L. (1991), 'The Genesis of Inflation and the Cost of Disinflation', *Journal of Money, Credit and Banking*, Aug., pp.439-51.

Bank Negara Malaysia (1989), *Money and Banking in Malaysia*, Bank Negara Malaysia.

The Banker Magazine: various issues.

Barro, R. (1989), 'The Neo-classical Approach to Fiscal Policy', *Modern Business Cycle Theory*, London: Basil Blackwell.

Bauer, P.T. (1984), *Reality and Rhetoric*, London: Weidenfeld Nicolson.

Bean, C.R. (1986), *Granger Causality and Econometric Exogeneity*, University of Warwick: Mimeo.

Bencivenca, V.R. and Smith, B.D. (1989), 'Some Consequences of Credit Rationing in an Endogenous Growth Model', *Journal of Economic*

Dynamics and Control, Vol.107(2), pp.773-84.

Beng, G.W. (1988), 'Monetary Policy and the Nominal Interest Rate in a Developing Country: The Case of Malaysia', *Singapore Economic Review*, Vol.33(1), pp.21-33.

Bhaduri, A. (1989), 'Moneylenders', in Eatwell, Milgate, and Newman (eds), *The New Palgrave Economic Development*, London: Macmillan, pp.243-47.

Bhatt, V.V. (1986), 'Improving the Financial Structure in Developing Countries', *Finance and Development*, June, pp.20-2.

Bhattachara, B.N. (1988), 'Development of Financial Infrastructure, An International Comparison', *Savings and Development*, Vol.12(4), pp.307-21.

Blanchard, O.J. and Fischer, S. (1989), *Lectures on Macroeconomics*, Cambridge, Mass.: MIT Press.

Blejer, M. and Cheasty, A. (1986), 'Using Fiscal Measures to Stimulate Savings in Developing Countries', *Finance and Development*, June, pp.16-9.

Blejer, M.I. and Guerrero, I. (1988), 'Stabilization Policies and Income Distribution in the Philippines', *Finance and Development*, Dec., pp.6-8.

Blejer, M. and Sagari, S.B. (1988), 'Sequencing the Liberalization of Financial Markets', *Finance and Development*, March, pp.18-20.

Bolnick, B. (1987), 'Financial Liberalization with Imperfect Markets: Indonesia during the 1970s', *Economic Development and Cultural Change*, Vol.35(3), pp.580-597.

Booth, A. (1989), 'Repelita V and Indonesian Medium Term Economic Strategy', *Bulletin of Indonesian Economic Studies*, Vol.25(2), pp.3-30.

Brunner, K. (1987), 'High-powered Money and the Monetary Base', Eatwell, Milgate and Newman (eds.), *The New Palgrave Money,* London: Macmillan, pp.175-78.

Brunner, K. and Meltzer, A. (1989), *Monetary Economics*, Oxford: Basil Blackwell.

Buffie, E.F. (1991), 'Credit Rationing and Capital Accumulation', *Economica*, Vol.58(231),pp.299-316.

Buffie, E. (1984),'Financial Repression, The New Structuralists, and Stabilization Policy in Semi-Industrialized Economies', *Journal of Development Economics*, Vol.14, pp.305-22.

Burkett, P. (1989),'Group Lending Programs and Rural Finance in Developing Countries', *Savings and Development*, Vol.13(4), pp.401-17.

Burkett, P. (1988), 'Informal Finance in Developing Countries: Lessons for Development of Formal Financial Intermediaries', *Journal of Economic*

Development, Vol.13(2), pp.81-109.

Burkett, P. (1986), 'Interest Rate Restrictions and Deposit Opportunities for Small-scale Savers in Developing Countries: An Analytical View', *Journal of Development Studies*, Vol.23(1), pp.77-91.

Burkett, P. and Vogel, R.C. (1992), 'Financial Assets, Inflation Hedges, and Capital Utilization in Developing Countries: An Extension of McKinnon's Complementarity Hypothesis', *Quarterly Journal of Economics*, Vol.107(2). pp.773-84.

Cargill, T.F., Cheng, H.S. and Hutchison, M.M. (1986), 'Financial Market Changes and Regulatory Reforms in Pacific-Basin Countries: An Overview', in Cheng. (ed.), *Financial Policy and Reform in Pacific-Basin Countries*, New York: Lexington Books, pp.17-41.

Chenery, H. and Srinivasan, T. (eds.)(1989), *Handbook of Development Economics Vol. I and II*, New York: North Holland.

Cheng, H.S. (ed.)(1988), *Monetary Policy in Pacific-Basin Countries*, Boston: Kluwer.

Cheng, H.S. (ed.)(1986), *Financial Policy and Reform in Pacific-Basin Countries*, New York: Lexington Books.

Cheng, H.S, and Glick, R. (1988), 'Monetary Policy Changes in Pacific Basin Countries', in Cheng. (ed.), *Monetary Policy in Pacific-Basin Countries*, Boston: Kluwer, pp.3-15.

Chiang, A.C. (1992), *Elements of Dynamic Optimization*, New York: McGraw-Hill.

Chiang, A.C. (1984), *Fundamental Methods of Mathematical Economics*, Third Edition, London: Mcgraw-Hill.

Chick, V. and Dow, S. (1988), 'A Post-Keynesian Perspective on the Relation Between Banking and Regional Development: Theories and Evidence', *The Greek Economic Review*, Vol.9(1), p.1-37.

Cho, K.R. (1990), 'Foreign Banking and Banking Market Concentration: The Case of Indonesia', *The Journal of Development Studies*, Vol.27(1), pp.98-109.

Cho, Y.J. (1989), 'Finance and Development: The Korean Approach', *Oxford Review of Economic Policy*, Vol.5(4), pp.88-102.

Cho, Y.J. (1986), 'Inefficiencies from Financial Liberalization in the Absence of Well-functioning Equity Markets', *Journal of Money, Credit and Banking*, Vol.18(2), pp.191-9.

Cho, Y.J. and Khatkhate, D. (1989), *Lessons of Financial Liberalization in Asia*, World Bank Discussion Paper No.50.

Chunanuntathum, S., Tambunlertychai, S. and Wattananukit, A. (1989), 'Thailand', in Page(ed.), *Trade, Finance and Developing Countries*,

London: Macmillan, pp.56-90.

Coats,W. and Khatkhate,D. (eds.)(1980), *Money and Monetary Policy in Less-Developed Countries*, Oxford: Pergamon Press.

Cole, D.C. (1988), 'Financial Development in Asia', *Asian-Pacific Economic Literature*, pp.26-47.

Cole, D., Chunanuntathum, S. and Loohawnchit, C. (1986), 'Modelling of Financial Markets in Thailand in an Asset-Demand and Institutional Framework', in Tan and Kapur (eds), *Pacific Growth and Financial Interdependence*, London: Allen and Unwin, pp.144-61.

Cole, D.C and Patrick, H.T.(1986), 'Financial Development in the Pacific Basin Market Economies', in Tan and Kapur (eds), *Pacific Growth and Financial Interdependence*, London: Allen & Unwin, pp.39-67.

Collier, P. and Mayer, C. (1989), 'The Assessment: Financial Liberalization, Financial Systems, and Economic Growth', *Oxford Review of Economic Policy*, Vol.5(4), pp.1-12.

Collins, S. and Park, W-A. (1989), 'South Korea', in Sachs and Collins (eds.), *Developing Country Debt and Economic Performance*, Chicago: University of Chicago Press, pp.153-325.

Corbo, V., de Melo, J. and Trybout, J. (1986),'What Went Wrong With The Recent Reforms In The Southern Cone', *Economic Development and Cultural Change*, Vol.34, pp.607-40.

Corsepius, U. and Fischer, B. (1988), 'Domestic Resource Mobilization in Thailand: A Success Case for Financial Deepening?', *The Singapore Economic Review*, Vol.33(2), pp.1-20.

Crushore, Koot, and Walker. (1990), 'Economic Stability and the Government Deficit', *Journal of Post-Keynesian Economics*, Vol.12(3), pp.390-403.

Cuthbertson, K. (1985), *The Supply and Demand for Money*, Oxford: Basil Blackwell.

Darrat, A.and Webb, M.A. (1986), 'Financial Changes and Interest Elasticity of Money Demand: Further Tests of the Gurley and Shaw Thesis', *Journal of Development Studies*, Vol.22(4), pp.724-29.

Davidson, P. and Weintraub, S. (1973), 'Money as Cause and Effect', *Economic Journal*, Vol.83(330), pp.1117-32.

de Grauwe, P. (1987),'Financial Deregulation in Developing Countries', *Tijdschrift Voor Economie en Management*, Vol.32(4), pp.381-401.

de Haan, J. and Zelhorst, D. (1990), 'The Impact of Government Deficits on Money Growth in Developing Countries', *Journal of International Money and Finance*, Vol.9, pp.455-69.

Deravi, M. and Hegi, C. (1990),'Monetary Regimes and Money Supply

Endogeneity', *Applied Economics*, Vol.22(10), pp.1355-64.

Desai, M. (1989), 'Endogenous and Exogenous Money', in Eatwell, Milgate and Newman (eds), *The New Palgrave Money*, London: Macmillan, pp.146-50.

Diaz-Alejandro, C. (1985), 'Goodbye Financial Repression, Hello Financial Crash', *Journal of Development Economics*, Vol.19, pp.1-24.

Dohner, R. and Intal, P. (1989), 'Philippines', in Sachs and Collins (eds), *Developing Country Debt and Economic Performance, Vol.3*, Chicago: University of Chicago Press, pp.373-450.

Dooley, M. and Mathieson, D. (1987), 'Financial Liberalization in Developing Countries', *Finance and Development*, Sept., pp.31-34.

Dornbusch, R, and Reynoso, A. (1989), 'Financial Factors in Economic Development', *American Economic Review*, Vol.79(2), pp.204-209.

Dow, A. and Dow, S. (1989), 'Endogenous Money Creation and Idle Balances', in Pheby, J. (ed.), *New Directions in Post-Keynesian Economics*, pp.147-64.

Dow, J.C.R. (1988), *Uncertainty and the Financial Process and its Consequences for the Power of the Central Bank*, National Institute of Economic and Social Research, Discussion Paper No. 135.

Dow, S. (1986), 'Post-Keynesian Monetary Theory for an Open Econmy', *Journal of Post-Keynesian Economics*, Vol.9(2). pp.237-57.

Earl, P.E. (1990), *Monetary Scenarios*, Aldershot: Edward Elgar.

Easterly, W. (1993), 'How Much Do Distortions Affect Growth?', *Journal of Monetary Economics*, Vol.32, pp.187-212.

Eatwell, J., Milgate, M. and Newman, P. (eds.) (1989), *The New Palgrave Money*, London: Macmillan Press.

Eatwell, J., Milgate, M. and Newman, P. (eds.)(1989a), *The New Palgrave Economic Development*, London: Macmillan Press.

Edwards, S. (1988), 'Financial Deregulation and Segmented Capital Markets: The Case of Korea', *World Development*, Vol.16(1), pp.185-94.

Engle, R.F. and Hendry, D.F. (1986), 'Testing Super Exogeneity and Invariance', Nuffield College Discussion Paper.

Engle, R., Hendry, D. and Richard, J.-F. (1983), 'Exogeneity', *Econometrica*, Vol.51(2), pp.277-304.

Eshag, E. (1989), 'Fiscal and Monetary Policies in Developing Countries', in Eatwell, Milgate, and Newman (eds), *The New Palgrave Economic Development*, London: Macmillan Press, pp.130-37.

Evans, D. (1988), 'Survey of Recent Developments', *Bulletin of Indonesian Economic Studies*, Vol.24(3), pp.3-30.

Eyzaguirre, N. (1989), 'Savings and Investment under External and Fiscal

Constraints', *Cepal Review*, Vol.38, pp.31-47.

Feige, E.L. and Pearce, D.K. (1979), 'The Casual Causal Relationship Between Money and Income: Some Caveats for Time Series Analysis', *Review of Economics and Statistics*, Vol.61, pp.521-33.

Fernando, N.A. (1988), 'The Interest Rate Structure and Factors Affecting Interest Rate Determination in the Informal Credit Market in Sri Lanka', *Savings and Development*, Vol.11(3), pp.249-265.

Fischer, A.M. (1989), 'Policy Regime Changes and Monetary Expectations: Testing for Super Exogeneity', *Journal of Monetary Economics*, Vol.24, pp.423-36.

Fischer, B. (1989), 'Savings Mobilization in Developing Countries: Bottlenecks and Reform Proposals', *Savings and Development*, Vol.13(2), pp.117-32.

Fisher, I. (1911), *The Purchasing Power of Money*, Rev. edn 1920, New York: Macmillan.

Friedman, B.M. and Hahn, F.H. (eds)(1990), *Handbook of Monetary Economics, Vol.1&2*, Amsterdam: North-Holland.

Friedman, M. (1989), 'Quantity Theory of Money', in Eatwell, Milgate and Newman.(eds), *The New Palgrave Money*, London: Macmillan, pp.1-40.

Friedman, M. (1971),'A Monetary Theory of Nominal Income', *Journal of Political Economy,* Vol.79, pp.323-37.

Friedman, M. (1968), 'The Role of Monetary Policy', *American Economic Review*, Vol.58, pp.1-17.

Fry, M.J. (1993a), *The Fiscal Abuse of Central Banks*, Mimeo: University of Birmingham.

Fry, M.J. (1993b), 'Financial Repression and Economic Growth', International Finance Group Working Paper, IFGWP-93-07, University of Birmingham.

Fry, M.J. (1993c), 'Flexibility and Finance in Developing Countries', International Finance Group Working Paper, IFGWP-93-06, University of Birmingham.

Fry, M.J. (1991), 'Domestic Resource Mobilization in Developing Asia: Four Policy Issues', *Asian Development Review*, Vol.9(1), pp.15-39.

Fry, M.J. (1991a), 'Mobilizing External Resources in Developing Asia: Structural Adjustment and Policy Reforms', *Asian Development Review*, Vol.9(2), pp.14-39.

Fry, M.J. (1989), 'Financial Development: Theories and Recent Experience', *Oxford Review of Economic Policy*, Vol.5(4), pp.13-27.

Fry, M.J. (1988), *Money, Interest, and Banking in Economic Development*, Baltimore: Johns Hopkins University Press.

Fry, M.J. (1987), 'Neo-Classical and Neo-Structuralist Models of Financial Development: Theories and Evidence', *The Greek Economic Review*, Vol.9(1), pp.1-37.

Fry, M.J. (1986), 'Financial Structure, Financial Regulation, and Financial Reform in the Philippines and Thailand, 1960-1984', in Cheng (ed.), *Financial Policy and Reform in Pacific-Basin Countries*, New York: Lexington Books, pp.160-83.

Fry, M.J. (1981),'Inflation and Economic Growth in Pacific-Basin Developing Countries', *Federal Reserve Bank of San Francisco Economic Review*, (Fall), pp.8-18.

Fry, M.J., Lilien, D. and Wadha, W. (1988), 'Monetary Policy in Pacific Basin Countries', in Cheng. (ed.),*Monetary Policy in Pacific-Basin Countries*, Boston: Klewer, pp.153-69.

Galbis, V. (1977), 'Financial Intermediation and Economic Growth in Less-Developed Countries: A Theoretical Approach', *Journal of Development Studies*, Vol.13(2), pp.58-72.

Ganjarerndee, S. (1986), 'Financial Reform in Thailand', in Cheng (ed.), *Financial Policy and Reform in Pacific-Basin Countries*, New York: Lexington Books, pp.185-89.

Gausden, R. (1986), *Real Wages and Employment - A Survey of Studies Based on the Granger-Causality Testing Approach*, National Institute of Economic and Social Research Discussion Papers, No.123.

Germidis, D. (1990), 'Interlinking the Formal and Informal Financial Sectors in Developing Countries', *Savings and Development*, Vol.14(1), pp.5-21.

Gerschenkron, A. (1962), *Economic Backwardness in Historical Perspective*, Cambridge Mass.

Gertler, M. and Gilchrist, S. (1993), 'The Role of Credit Market Imperfections in the Monetary Transmission Mechanism: Arguments and Evidence', *Scandinavian Journal of Economics*, Vol.95(1), pp.43-64.

Geweke, J. (1978),'Testing the Exogeneity Specification in the Complete Dynamic Simultaneous Equations Model', *Journal of Econometrics*, Vol.7, pp.163-85.

Geweke, J., Meese, R. and Dent, W. (1983), 'Comparing Alternative Tests of Causality in Temporal Systems', *Journal of Econometrics*, Vol.21, pp.161-94.

Ghatak, S. (1981), *Monetary Economics in Developing Countries,* London: Macmillan.

Gilbert, C.L. (1986), 'Professor Hendry's Econometric Methodology', *Oxford Bulletin of Economics and Statistics*, Vol.48(3), pp.283-307.

Gill, D. and Tropper, P. (1988), 'Emerging Stock Markets in Developing Countries', *Finance and Development*, Dec., pp.28-31.

Ginsberg, V.A. (1973), 'A Further Note on the Derivation of Quarterly Figures Consistent with Annual Data', *Applied Statistics*, Vol.21, pp.368-75.

Glick, R. (1988), ' Financial Market Changes and Monetary Policy in Pacific-Basin Countries', in Cheng. (ed.), *Monetary Policy in Pacific-Basin Countries*, pp.17-41.

Goldsmith, R. (1969), *Financial Structure and Development*, New Haven.

Goodhart, C. (1989), *Money, Inflation, and Uncertainty*, Second edn, London: Macmillan.

Goodhart, C. (1989a), 'Monetary Base', in Eatwell, Milgate and Newman (eds), *The New Palgrave Money*, London: Macmillan, pp.206-11.

Granger, C.W.J. (1988), 'Some Recent Developments in the Concept of Causality', *Journal of Econometrics*, Vol.39, pp.199-211.

Granger, C.W.J. (1969), 'Investigating Causal Relationships by Econometric Models and Cross-Spectoral Methods', *Econometrica,* Vol.37, pp.424-38.

Green, R. (1989), 'The Real Bills Doctrine', in Eatwell, Milgate and Newman (eds), *The New Palgrave Money*, London: Macmillan, pp.310-13.

Greenaway, D. and Morrissey, O. (1992), *Structural Adjustment and Liberalisation in Developing Countries: What Lessons Have We Learned?* University of Nottingham: Mimeo.

Greenwood, J.G. (1988), 'Monetray Policy in Thailand', in Cheng. (ed.), *Monetary Policy in Pacific-Basin Countries*, Boston: Kluwer, pp.303-19.

Greenwood, J.G. (1986), 'Financial Liberalization and Innovation in Seven-East Asian Economies', in Suzuki and Yomo (eds.), *Financial Innovation and Monetary Policy: Asia and the West*, Tokyo: University of Tokyo, pp.79-105.

Gupta, S. and Moazzami. (1989), 'Demand for Money in Asia', *Economic Modelling*, Vol.6(4), pp.467-73.

Hamilton, C. (1989), 'The Irrelevance of Economic Liberalization in the Third World', *World Development*, Vol.17(10), pp.1523-30.

Hamilton, J. (1989), 'The Long-run Behaviour of the Velocity of Circulation: A Review Essay', *Journal of Monetary Economics*, Vol.23, pp.335-49.

Harris, L. (1985), *Monetary Theory*, McGraw-Hill int.editions.

Hedgi, C. (1990), 'Policy Implications of an Endogenous Money Supply', *Economic Notes*, Vol.2, pp.246-59.

Hendry, D.F. (1979), 'Predictive Failure and Econometric Modelling in Macroeconomics: The Transactions Demand for Money', in Omerod, P.

(ed.), *Modelling the Economy*, London: Heinemann.

Holmes, J. and Hutton, P.A. (1992), 'A New Test of Money-Income Causality', *Journal of Money, Credit and Banking*, Vol.24(3), pp.338-55.

Hong, W. (1986), 'Institutionalized Monopsonistic Capital Markets in a Developing Country', *Journal of Development Economics*, Vol.21, pp.353-9.

Hong, W.and Park, Y.C. (1986), 'The Financing of Export-Oriented Growth in Korea', in Tan and Kapur (eds),*Pacific Growth and Financial Interdependence*, pp.163-82.

Horrigan, B. (1988), 'Are Reserve Requirements Relevant for Economic Stabilization?', *Journal of Monetary Economics*, Vol.21, pp.97-105.

Husnan, S. and Theobald, M. (1991), 'Financial Sector Reforms, Corporate Financing and the Tax System in Indonesia', Savings and Development, Vol.15(2), pp.97-108.

Hutchison, M. (1986), 'Financial Effects of Budget Deficits in the Pacific Basin', in Cheng, H. (ed.), *Financial Policy and Reform in Pacific-Basin Countries*, pp.310-33.

IMF International Financial Statistics. Various issues.

Jaffee, D. and Stiglitz,J. (1990), 'Credit Rationing', in Friedman and Hahn (eds), *Handbook of Monetary Economics Vol. II*, New York: North-Holland, pp.838-88.

Jao, Y.C. (1989), 'Money Supply Exogeneity and Endogeneity:A Review of the Monetarist-Post-Keynesian Debate', *Greek Economic Review*, Vol.11(2), pp.204-34.

Jao, Y.C. (1985), 'Financial Deepening and Economic Growth: Theory, Evidence, and Policy', *Greek Economic Review*, Vol.7(3), pp.187-217.

Jappelli, T. and Pagano, M. (1991), *Saving, Growth, and Liquidity Constraints*, Naples: Instituto Universario Navale, Instituto Di Studi Economici, Dec..

Jayasuriya, S. and Manning, C. (1988), 'Survey of Recent Developments', *Bulletin of Indonesian Economic Studies*, Vol.24(2), pp.3-41.

Johannes, J.M. and Rasche, R.H. (1987), *Controlling the Growth of Monetary Aggregates*, Boston: Kluwer Academic Publishers.

Johansen, S. (1988), 'Statistical Analysis of Co-integration Vectors', *Journal of Economic Dynamics and Control*, Vol.12.

Jung, W.S. (1986), 'Financial Development and Economic Growth: International Evidence', *Economic Development and Cultural Change*, Vol.34(2), pp.333-46.

Kaldor, N. (1982), *The Scourge of Monetarism*, Oxford: Oxford University Press.

Kalecki, M. (1971), *Selected Essays on the Dynamics of the Capitalist Economy 1933-1970*, Cambridge: Cambridge University Press.

Kanath, S. (1985), 'Monetary Aggregates, Income, and Causality in a Developing Country', *Journal of Economic Studies*, Vol. 12(3), pp.36-53.

Kapur, B.K. (1990), 'Formal and Informal Financial Markets, and the Neo-structuralist Critique of the Financial Liberalization Strategy in Less Developed Countries', *Journal of Development Economics*, Vol.38, pp.63-77.

Kapur, B.K. (1989), 'Inflation and Financial Deepening', *Journal of Development Economics*, Vol.13, pp.379-96.

Kapur, B.K. (1976), 'Alternative Stabilization Policies for Less Developed Countries', *Journal of Political Economy*, Vol.84(4), pp.777-795.

Katseli, L.T. (1983), 'Devaluation: A Critical Appraisal of the IMF's Policy Prescription', *American Economic Review*, Vol.73(2), pp.359-363.

Keynes, J.M. (1936), *The General Theory of Employment, Interest, and Money*, London: Macmillan.

Keynes, J.M. (1930), *A Treatise on Money*, London: Macmillan.

Kharadia, V.C. (1988), 'The Behavior of Income Velocity of Money in India: Implications for Monetary Theory and Policy', *Indian Economic Journal*, Vol.36(1), pp.1-17.

Kharas, H.J. and Kiguel, M.A. (1988), 'Monetary Policy and Foreign Debt: The Experiences of the Far East Countries', in Cheng (ed.), *Monetary Policy in Pacific-Basin Countries*, pp.95-123.

Kim, H.N. (1989), 'Foreign Banks in Korea', *Korea Exchange Bank Monthly Review*, Vol.23(4), pp.3-12.

Kim, K. (1989), 'Korean Experience in Development', *The Bank of Korea Quarterly Economic Review*, June, pp.3-21.

Kim, K.S. (1989), 'Korea's Capital Market International Plan for 1989-1992', *Korea Exchange Bank Monthly*, Vol.23(2), pp.3-14.

Kim, T. (1990), 'Internationalization of Banking', *Journal of Economic Development*, Vol.15(1), pp.63-81.

Kim, W.W. (1988), 'Recent Interest Rate Liberalization in Korea', *Korea Exchange Bank Monthly Review*, Vol.22(12), pp.3-13.

Kim, Y.S. (1988), 'Financial Market Behaviour and the Balance of Payments During the Periods of Partial Financial Reform in Korea, 1976-81', *The Developing Economies*, Vol.26(3), pp.247-63.

Kincaid, G.R. (1988), 'Policy Implications of Structural Changes in Financial Markets', *Finance and Development*, Mar., pp.2-5.

King, R. and Levine, R. (1993),'Finance and Growth: Schumpeter Might Be Right', *Quarterly Journal of Economics*, Vol.58(3), pp.717-35.

Kohsaka, A. (1987), 'Financial Liberalization in Asian NIC's: A Comparative Study of Korea and Taiwan in the 1980s', *The Developing Economies*, Vol.25(4), pp.324-44.

Kwack, S. and Chung, U. (1986), 'The Role of Financial Policies and Institutions in Korea's Economic Development Process', in Cheng (ed.), *Financial Policy and Reform in Pacific-Basin Countries*, New York: Lexington Books, pp.115-35.

Lahiri, A. (1989), 'Dynamics of Asian Savings: The Role of Growth and Age Structures', *IMF Staff Papers*, Vol.36(1), pp.228-51.

Laidler, D. (1991), 'The Quantity Theory is Always and Everywhere Controversial - Why?', *The Economic Record*, Vol.67(199), pp.289-305.

Laidler, D. (1989), 'The Bullionist Controversy', in Eatwell, Milgate and Newman (eds.), *The New Palgrave Money*, London: Macmillan, pp.60-72.

Laumus, P. (1990), 'Monetization, Financial Liberalization, and Economic Development', *Economic Development and Cultural Change*, Vol.38(2), pp.377-87.

Lavoie, M. (1984),'The Endogenous Flow of Credit and the Post-Keynesian Theory of Money', *Journal of Economic Issues*, Vol. 18(3), pp.771-97.

Layman, T.A. (1988), 'Monetary Policy and Financial Reform in Korea', in Cheng. (ed.), *Monetary Policy in Pacific-Basin Countries*, pp.353-77.

Lee, C.-K. (1986), 'Financial Reform Experiences in Korea', in Cheng (ed.), *Financial Policy and Reform in Pacific-Basin Countries*, New York: Lexington Books, pp.137-42.

Lee, S.Y. and Li,W.K. (1985), 'The Lead-Lag Relationship of Money Income and Prices, in Malaysia', *Singapore Economic Review*, Vol.30(1), pp.68-76.

Lee, S.Y. and Li, W.K. (1983), 'Money, Income and Prices and their Lead-Lag Relationships in Singapore', *Singapore Economic Review*, Vol.20(1), pp.73-87.

Lee, T.H. and Han, S. (1990), 'On Measuring the Relative Size of the Unregulated to the Regulated Money Market Over Time', *Journal of Development Economics*, Vol.33, pp.53-65.

Lee, Y.-P. (1980), 'Inflation Hedges and Economic Growth in a Monetary Economy', PhD Stanford University.

Leite, S.P. and Makonnen, D. (1986), 'Savings and Interest Rates in BCEAO Countries: An Empirical Analysis', *Savings and Development*, Vol.10(3), pp.219-32.

Leite, S.P. and Sundararajan, V. (1990), 'Issues in Interest Rate Management and Liberalization', *IMF Staff Papers*, Vol.37(4), pp.735-51.

Lewis, J. and Kapur, D. (1990), 'An Updating Country Study: Thailand's

Needs and Prospects in the 1990s',*World Development*, Vol.18(10), pp.1363-78.

Li, K.W. and Skully, M. (1991), 'Financial Deepening and Institutional Development, Some Asian Experiences', *Savings and Development*, Vol.15(2), pp.147-64.

Lim, J. (1987), 'The New Structuralist Critique of the Monetarist Theory of Inflation', *Journal of Development Economics*, Vol.25, pp.45-61.

Lin, C.C. and Chu,Y.-P. (1989), 'Interest Rate Interactions Between Dual Financial Markets', *Journal of Economic Development*, Vol.14(2), pp.107-15.

Lirio, R.P. (1988), 'Domestic Resource Mobilization in the Seacean Countries: The Philippines', *Central Bank of the Philippines: CB Review*, Vol.40(1), pp.16-37.

Lizondo, J. and Montiel, P. (1989), 'Contractionary Devaluation in Developing Countries', *IMF Staff Papers*, Mar., pp.182-223.

LLanto, G.M. (1990), 'Asymmetric Information in Rural Financial Markets and Interlinking of Transactions through Self-help Groups', *Savings and Development*, Vol.14(2), pp.137-52.

Long, M. and Evinhouse, E. (1989), 'Restructuring Distressed Financial Systems', *Finance and Development*, Sept., pp.5-7.

Loong, P. (1989), 'Malay Banks Come Out Of The Doldrums', *Euromoney*, July, pp.90-92.

Lowenstein, J. (1989), 'Indonesia: Reaping the Rewards of Reform', *Euromoney*, Dec., pp.2-36.

Lowenstein, J. (1989a), 'After Chaos, Some Calm', *Euromoney*, July, pp.85-90.

Lucas, R.E. (1976), 'Econometric Policy Evaluation: A Critique', in Brunner and Meltzer (eds.), *Carnegie Rochester Conferences on Public Policy Vol.1*, Supplementary series to *Journal of Monetary Economics*, pp.19-46.

Mackie, J. (1989), 'Survey of Recent Developments', *Bulletin of Indonesian Economic Studies*, Vol.25(3), pp.3-34.

Maddala, G.S. (1989), *Introduction to Econometrics*, New York: Maxwell Macmillan International Editions.

Mahdavi, S. (1989), 'The Effects of External Trade, Foreign Resources and Domestic Policies on Domestic Savings in Some Developing Countries: A Regression Analysis', *De Economist*, Vol.132(2), pp.217-31.

Marshall, A. (1923), *Money, Credit and Commerce*, London: Macmillan.

Mascaindro, D. and Tabellini, G. (1988), 'Monetary Regimes and Fiscal Deficits: A Comparative Analysis', in Cheng, H. (ed.), *Monetary Policy in Pacific-Basin Countries*, pp.125-43

Mathieson, D.J. (1989), 'Exchange Rate Arrangements and Monetary Policy', *Finance and Development*, March, pp.21-4.

Mathieson, D.J. (1988), 'Exchange Rate Arrangements and Monetary Policy', in Cheng, H.(ed.), *Monetary Policy in Pacific-Basin Countries*, Boston: Kluwer, pp.44-79.

Mathieson, D.J. (1980), 'Financial Reform and Stabilization Policy in a Developing Economy', *Journal of Development Economics*, Vol.7., pp.359-95.

Mathieson, D.J. (1979), 'Financial Reform and Capital Flows in a Developing Economy', *IMF Staff Papers*, Vol.26, pp.450-89.

McKinnon, R.I. (1993), 'Gradual Versus Rapid Liberalization in Socialist Economies: Financial Policies and Macroeconomic Stability in China and Russia Compared', Paper for World Banks Annual Conference on Development Economics.

McKinnon, R.I. (1989), 'Financial Liberalization and Economic Development: A Reassessment of Interest Rate Policies in Asia and Latin-America', *Oxford Review of Economic Policy*, Vol.5(4), pp.29-54.

McKinnon, R.I. (1986), 'Issues and Perspectives: An Overview of Bank Regulation and Monetary Control', Tan and Kapur (eds), *Pacific Growth and Financial Interdependence*, pp.319-36.

McKinnon, R.I. (1973), *Money and Capital in a Developing Country*, Washington: Brookings.

Mcleod, R. (1991), 'Informal and Formal Sector Finance in Indonesia: The Financial Evolution of Small Business', *Savings and Development*, Vol.15(2), pp.187-209.

Minsky, H. (1986), *Stabilizing An Unstable Economy*, New York: Yale University Press.

Minsky, H. (1982), *Can 'it' Happen Again? Essays on Instability and Finance*, Chicago: University of Chicago Press.

Modigliani, F. (1987), 'The Economics of Public Deficits', in Razin, and Sadka, (eds), *Economic Theory and Practice*, London: Macmillan Press, pp.3-43.

Molho, L.E. (1986), 'Interest Rates, Savings, and Investment in Developing Countries: A Re-examination of the McKinnon-Shaw Hypothesis', *IMF Staff Papers*, Vol.33(1), pp.90-116.

Monticelli, C. (1987), 'Stabilization Priorities and Optimal Monetary policy', *Greek Economic Review*, Vol.9(2), pp.210-23.

Montiel, P. (1991), 'The Transmission Mechanism for Monetary Policy in Developing Countries, *IMF Staff Papers*, Vol.38(1), pp.83-107.

Moore, B.J. (1991), 'Money Supply Endogeneity', *Journal of Post Keynesian Economics*, Vol.13(3), pp.404-13.

Moore, B.J. (1991a), 'Has the Demand for Money been Mislaid?', *Journal of Post Keynesian Economics*, Vol.14(1), pp. 125-34.

Moore, B.J. (1988), 'Unpacking the Post-Keynesian Black-Box: Wages, Bank Lending, and the Money Supply', in Arestis, P. (ed.), *Post-Keynesian Monetary Economics*, Aldershot: Edward Elgar, pp.122-51.

Moore, B.J. (1988a), *Horizontalists and Verticalists*, Cambridge: Cambridge University Press.

Morisset, J. (1993), 'Does Financial Liberalization Really Improve Private Investment in Developing Countries?', *Journal of Development Economics*, Vol.40, pp.133-50.

Myrdal, G. (1939), *Monetary Equilibrium*, London: William Hodge.

Odedokun, M.O. (1989), 'Causalities Between Financial Aggregates and Economic Activities in Nigeria:The Results from Granger's Test', *Savings and Development*, Vol.13(1), pp.101-9.

Okuda, H. (1990), 'Financial Factors in Economic Development: A Study of Financial Liberalization Policy in the Philippines', *The Developing Economies*, Vol.28(3), pp.240-70.

Osband, K. and Villanueva, D. (1993), 'Independent Currency Authorities', *IMF Staff Papers*, Vol.40(1), pp.202-16.

Owen, P. and Solis-Fallas, (1989), 'Unorganized Money Markets and Unproductive Assets in the New Structuralists' Critique of Financial Liberalization', *Journal of Development Economics*, Vol.31, pp.341-55.

Page, S. (ed.) (1989), *Trade, Finance and Developing Countries*, London: Macmillan.

Palley, T.I. (1991), 'Endogenous Money System', *Journal of Post Keynesian Economics*, Vol.13(3), pp.397-403.

Papademos, L. and Modigliani, F. (1990), 'The Supply and Demand of Money and the Control of Nominal Income', in Friedman, B. and Hahn, F.(eds), *Handbook of Monetary Economics Vol.1*, pp.399-494.

Park, S.P. (1989), 'Financial Repression and Liberalization in Korea', *Korea Exchange Bank Monthly Review*, Vol.23(10), pp.3-23.

Park, Y.C. (1987), 'Evaluating the Performance of Korea's Government-Invested Enterprises', *Finance and Development,* June, pp.25-7.

Parkin, M. (1987), 'The Quantity Theory of Money, Rational Expectations and the Relationship between Money,Income and Prices', *Greek Economic Review*, Vol.9(1), pp.57-87.

Patalinghug, E. (1987), 'Rediscounting, Savings Mobilization, and the Rural Banking System', *Philippine Review of Economics and Business*,

Vol.14(1,2), pp.103-23.

Patinkin, D. (1989), 'Neutrality of Money', in Eatwell, Milgate and Newman (eds.), The *New Palgrave Money*, London: Macmillan, pp.273-87.

Patrick, H. (1966), 'Financial Development and Economic Growth in Underdeveloped Countries', *Economic Development and Cultural Change*, Jan., pp.174-89.

Perman, R. (1991),'Cointegration: An Introduction to the Literature', *Journal of Economic Studies*, Vol.18(3), pp.3-30.

Pheby, J. (ed.) (1989), *New Directions in Post-Keynesian Economics*, Aldershot: Edward Elgar.

Phelps, E.S. (1968), 'Money-Wage Dynamics and Labour Market Equilibrium', *Journal of Political Economy*, Vol.76, pp.678-711.

Phillips, A.W. (1958), 'The Relation Between Unemployment and the Rate of Change of Money Wage Rates in the United Kingdom, 1861-1957', *Economica*, Vol.25, pp.283-99.

Pierce, D. and Haugh, L. (1977), 'Causality in Temporal Systems', *Journal of Econometrics*, Vol.5, pp.101-09.

Pigou, A.C. (1917),'The Value Of Money', *Quarterly Journal of Economics*, Vol.32. pp.38-65.

Please, S. (1971), 'Mobilizing Internal Resources through Taxation', in Robinson, R. (ed.), *Developing the Third World: Experiences of the 1960s*, London: Cambridge University Press.

Pollin, R. (1991), 'Two Theories of Money Supply Endogeneity', *Journal of Post Keynesian Economics*, Vol.13(3), pp.366-96.

Polvorosa, C.G. (1988), 'The Financial System and the Impact of Central Bank Policies', *Central Bank of the Philippines: CB Review*, Vol.40(5), pp.11-6.

Powell, A. (1989), 'The Management of Risk in Developing Country Finance', *Oxford Review of Economic Policy*, Vol.5(4), pp.69-85.

Rana, P.B. (1987), 'Foreign Capital, Exports, Savings and Growth in the Asian Region', *Savings and Development*, Vol.11(1), pp.5-28.

Ransom, B. (1983), 'The Unrecognized Revolution in the Theory of Capital Formulation', *Journal of Economic Issues*, Vol.17(4), pp.901-13.

Remula, E. and Lanberte, M. (1986), 'Financial Reforms and the Balance of Payments Crises: The Case of the Philippines 1980-83', *Philippine Review of Economics and Business*, Vol.24(1&2), pp.101-141.

Robinson, J. (1970), 'Quantity Theories Old and New: A Comment', *Journal of Money, Credit, and Banking*, Nov., pp.727-734.

Roubini, N. and Sala-i-Martin, X. (1992), 'Financial Repression and

Economic Growth', *Journal of Development Economics*, Vol.39, pp.5-30.

Rousseaus, S. (1986), *Post Keyensian Monetary Economics*, London: Macmillan.

Sachs, J. and Collins, S. (eds.)(1989), *Developing Country Debt and Economic Performance Vol. 3*, Chicago: University of Chicago Press for NBER.

Sargent, T. and Wallace, N. (1981), 'Some Unpleasant Monetarist Arithmetic', *Federal Reserve Bank of Minneapolis Quarterly Review*, Vol.5.

Schumpeter, J. (1911, 1935), *Theorie der Wirtschapelichen Entwicklung*, Berlin. English edition entitled *Theory of Economic Development*, translated Opie, R., Cambridge, Mass.

Shahin, W. (1990), 'Unorganized Markets and Monetary Policy Instruments', *World Development*, Vol.18(2), pp.325-32.

Shanmugam, B. (1989), 'Development Strategy and Mobilising Savings Through ROSCAs: The Case of Malaysia', *Savings and Development*, Vol.13(4), pp.351-65.

Shaw, E. (1973), *Financial Deepening in Economic Development*, New York: Oxford University Press.

Sheng, A. (1989), *Bank Restructuring in Malaysia, 1985-88*, World Development Report Working Papers: WPS 54.

Shin, H. (1978), 'Money, Income, and Causality', *Asian Economies*, pp.13-28.

Sicat, G. (1985), 'A Historical and Current Perspective of Philippine Economic Problems', *The Philippine Economic Journal*, Vol.24(1), pp.24-63.

Sidrauski, M. (1966), 'Inflation and Economic Growth', *Journal of Political Economy*, Vol.75(6), Dec., pp.776-810.

Sikorski, T. (1992), *Economic Causality: Income and Money - Some Results for South-East Asian Economies*, Glasgow: Mimeo.

Simmons, R. (1992), 'An Error-Correction Approach to Demand for Money in Five African Developing Countries', *Journal of Economic Studies*, Vol.19(1), pp.29-47.

Sims, C.A. (1972), 'Money, Income and Causality', *American Economic Review*, Vol.62, pp.540-51.

Sines, R.H. (1979), '"Financial Deepening" and Industrial Production: A Microeconomic Analysis of the Venezuelan Food Processing Sector', *Social and Economic Studies*, Vol.28(2), pp.450-74.

Sirivedhin, T. (1988), 'The Role of the Bank of Thailand in Development', *Bank of Thailand Quarterly Review*, Vol.28(1&2), pp.13-9.

Snowden, P.N. (1987), 'Financial Market Liberalization in LDCs: The Incidence of Risk Allocation Effects of Interest Rate Increases', *Journal of Development Studies*, Vol.24(1), pp.83-93.

Solimano, A. (1986), 'Contractionary Devaluation in the Southern Cone: Chile', *Journal of Development Economics*, Vol.23, pp.135-52.

Somogyi, J.(1991), 'Malaysia's Successful Reform Experience', *Finance and Development*, Mar., pp.35-8.

Sta. Romano, E.R. (1989), 'The Philippine State's Hegemony and Fiscal Base, 1950-1985', *The Developing Economies*, Vol.27(2), pp.185-205.

Stern, N. (1989), 'The Economics of Development: A Survey', *Economic Journal*, Vol.99, pp.597-684.

Stiglitz, J.E. (1989), 'Financial Markets and Development', *Oxford Review of Economic Policy*, Vol.5(4), pp.55-67.

Stiglitz, J. and Weiss, A. (1992), 'Asymmetric Information in Credit Markets and its Implications for Macro-Economics', *Oxford Economic Papers*, Vol.44, pp.694-724.

Stiglitz, J. and Weiss, A. (1981),'Credit Rationing in Markets with Imperfect Information', *American Economic Review*, Vol.71, pp.133-52.

Streeten, P. (1984), 'Development Dichotomies', in Meier, and Seers, (eds), *Pioneers in Development*, New York: Oxford University Press, pp.337-61.

Sundararajan, V. (1985), 'Debt-Equity Ratios of Firms and Interest Rate Policy', *IMF Staff Papers*, Vol.32(3), pp.430-73.

Sundararajan, V. and Molho, L. (1988), 'Financial Reform and Monetary Control in Indonesia', in Cheng, H. (ed.), *Monetary Policy in Pacific Basin Countries*, pp.320-51.

Sundararajan, V. and Molho, L. (1988a), 'Financial Reform in Indonesia', *Finance and Development*, Dec., pp.43-5.

Sundaravej, T. and Trairatvorakul, P. (1989), *Experiences of Financial Distress in Thailand*, World Development Report Working Papers, WPS 283.

Sutuntivorakoon, P. (1989), 'Banking Regulations in Thailand - an Overview of the Commercial Banking Act B.E.2505(1962) and its Amendments', *Journal of International Banking Law*, Vol. 4(5), pp.226-33.

Suzuki, Y. and Yomo, H. (eds.) (1986), *Financial Innovation and Monetary Policy: Asia and the West*, Tokyo: University of Tokyo Press.

Tan, A.H. and Kapur, B. (eds.) (1986), *Pacific Growth and Financial Interdependence*, London: Allen & Unwin.

Tanzi, V. (1987), 'Quantitative Characteristics of the Tax Systems of

Developing Countries' in Newbury, and Stern, N. (eds.), *The Theory of Taxation for Developing Countries*, New York: Oxford University Press.

Taylor, L. (1983), *Structuralist Macroeconomics: Applicable Models for the Third World*, New York: Basic Books.

Thornton, J. (1991), 'The Financial Repression Paradigm: A Survey of Empirical Research', *Savings and Development*, Vol.15(1),

Tobin, J. (1965), 'Money and Economic Growth', *Econometrica*. Vol.33(4), pp.671-84.

Todaro, M.P. (1989), *Economic Development in the Third World*, Fourth edn, London:Longman.

Tolentino, V.B.J. (1989), 'The Political Economy of Credit Availability and Financial Liberalization: Notes on the Philippine Experience', *Savings and Development*, Vol.13(4), pp.321-36.

Tooke, T. (1844), *An Enquiry into the Circulation of Money*. Reprinted London School of Economics Press (1959).

Tsang, S.K. (1986), 'Testing Money - Income Causality in South Korea', *Hong Kong Economic Papers*, Vol.17, pp.34-50.

Tseng, W. and Corker, R. (1991), 'Financial Liberalization, Money Demand, and Monetary Policy in Asian Countries', *IMF Occasional Papers 84*.

van Wijnbergen, S. (1985), 'Macroeconomic Effects of Changes in Bank Interest Rates', *Journal of Development Economics*, Vol.18, pp.541-54.

van Wijnbergen, S. (1983), 'Interest Rate Management in LDCs', *Journal of Monetary Economics*, Vol.12, pp.433-52.

van Wijnbergen, S. (1982), 'Stagflationary Effects on Monetary Stabilization Policies', *Journal of Development Economics*, Vol.10, pp.133-69.

Villanueva, D. (1988), 'Issues in Financial Sector Reform', *Finance and Development*, March, pp.14-16.

Villanueva, D. and Mirakhor, A. (1990), 'Strategies for Financial Reforms', *IMF Staff Papers*, Vol.37(3), pp.509-36.

Virmani, A. (1989), 'Credit Markets and Credit Policy in Developing Countries: Myths and Reality', *Greek Economic Review*, Vol.11(1), pp.49-67.

Wallich, H.C. (1986), 'A Broad View of Deregulation', in Cheng, H.(ed.), *Financial Policy and Reform in Pacific-Basin Countries*, New York: Lexington Books, pp.3-36.

Weintraub, S. (1978), *Keynes, Keynesians, and Monetarists*, Philadelphia: University of Pennsylvania Press.

Wolfson, M.H. (1990), 'The Causes of Financial Instability', *Journal of Post-Keynesian Economics*, Vol.12(8), pp.333-53.

Woo, T.W. and Nasution, A.(1989), 'Indonesia', in Sachs and Collins (eds.), *Developing Country Debt and Economic Performance Vol.3*, pp.19-100.

The World Bank, (1989), *World Development Report 1989: Financial Systems and Development*, New York: Oxford University Press.

Wray, L.R. (1993), 'Money, Interest Rates and Monetarist Policy', *Journal of Post Keynesian Economics*, Vol.15(4), pp.541-70.

Wray, L.R. (1992), 'Commercial Banks, the Central Bank and Endogeneity', *Journal of Post Keynesian Economics*, Vol.14(3), pp.297-310.

Yototopolus, P. and Floro, S.L. (1992), 'Income Distribution, Transaction Costs and Market Fragmentation in Informal Credit Markets', *Cambridge Journal of Economics*, Vol. 16(3), pp.303-27.

Zellner, A. (1988), 'Causality and Causal Laws in Economics', *Journal of Econometrics*, Vol. 39, pp.7-21.

Index

304